A
Functioning
Society

Chosen and edited by the author

Peter F. Drucker

A Functioning Society

Selections from Sixty-Five Years of
Writing on Community, Society, and Polity

Routledge
Taylor & Francis Group

LONDON AND NEW YORK

First published 2003 by Transaction Publishers

Published 2017 by Routledge
2 Park Square, Milton Park, Abingdon, Oxon OX14 4RN
711 Third Avenue, New York, NY 10017, USA

Routledge is an imprint of the Taylor & Francis Group, an informa business

Library of Congress Catalog Number: 2002073265

Library of Congress Cataloging-in-Publication Data

Drucker, Peter Ferdinand, 1909-
    A functioning society : selections from sixty-five years of writing on community, society, and polity / Peter F. Drucker ; chosen and edited by the author.
        p. cm.
    Includes bibliographical references and index.
    ISBN 0-7658-0159-0 (alk. paper)
    1. Community. 2. Social institutions. 3. State, The. 4. Organization. 5. Social change. 6. Information society. I. Title: Community, society, and polity. II. Title.

HM756 .D78 2003
307—dc21

                                                        2002073265

ISBN 13: 978-1-4128-1845-2 (pbk)
ISBN 13: 978-0-7658-0159-3 (hbk)

Contents

Introduction

Community, Society, Polity

I am best known, especially in The United States, as a writer on management. But management was neither my first nor has it been my foremost concern. I only became interested in it because of my work on community and society.

More of my books deal actually with community, society, and polity than deal with management. And even of my fifteen management books only two are "business" books: my 1964 book *Managing for Results*—the first book to deal with what a few years later became known as "strategy"—and my 1985 book *Innovation and Entrepreneurship*. All my other management books deal with the corporation as *human effort* and as *social institution*—the titles of the two main parts of my first book on the corporation, my 1946 book *Concept of the Corporation* (an excerpt from which can be found in part 5 of this volume).

My interest in, and concern for, community, society, and polity, goes back a very long time, all the way back to 1927 and 1928. Having finished high school (*Gymnasium*) in 1927 in my native Vienna, I went to Hamburg in Germany as a trainee in an export firm, enrolling at the same time in the local university's law faculty. Work in the firm began at 7 and ended at 3 or 3:30; and it was neither stimulating nor taxing, consisting mostly of copying invoices into a ledger book. The university offered very few classes after 4 P.M. My student pass entitled me to only one free ticket a week either at the municipal theater or at the municipal opera. And so I was free most afternoons and evenings to read in the excellent and multilingual public library.

Those fifteen or sixteen months in Hamburg—I left in early 1929—were my real education; I certainly learned a great deal more reading in the public library than I had learned in twelve years of school, or was going to learn in several university years.

I read voraciously, without plan or direction. But I found myself gravitating increasingly to books on political and social theory and policy. And two of the hundreds of books I devoured in those months permanently changed my life. They were Edmund Burke's 1790 *Reflections on the French Revolution* and the 1887 German sociological classic *Gemeinschaft und Gesellschaft (Community and Society)* by Ferdinand Toennies.

That Germany, and indeed all of Continental Europe, had been in a revolutionary period ever since World War I and the Russian Revolution, every one of us younger people *knew*—only people who had grown to adulthood before 1914 thought possibly a return to "prewar" and actually wanted it. And so Burke's main thesis: that to find in such a period the balance between *continuity* and *change* is the first task of politics and politicians, immediately resonated with this eighteen-year-old reader, 140 years after the book had been written. It immediately became central to my own politics, to my own world-view and to all my later work.

Equally great was the impact of Toennies' book. He himself was still alive although already retired (he died in 1936, eighty-one years old). But the book itself was, of course, forty years old. And it was obvious even to a totally ignorant eighteen year old that the "organic" community which Toennies hoped to save with his book— the rural community of pre-industrial days—was gone for good beyond any hope of renewal.

As my own work on community and society evolved over the next few years, my concepts of both became very different from Toennies' pre-industrial and indeed, pre-capitalist views with their roots in eighteenth-century German romanticism. But what I learned from Toennies—and never forgot—is the need for both, a community in which the individual has status, and a society in which the individual has function.

A few years later, in 1931-32, I found myself in Frankfurt, a senior writer at a major daily paper. But by that time I had also acquired a doctorate in international law and political theory, had become a post doc assistant in the seminars on international law and in jurisprudence, and was preparing for my *Habilation* at the university—the (unpaid) lectureship that was (and still is) the first step up the Continental-European academic ladder. In fact, the outline of my *Habilitations Schrift* (thesis) had already been accepted by the appropriate committee at the university. It was to deal with the origins of the *Rechtsstaat* ("state under the law" is the nearest English translation) and with the three German political thinkers who created it between 1800 and 1850 and who thereby laid the foundations on which Bismarck, then, in 1871, built a unified Germany and designed its unique constitution. Primarily a book on the history of ideas, its main theme was the balance between continuity and change which these men achieved—each in his own and very different way—the balance between a still pre-industrial, rural and solidly monarchical eighteenth-century society and polity and the world created by the French Revolution, the Napoleonic Wars, urbanization, capitalism, and the Industrial Revolution—a balance which France, for instance, never achieved until a hundred years later, under de Gaulle.

The only part of this project that was ever finished, was a short essay on the last of these three men, Friedrich Julius Stahl (1804-1861). I only published it because Stahl, for thirty years the leader of Prussia's Conservatives, was a (baptized) Jew—with a role, by the way not too dissimilar from that of Disraeli, another baptized Jew, in Queen Victoria's England. And an essay on the Jew, Stahl, as the great Conservative, was meant by me to be a direct attack on the Nazis—and to my delight fully understood by them as such. Written in the summer of 1932 it was accepted for publication in December of that year by Germany's most prestigious publisher of political theory, sociology and law, Mohr (in Tübingen). It was published in April 1933—two months after Hitler had come to power—as no. 100 in the highly prestigious series *Recht und Staat in Geschichte und Gegenwart* (Law and Government in History and in the Present). It was immediately banned by the Nazis and all copies ordered to be destroyed.

It has not been republished since, until last summer when *Society* magazine in its July/August 2002 issue published an English translation under the title "Conservative Theory of the State and Historical Development."

With the Nazis coming to power there was of course no more continuity—and so I abandoned that book.

Instead I started work on a book to explain the rise of totalitarianism, that is on the total collapse of European society. This became my first published book, *The End of Economic Man*, brought out in the U.K. in the last weeks of 1938 and in the U.S. in the first weeks of 1939 (with excerpts from it to be found in part II of this volume).

The End of Economic Man reached the conclusion that totalitarianism—whether Communist, Nazism, or Mussolini's Fascism—was
certain to fail—a conclusion by no means generally accepted in those
days. But this conclusion then led me to ask: what will, what can
take the place of the "organic" community of Toennies' rural society? What can again integrate individual, community and society in
an Industrial Age? This is the theme of my second book *The Future
of Industrial Man*, written in 1940 and 1941 with Europe already at
war (and with the U.S. inching toward war day by day)—and published in early 1942. (Excerpts from it are the prologue and part 1 of
this volume). In working on this book I began to realize that totally
new—indeed unprecedented—social institutions were rapidly evolv-
ing, totally new and unprecedented power centers within industrial
society and nation-state. The first—and the most visible one—was
the business corporation, invented—without any real antecedents—
around 1860 or 1870. I began to see that management is a new
social function and that it is the generic function of this new institution. This led to my third book *Concept of the Corporation* (written
in 1943 and 1944 and published in early 1946, a few months after
World War II had ended with Japan's surrender). (A short excerpt
from it can be found in part 5 of this volume.) Within a few years I
then realized that the business corporation was only the earliest of
these new organizations, within industrial society—each an autonomous power center in its own right—so that society was becoming a
Society of Organizations (the title of chapter 11 of this volume).

And I also began to realize that each of these new organizations,
unlike any earlier power center, was based on knowledge and that,
as a result society and economy were rapidly becoming knowledge
society and knowledge economy, with knowledge workers the center of population and work force—excerpts from my writings on
these topics can be found in parts 4 and 6 of this volume. And since
Concept of the Corporation I have alternated between books on
community, society, and polity, and books on management for over
fifty years.

In selecting the excerpts for *A Functioning Society*, I have not
tried to be chronological but topical. The excerpts themselves were
picked because each seemed to me to represent a basic theme. I
have abridged; but I have not changed the text, not added to it, not
updated it. Each chapter is clearly dated; the reader will therefore
know that a reference to "three years ago" in a chapter originally

published in 1957 refers to 1954. And I have looked for texts that not only inform but that are also easy, if not a pleasure, to read.

Peter F. Drucker
Claremont California
Summer 2002

Acknowledgements

The impetus for this book came from my friend and editor, Professor Irving Louis Horowitz, distinguished sociologist and historian of ideas, chairman and editorial director of Transaction Publishers, and publisher/editor of *Society* magazine. He has urged me for years to select and edit an anthology of my works on community, society, and polity. And he has helped greatly both, in selecting and in editing the excerpts printed in this volume. My readers and I owe Professor Horowitz profound thanks.

But thanks are due also to my long-time Japanese editor and translator, Professor Atsuo Ueda. Quite independently he conceived in 1998 the idea of selecting and editing a three-volume *Essential Drucker*—volume one on "The Individual," volume two on "Management," volume three on "Society." This three-volume edition was published in Japanese in the year 2000. It has since also been published (in the respective languages) in Korea, Taiwan; Mainland China; Argentina; Mexico and Spain; and in Brazil. A one-volume *The Essential Drucker on Management*—using the excerpts which Professor Ueda had originally picked for the second volume of the Japanese edition—was published in English in the U.S. and the U.K. in the year 2001, and has since been published in translations in the Scandinavian countries, in Holland, in Poland, in the Czech Republic; in German, in France, and in Italy.

This present volume uses a few—a very few—of Professor Ueda's selections—and they are edited quite differently. But most selections were picked for this volume only. They are chosen expressly for an American audience and edited for it.

Prologue

What is a Functioning Society?
(from *The Future of Industrial Man*, 1942)

Man in his social and political existence must have a functioning society just as he must have air to breathe in his biological existence. However, the fact that man has to have a society does not necessarily mean that he has it. Nobody calls the mass of unorganized, panicky, stampeding humanity in a shipwreck a "society." There is no society, though there are human beings in a group. Actually, the panic is directly due to the breakdown of a society; and the only way to overcome it is by restoring a society with social values, social discipline, social power, and social organization.

Social life cannot function without a society; but it is conceivable that it does not function at all. The evidence of the last twenty-five years of Western civilization hardly entitles us to say that our social life functioned so well as to make out a prima-facie case for the existence of a functioning society.

It is not true that a society must grow out of the material reality around it. There can be a social organization of a physical reality on the basis of values, disciplines, ideals, conventions and powers which belong completely to another social reality. Take, for instance, Robinson Crusoe and his man Friday. Undoubtedly they had a society. Nothing is more ridiculous than the traditional view of Robinson as the isolated individualist Economic Man. He had social values, conventions, taboos, powers. His society was not one developed according to the demands of life on a subtropical islet in the southern Pacific Ocean, but basically that of Calvinist Scotsmen developed on the cold shores of the North Atlantic. What is so marvelous in Robinson Crusoe is not the extent to which he adapted himself, but the almost complete absence of adaptation. Had he been of a different class and a different time, he would surely have dressed for dinner in the evening. Here we have a case where a successful social life was built on the values and concepts of a society quite different in its physical reality and problems from those to which it was adapted.

A society may be based on concepts and beliefs developed to organize a specific physical reality. Or it may rest on foundations as alien to its surroundings as were those of Robinson Crusoe's society to San Juan Fernandez. But it must always be capable of organizing the actual reality in a social order. It must master the material world, make it meaningful and comprehensible for the individual; and it must establish legitimate social and political power.

The reality of the industrial system, though it grew out of the mercantile society and the market, was from the start different from, and often incompatible with, the basic assumptions on which the mercantile society rested. Yet during the entire nineteenth century the mercantile society succeeded in mastering, organizing, integrating the growing industrial reality. There was tension even in the early years. The history of the conflict between mercantile assumptions and industrial reality, between Jeffersonian policies and Hamiltonian facts, between the market and the system of industrial production is very largely the social history of the hundred years before the First World War. During the closing years of the last century it became increasingly clear that the mercantile society was disintegrating, and that the industrial system was getting out of hand socially. But it was not until after 1918—maybe not until after 1929—that the mercantile society broke down. By now, however, it has ceased to be a functioning society.

To define what a society is, is just as impossible as to define life. We are so close to it that the basic simple characteristics disappear behind a bewildering and complex mass of details. We are also so much a part of it that we cannot possibly see the whole. And finally, there is no sharp line, no point where nonlife turns definitely into life, nonsociety definitely into society. But, although we do not know what life is, all of us know when a living body ceases to be a living body and becomes a corpse. We know that the human body cannot function as a living body if the heart has ceased to beat or the lungs stopped breathing. As long as there is a heartbeat or a breath, there is a live body; without them there is only a corpse. Similarly the impossibility of a normative definition of society does not prevent us from understanding society functionally. No society can function as a society unless it gives the individual member social status and function, and unless the decisive social power is legitimate power. The former establishes the basic frame of social life: the purpose and meaning of society. The latter shapes the space within the frame: it makes society concrete and creates its institutions. If the individual is not given social status and function, there can be no society but only a mass of social atoms flying through space without aim or purpose. And unless power is legitimate there can be no social fabric; there is only a social vacuum held together by mere slavery or inertia.

It is only natural to ask which of these criteria is more important or which of these principles of social life comes first. This question is as old as political thinking itself. It was the basis for the first sharp cleavage in political theory, that between Plato and Aristotle, between the priority of the purpose of society and that of its institutional organization. But though hallowed by antiquity and great names, it is a meaningless question. There can be no question of primacy—neither in time nor in importance—between basic political concepts and basic political institutions. Indeed, it is the very essence of political thought and action that they have always one pole in the conceptual realm of beliefs, aims, desires, and values, and one in the pragmatic realm of facts, institutions, and organizations. The one without the other is not politics. The exclusively conceptual may be sound philosophy or sound ethics; the exclusively pragmatic, sound anthropology or sound journalism. Alone, neither of them can make sound politics or, indeed, politics at all.

Social status and function of the individual is the equation of the relationship between the group and the individual member. It symbolizes the integration of the individual with the group, and that of the group with the individual. It expresses the individual purpose in terms of the society, and the social purpose in terms of the individual. It thus makes comprehensible and rational individual existence from the point of the group, and group existence from that of the individual.

For the individual there is no society unless he has social status and function. Society is only meaningful if its purpose, its aims, its ideas and ideals make sense in terms of the individual's purposes, aims, ideas and ideals. There must be a definite functional relationship between individual life and group life.

This relationship might lie in an identity of purpose under which there would be no individual life other than social life, and under which the individual would have none but social aims. This was basically the position of the great Greek political philosophers, especially of Plato; and the Socratic attack against the Sophists was largely directed against an "individualist" concept of personality. The "polis" of the Socratic school is absolutely collectivist in the sense that there is no possibility of distinction between group purpose and individual purpose, group virtue and individual virtue, group life and individual life. But it is just as possible to assume no group purpose and no social life except in individual purpose and individual life—the position of the extreme, early-nineteenth-century individualists.

There need not even be an assumption of identity between individual and social purposes. Indeed, one of the most rigid of all theories of functional relationship between group and individual is the class-war theory of the Marxists, which assumes a permanent conspiracy of the propertied minority against the property-less majority. Organized society in the Marxist pattern is the instrument of oppression. And to this assumption of conflict, Marxism—otherwise discredited and disproved—owed its appeal during the Depression years; it alone seemed able to explain rationally what was happening at a time when the traditional theories of harmony between individual and social purposes could not make sense at all.

For the individual without function and status, society is irrational, incalculable and shapeless. The "rootless" individual, the outcast—for absence of social function and status casts a man from the society of his fellows—sees no society. He sees only demonic forces, half sensible, half meaningless, half in light and half in darkness, but never predictable. They decide about his life and his livelihood without possibility of interference on his part, indeed without possibility of his understanding them. He is like a blindfolded man in a strange room, playing a game of which he does not know the rules; and the prize at stake is his own happiness, his own livelihood, and even his own life. That the individual should have social status and function is just as important for society as for him. Unless the purpose, aims, actions and motives of the individual member of integrated with the purpose, aims, actions and motives of society, society cannot understand or contain him. The asocial, uprooted, unintegrated individual appears not only as irrational but as a danger; he is a disintegrating, a threatening, a mysteriously shadowy force. It is no coincidence that so many of the great myths—the Wandering Jew, Dr. Faustus, Don Juan—are myths of the individual who has lost or repudiated social function and status. Lack of social status and function, and absence of a functional relationship between society and individual are at the bottom of every persecution of minorities which either are without social status and function—that is, not integrated into society (like the Negro in America)—or are made the scapegoat for the lack of integration in society (like the Jew in Nazi Germany).

That the individual must have definite social status in society does not mean that he must have a *fixed* social status. To identify "definite" with "frozen" was the great mistake of the early-nineteenth-century Liberals such as Bentham. It was a tragic misunderstanding as it led to a social atomism which repudiated social values altogether. Of course, a society may have fixed status and function to the individual. The Hindu caste system is the expression of a definite functional relationship between the group and the individual, integrating them in a religious purpose. It obtains its rationality from the religious doctrine of perpetual rebirth until complete purification. On that basis even the Untouchables have a social status and function which make society and their individual life in it meaningful to them, and their life meaningful and indeed necessary to society. It is only when this religious creed itself disintegrates that the Hindu social system loses its rationality for both, individual and society.

On the other hand, in the society of the American frontier with its complete fluidity, the individual had just as much definite social status and function as the untouchable or the Brahmin in the Hindu society with its absolutely rigid castes. It may even be said that no society ever succeeded as perfectly in integrating its members in a functional relationship between individual and group as the frontier of Jackson, Henry Clay, or Lincoln. What counts is that the status is definite, functionally understandable and purposefully rational, and not whether it is fixed, flexible or fluid. To say that every boy has an equal chance to become president is just as much a definition of a functional relationship between group and individual as to say that the individual is born only that he may try to escape being reborn in the same caste.

It will be clear from the foregoing that the type and form of the functional relationship between society and individual in any given society depends upon the basic belief of this society regarding the nature and fulfillment of man. The nature of man may be seen as free or unfree, equal or unequal, good or evil, perfect, perfectible or imperfect. The fulfillment may be seen in this world or in the next; in immortality or in the final extinction of the individual soul which the religions of the East preach; in peace or in war; in economic success or in a large family. The belief regarding the nature of man determines the purpose of society; the belief regarding this fulfillment, the sphere in which realization of the purpose is sought.

Any one of these basic beliefs about the nature and fulfillment of man will lead to a different society and a different basic functional relationship between society and the individual. Which of these beliefs is the right one, which is true or false, good or evil, Christian or anti-Christian, does not occupy us here. The point is that any one of these beliefs can be the basis for a working and workable society; that is, for one in which the individual has social status and function. And conversely, any society, regardless of the nature of its basic beliefs, can work only as long as it gives the individual a social status and function.

Legitimate power stems from the same basic belief of society regarding man's nature and fulfillment on which the individual's social status and function rest. Indeed, legitimate power can be defined as rulership which finds its justification in the basic ethos of the society. In every society there are many powers which have nothing to do with such a basic principle, and institutions which in no way are either designed or devoted to its fulfillment. In other words, there are always a great many "unfree" institutions in a free society, a great many inequalities in an equal society, and a great many sinners among the saints. But as long as that decisive social power which we call rulership is based upon the claim of freedom, equality or saintliness, and is exercised through institutions which are designed toward the fulfillment of these ideal purposes, society can function as a free, equal or saintly society. For its institutional structure is one of legitimate power.

This does not mean that it is immaterial whether non-decisive powers and institutions of a society are in contradiction to its basic principles. On the contrary, the most serious problems of politics arise from such conflicts. And a society may well feel that a nondecisive institution or power relationship is in such blatant contrast to its basic beliefs as to endanger social life in spite of its nondecisive character. The best case in point is that of the American Civil War when the chattel-slavery of the South was felt to endanger the whole structure of a free society. Yet the decisive power of antebellum America was undoubtedly legitimate power deriving its claim from the principle of freedom, and exercised through institutions designed and devoted to the realization of freedom. American society did thus function as a free society. It was indeed only because it functioned as such that it felt slavery as a threat.

What is the decisive power, and the decisive institutional organization in any society cannot be determined by statistical analysis.

Nothing could be more futile than to measure a society by counting noses, quoting tax receipts or comparing income levels. Decisive is a political, and that means a purely qualitative, term. The English landed gentry comprised never more than a small fraction of the population; furthermore, after the rise of the merchants and manufacturers it had only a very modest share of the national wealth and income. Nevertheless, down to our times it held the decisive social power. Its institutions were the decisive institutions of English society. Its beliefs were the basis for social life; its standards the representative standards; its way of life the social pattern. And its personality ideal, the gentleman, remained the ideal type of all society. Its power was not only decisive; it was legitimate power.

Equally, laws and constitutions will rarely, if ever, tell us where the decisive power lies. In other words, rulership is not identical with political government. Rulership is a social, political government largely a legal category. The Prussian Army between 1870 and 1914 was, for instance, hardly as much as mentioned in the Imperial German Constitution; yet it undoubtedly held decisive power and probably legitimately. The government was actually subordinated to the army, in spite of a civilian and usually antimilitaristic Parliament.

Another example is that of British "indirect rule" in certain African colonies. There the socially decisive power is within the tribes. At least in theory the government of the white man wields no social power at all; it confines itself to mere police matters designed to support and to maintain the social organization of the tribes within a loose and purely normative framework of "law and order." Yet, constitutionally, the governor and his council have absolute power.

Finally, it should be understood that legitimacy is a purely functional concept. There is no absolute legitimacy. Power can be legitimate only in relation to a basic social belief. What constitutes "legitimacy" is a question that must be answered in terms of a given society and its given political beliefs. Legitimate is a power when it is justified by an ethical or metaphysical principle that has been accepted by the society. Whether this principle is good or bad ethically, true or false metaphysically, has nothing to do with legitimacy, which is as indifferent ethically and metaphysically as any other formal criterion. Legitimate power is socially functioning power; but why it functions and to what purpose is a question entirely outside and before legitimacy.

Failure to understand this was responsible for the confusion which made "legitimism" the name of a political creed in the early-nineteenth century. The European reactionaries of 1815 were, of course, absolutely within their rights when they taught that no society could be *good* except under an absolute monarch; to have an opinion on what is desirable or just as basis of a society is not only a right, it is a duty, of man. But they were simply confusing ethical choice with functional analysis, when they said that no society could *function* unless it had an absolute monarch. And they were provably wrong when they proclaimed the dogma that only absolute monarchy was *legitimate*. Actually, after the Napoleonic Wars, absolute monarchy was illegitimate in Europe; the dynastic principle had ceased to be a legitimate claim to decisive power. The revolutionary half century before 1815 had resulted in a change in basic beliefs which made illegitimate any but constitutionally limited government. This change may have been desirable or deplorable; but it was a fact. The Legitimists might have tried to make undone this change in beliefs. They might have maintained that it would be better for the individual and for society to have an illegitimate absolute rule than a legitimate constitutional one. Or they might have invoked a "right of resistance," of secession or of revolution. The only basis on which their claim could not be based politically was that of legitimacy.

The functional analysis as to what is legitimate power does not in any way prejudge the ethical question of the individual's right or duty to resist what he considers pernicious power. Whether it is better that society perish than that justice perish is a question outside and before functional analysis. The same man who maintains most vigorously that society can function only under a legitimate power may well decide that society is less of a value than certain individual rights or beliefs. But he cannot decide, as the Legitimists did, that his values and beliefs *are* the socially accepted values and beliefs because they *ought* to be.

Illegitimate power is a power which does not derive its claim from the basic beliefs of the society. Accordingly, there is no possibility to decide whether the ruler wielding the power is exercising it in conformity with the purpose of power or not; for there is no social purpose. Illegitimate power cannot be controlled; it is by its nature uncontrollable. It cannot be made responsible since there is no criterion of responsibility, no socially accepted final authority for its justification. And what is unjustifiable cannot be responsible.

For the same reason, it cannot be limited. To limit the exercise of power is to fix the lines beyond which power ceases to be legitimate; that is, ceases to realize the basic social purpose. And if power is not legitimate to begin with, there are no limits beyond which it ceases to be legitimate.

No illegitimate ruler can possibly be a good or wise ruler. Illegitimate power invariable corrupts; for it can be only "might," never authority. It cannot be a controlled, limited, responsible, or rationally determinable power. And it has been an axiom of politics— ever since Tacitus in his history of the Roman emperors gave us one case study after another—that no human being, however good, wise or judicious, can wield uncontrolled, irresponsible, unlimited or rationally not determinable power without becoming very soon arbitrary, cruel, inhuman and capricious—in other words, a tyrant.

For all these reasons a society in which the socially decisive power is illegitimate power cannot function as a society. It can only be held together by sheer brute force—tyranny, slavery, civil war. Of course, force is the ultimate safeguard of every power; but in a functioning society it is not more than a desperate remedy for exceptional and rare diseases. In a functioning society power is exercised as authority, and *authority is the rule of right over might.* But only a legitimate power can have authority and can expect and command that social self-discipline which alone makes organized institutional life possible. Illegitimate power, even if wielded by the best and the wisest, can never depend upon anything but the submission to force. On that basis a functioning, institutional organization of social life cannot be built. Even the best tyrant is still a tyrant.

Part 1

Foundations

Introduction to Part 1

The Future of Industrial Man (1942) was my second book. But it was the first one conceived and written in its entirety in the U.S., that is, after I had come to New York from London in early 1937 as American feature writer for a group of British newspapers. The book's predecessor, *The End of Economic Man* (excerpted in part 2 of this volume), was published in the U.K. in late fall 1938 and in the U.S. in early spring 1939. But it was only finished in the U.S. Most of it had already been written before I left Europe. In fact, an excerpt (predicting Hitler's "Final Solution," that is, the extermination of the Jews) was actually published in 1936 in an Austrian Catholic, anti-Nazi magazine.

The American economy in 1937 was in deep depression—far deeper than the economy of the England I had left. But what immediately struck me—it was a profound shock—was the vibrant health of American society. Today, more than sixty years later, the New Deal is often condemned for doing absolutely nothing to revive the American economy. In fact, the U.S. economy was in worse shape in 1937 than it had been in 1932 before Franklin D. Roosevelt had taken over. It seems inconceivable today with our slogan "It's the Economy, Stupid." But the New Deal consciously, deliberately, publicly put "reform," that is, society, ahead of "recovery," that is, the economy. That was indeed the Republicans' complaint and their criticism of the New Deal. But the voters overwhelmingly approved, again and again.

In respect to the economy, the U.S. looked backwards as much as did Europe. "Pre-Depression" was the measure of all things economic. But society in the U.S. looked forward—and by no means only (or even primarily) in terms of government action. Every American college, even the smallest "cow college," was engaged in educational reform and educational experimentation—ranging all the way from the return to the Medieval Trivium preached by Mortimer Adler at the University of Chicago, to the abolition of all disciplines

3

in favor of "doing one's own thing" preached with equal fervor and equal fanfare in such places as Black Mountain College. Reinhold Niebuhr and Paul Tillich galvanized the Protestant churches, Jacques Maritain and the Neo-Thomists, the Catholic ones. A few pioneers—Massachusetts General in Boston, Presbyterian and Mt. Sinai in New York—were converting the hospital from a place for the poor to die into a science-based place to diagnose and heal. Every museum was reforming itself with New York's Museum of Modern Art in the lead. And even quite small cities—Palo Alto in California, for instance—were forming their own symphony orchestras. Economically the U.S. was in a deep depression. Socially it experienced a veritable renaissance.

This then raised the question in my mind to which *The Future of Industrial Man* addresses itself: What is a functioning society? And what are the institutions that could recreate the community the collapse of which in Europe had produced totalitarianism? *The Future of Industrial Man* did not answer these questions—I am still asking them. But it laid the foundations for all my work since then on community, society, and polity.

1

From Rousseau to Hitler

(From *The Future of Industrial Man*, 1942)

It is almost an axiom in contemporary political and historical literature that our freedom has its roots in the Enlightenment and the French Revolution. So general is this belief, so complete its acceptance, that the descendants of the eighteenth-century rationalists have preempted for themselves the very name of Liberty in their designation as Liberals.

It cannot be denied that the Enlightenment and the French Revolution contributed to the freedom of the nineteenth century. But their contribution was entirely negative; they were the dynamite that blew away the debris of the old structure. In no way, however, did they contribute to the foundation of the new structure of freedom on which the nineteenth-century order was built. On the contrary: The Enlightenment, the French Revolution, and their successors down to the rationalist Liberalism of our days are in irreconcilable opposition to freedom. Fundamentally, rationalist Liberalism is totalitarian.

And every totalitarian movement during the last two hundred years of Western history has grown out of the Liberalism of its time. There is a straight line from Rousseau to Hitler—a line that takes in Robespierre, Marx, and Stalin. All of them grew out of the failure of the rationalist Liberalism of their times. They all retained the essence of their respective liberal creeds, and all used the same mechanism to convert the latent and ineffective totalitarianism of the rationalist into the open and effective totalitarianism of the revolutionary despot. Far from being the roots of freedom, the Enlightenment and the French Revolution were the seeds of the totalitarian despotism which threatens the world today. The fathers and grandfathers of Hitlerism are not medieval feudalism or nineteenth-century romanticism but

5

Bentham and Condorcet, the orthodox economists, and the liberal constitutionalists, Darwin, Freud, and the Behaviorists.

The great discovery of the Enlightenment was that human reason is absolute. On this discovery were based not only all subsequent liberal creeds but also all subsequent totalitarian creeds from Rousseau on. It was no accident that Robespierre installed a Goddess of Reason; his symbolism was cruder than that of the later revolutionaries but not really very different. Nor was it an accident that the French Revolution chose a living person to act the role of Goddess of Reason. The whole point of the rationalist philosophy is that it attributes to actual living men the perfection of absolute reason. The symbols and slogans have changed. Where the "scientific philosopher" was supreme in 1750, it was the sociologist with his economic utilitarianism and the "pleasure-pain calculus" a hundred years later. Today it is the "scientific psycho-biologist" with his determinism of race and propaganda. But we fight today basically the same totalitarian absolutism that first was formulated by the Enlighteners and Encyclopedists—the rationalists of 1750—and that first led to a revolutionary tyranny in the Terror of 1793.

It must be understood that not everything that is called liberalism is of necessity an absolutist creed. Every liberal movement, it is true, contains the seeds of a totalitarian philosophy—just as every conservative movement contains a tendency to become reactionary. On the continent of Europe there never were any liberal movements or parties which were not totalitarian in their fundamental beliefs. In the United States the totalitarian element was strongly represented from the start—based as much upon the influence from Europe as upon the Puritan tradition. And since the last war liberalism everywhere has become absolutist. Today it is true, almost without reservation, that the liberal is an absolutist in his objective creed.

But for a hundred years before 1914 Great Britain had a liberal movement that was not absolutist, not incompatible with freedom and not based upon a man-made absolute reason. The United States had during the same period a liberal tradition which was as much opposed to absolutist liberalism as it was close to English liberalism. This free and antitotalitarian tradition, which was expressed in its most lucid form by Mr. Justice Holmes, was usually not the dominant liberal tradition in America. It was often completely overshadowed by the absolutist liberalism of which the Abolitionists and the radical Republicans of the Reconstruction Period are the outstanding representatives. It produced, however, in Lincoln the nineteenth century's greatest symbol of an anti-absolutist and truly liberal liberalism. It became politically effective in Populism—the most indigenous American political movement since the early days of the republic. And the New Deal, though very largely dominated by rationalism, owed its appeal and political effectiveness to its populist heritage.

The fundamental difference between the free and constructive Anglo-American liberalism of the nineteenth century, and the absolutist and destructive liberalism of the Enlightenment and of our Liberals today, is that the first is based on religion and Christianity, while the second is rationalist. The true liberalism grew out of a religious renunciation of rationalism. The English Liberal party of the nineteenth century was based partly on the tradition of the settlement of 1688. But the main element was the "Nonconformist Conscience." The first was a reaffirmation of freedom against the rationalist absolutism of both, Cromwellian theocracy and centralized monarchy. The second sprang from the great religious revivals of the eighteenth century, notably Wesley's Methodism and Low Church Evangelism. Both were appeals to Christian love, faith, and humility. And both were directed against the rationalism of their time—Methodism against Enlightenment, the Evangelical movement against the utilitarianism of Bentham and the classical economists.

In the United States similarly the true and genuinely "liberal" liberalism traces back to a religious protest against rationalist absolutism. Its forefather, Roger Williams, attacked in the name of Christian freedom the rationalist theocracy of the New England divines who had set up their scripture learning as absolute reason. And the Populist movement—whatever its economic causes—rested squarely upon an evangelical protest against rationalist utilitarianism and orthodox economists. It was an invocation of the dignity of man against the tyranny of absolute reason and of "inevitable economic progress."

That objectively the rationalist's creed is incompatible with freedom is no denial of the individual rationalist's or liberal's good will or good faith. Doubtless the individual rationalist liberal believes sincerely that he, and he alone, stands for freedom and against tyranny. There is also no doubt that he subjectively abhors totalitarian tyranny and all it represents. And in turn, he is the first victim of the despots.

But these antitotalitarian sentiments of the individual rationalist are entirely ineffective in politics. Altogether rationalism is incapable of positive political action. It can function only in opposition. It can never make the step from negative critique to constructive policy. And it always opposes the free institutions of society fully as much as the unfree and oppressive ones.

The rationalist liberal sees his function in the opposition to the injustices, superstitions and prejudices of his time. But this opposition to injustice is only a part of a general hostility to all institutions of society including free and just ones. The Enlighteners, for instance, swept away aristocratic privileges, serfdom and religious intolerance. They also destroyed provincial autonomies and local self-government; and no country on the continent of Europe has ever fully recovered from this blow to freedom. They attacked clerical abuses, privileges, and oppression. They also degraded the churches of Europe into administrative arms of the political government. They did their best to deprive religious life of its social autonomy and moral authority. And the full force of Enlightened scorn was directed against independent courts and against the common law. The insistence of the eighteenth-century rationalist on a "rationally perfect" law code and on state-controlled courts leads straight to the omnipotent total state. It is no accident that the "free" Anglo-American liberalism of the nineteenth century was based to a large extent on these very institutions which the Enlighteners had repudiated: local self-government, free autonomous churches, the common law, and an independent judiciary.

The rationalist not only destroys and opposes existing institutions; he is completely incapable of developing new institutions for the old ones which he destroys. He does not even see the need for constructive activity. For to him the good is only the absence of evil. He thinks that he has done his job if he has criticized away bad or oppressive institutions. But in political and social life nothing is effective unless it is given institutional realization. Society must be organized on the basis of functional power-relations. To subvert is only legitimate in politics if it leads to the construction of something better. But just to sweep away something—however bad—is no solution. And unless a functioning institution is put into the place of the destroyed institution, the ensuing collapse of social life will breed evils which may be even worse than the one that was originally destroyed.

Wherever the rationalist liberal has come to power, he always failed. The fate of Kerenski's Liberal government in Russia, which collapsed into Bolshevism after half a year of political paralysis, is only the most obvious case. The German Social Democrats were equally incapable of political action when they came to power in 1918. They had been an extremely useful opposition under the Kaiser. There is no doubt that their leaders were sincere and honorable, that they were capable administrators, personally courageous and popular. Yet what is amazing is not that they failed but that they lasted as long as they did. For by 1922 or 1923 they had become completely bankrupt. The same is true of French Radicals, of Italian Liberals, or of Spanish Democrats. And the "reformer" in the United States also normally ended in frustration. The history of every city government in America shows the political ineffectiveness of these well-meaning rationalists.

It is impossible to explain so extraordinary and consistent a record of failure as one of circumstances and accidents. The real reason is that rationalist liberalism is by its very nature condemned to political sterility. It lives in constant conflict with itself. It is based on two principles which exclude each other. It can only deny but it cannot act.

On the one hand the rationalist believes in an absolute reason. Yesterday it was inevitable progress or national harmony between individual self-interest and the common weal. Today it is the creed that libido, frustration, and glands explain all personal or group conflicts. On the other hand rationalist liberalism believes that its absolutes are the result of rational deduction, are provable and rationally incontrovertible. It is the essence of rationalist liberalism that it proclaims its absolutes to be rationally evident.

Absolute reason can, however, never be rational; it can never be proved or disproved by logic. Absolute reason is by its very nature above and before rational argument. Logical deduction can and must be based upon an absolute reason but can never prove it. If truly religious, an absolute principle is superrational—a true metaphysical principle which gives a valid basis of rational logic. If man-made and man-proclaimed, absolute reason must be irrational and in insoluble conflict with rational logic and rational means.

All the basic dogmas of rationalism during the last hundred and fifty years were not only irrational but basically antirational. This was true of the philosophical rationalism of the Enlighteners who proclaimed the inherent reasonableness of man. It was true of the utilitarian rationalism of the generation of 1848 which saw in the individual's greed the mechanism through which the "invisible hand" of nature promoted the common good. It is particularly true of the twentieth-century rationalism which sees man as psychologically and biologically determined. Every one of these principles denies not only free will. It denies human reason. And every one of the these principles can be translated into political action only by force and by an absolute ruler.

But this the rationalist cannot admit. He must maintain that his principles are rational and that they can be made effective by rational means. He maintains as a dogma that his principles are rationally evident. Hence the rationalist liberal cannot attempt to translate them into political action except through rational conversion—which attempt must fail. On the one had he cannot respect any opposition, for it can only be opposition to absolute truth. On the other hand, he cannot fight it. For error—and all opposition to his absolute truth must be error to a rationalist—can only be due to lack of information. Nothing shows this better than the saying current during the twenties and early thirties in Europe as well as in the United States that an *intelligent* person must be on the Left. And today the belief in the omnipotence of propaganda expresses openly and clearly the absolutist basis and the self-contradiction of the rationalist creed.

On the one hand, the rationalist liberal cannot compromise. His is a perfectionist creed which allows of no concession. Anyone who refuses to see the light is an unmitigated blackguard with whom political relations are impossible. On the other hand, the rationalist cannot fight or suppress enemies. He cannot admit their existence. There can be only misjudged or misinformed people who, of necessity, will see reason when the incontrovertible evidence of the rational truth is presented to them. The rationalist liberal is caught between holy wrath at conspirators and educational zeal for the misinformed. He always knows what is right, necessary, and good—and it always is simple and easy. But he can never do it. For he can neither compromise for power nor fight for it. He is always paralyzed politically: ultra-bold in theory and timid in action, strong in opposition and helpless in power, right on paper but incapable in politics.

It is the tragedy of the rationalist liberal that there is only one way from his position to political effectiveness: totalitarianism. His subjectively sincere belief in freedom can objectively lead only to tyranny. For there is only one way out of the political sterility of the rationalist liberal: to drop the rationalism and to become openly to-talitarian, absolutist and revolutionary.

During the Enlightenment it was Rousseau who made the fatal step from rationalism and pretended rationality to openly irrational and antirational totalitarianism. There is no pretense that the "general will" is rationally ascertainable or rationally realizable. It is admittedly an irrational absolute which defies rational analysis and which is outside and beyond rational comprehension. It exists—but how, where and why no one knows. It must prevail—naturally, since it is perfect and absolute. Whoever is in possession of reason, whoever understands the supreme will of society, is entitled and, indeed, is duty bound to enforce it upon majority, minority and individual alike. Freedom lies only in the perfect realization of the *volunté générale*. There is no pretense in Rousseau of individual reason or individual freedom.

It is true that Rousseau insisted upon the small unit of the city-state with its direct, nonrepresentative democracy as the only perfect form of government. And he laid down an inalienable right of the individual to disagree by leaving his society. This has been taken as an indication of his desire for individual freedom. But in a world in which these conditions were as impossible of fulfillment as in that of the middle-eighteenth century, they can hardly be taken as anything but romantic flourishes in an otherwise unyieldingly realistic and unromantic totalitarianism. Otherwise Hitler's "offer" of emigration to the Jews would also be "freedom."

Rousseau's plunge into the irrational absolute made the basic concepts of the Enlightenment politically effective. Rousseau was right when he saw in the repudiation of rationalism the basic difference of his system from that of the *philosophes*. His open irrationalism enabled him to shake off the fetters which had condemned the Encyclopedists to political ineffectiveness. Where they believed in the slow and painstaking rational process of education and scientific investigation, he believed in the inner light of revelation. They tried to define man as within the laws of physics. But Rousseau saw man as a political being acting upon impulse and emotion. Where they saw the gradual rationalist improvement, he believed in the millennium that could and would be established by that most irrational of forces: the revolution. No doubt he knew more about politics and society than all the Enlighteners taken together. His view of man in society was realistic where the rationalist Enlighteners had been hopelessly and pathetically romantic.

In fact, Rousseau can be fought only if his basis is attacked: the belief in a man-made absolute reason, the belief that he himself possessed it and that whoever has absolute reason has the right and the duty to enforce it.

Because Rousseau threw overboard the rationalism of the Enlightenment, he became the great political force he has been to our day. Because he retained the Enlighteners' belief in human perfectibility, he denied human freedom and became the great totalitarian and revolutionary who lit the fuse for a universal blaze equaled only by our generation.

Rousseau's method has been followed every time a politically sterile, because rationalist, liberalism was converted into a politically effective nonrationalist totalitarianism. The first to follow in his footsteps was Karl Marx. Just as Rousseau appeared when the Enlighteners of the early eighteenth century had shown their political ineffectiveness, so Marx began when the utilitarian rationalists of the early nineteenth century had foundered politically. In 1848 rationalist liberalism was bankrupt. It had had power thrust into its lap through the breakdown of reactionary monarchy in France, Austria, Germany, and Spain; and, without exception, it proved completely incapable of doing anything with it except lose it again.

Marx converted the impotent rationalist liberalism of his time into a politically potent force by dropping its rationalism and adopting an openly irrational absolutism. He kept the absolute of the contemporary liberals, the thesis of economic determination which sees man as rational Economic Man. But he eliminated the rationalism which expected the attainment of the perfect economic society from the free and rational economic action of the individual. Instead he proclaimed an irrational principle: that of the determination of human action by the class situation of the individual. This principle denies man's capacity for rational action, thinking, and analysis. Everybody's deeds and thoughts are the result of a class situation which is beyond the individual's control and understanding. Marx kept the utilitarian's historical materialism; but for the materialism of inevitable harmony he substituted that of the equally inevitable class struggle. He kept the rationalist belief in the essential perfection of man. But he confined perfection to the one proletarian class.

Marx went one step further than Rousseau. To Rousseau the revolution was necessary as it must indeed be to every totalitarian. But it was not inevitable. Rousseau left an element of doubt; Marx left none. In a truly apocalyptic vision he saw the inevitability of the revolution which would usher in the millennium. Rationally, the Marxist belief that the future will inevitably belong to the perfect classless society *because* all the past has been one of class societies is blatant, arrant, and mystical nonsense. Politically, the very antirationality of this article of faith was its strength. It not only gave belief; it also made possible the mastermind, the revolutionary philosopher-tyrant who, schooled in the dialectics of the inevitable, could claim absolute knowledge at every time.

Rousseau became a tremendous political force because the revolution did happen. Marx—though much inferior to Rousseau as a politician, a psychologist, and a philosopher—became a force of equal strength even though the revolution did not happen; it was sufficient that, unlike Rousseau's, Marx's revolution was inevitable.

But while Marxism failed as a revolutionary creed in the industrial countries, it made a lasting impact on political beliefs on the Continent of Europe. It prepared the great masses for totalitarianism. It made them ready to accept the logic of man-made, absolutist, apocalyptic visions. For this alone Marxism deserves to be called the father of Hitlerism. It also bequeathed to the totalitarianism of our time the mold and the structure of ideas and political thought. What Marx did with the broken-down rationalist liberalism of his time—the liberalism of the classical economists and of the utilitarians—Hitler has been doing with the broken-down rationalism of our time—that of the natural scientists and psychologists.

2

The Conservative Counter-Revolution of 1776

(from *The Future of Industrial Man*, 1942)

Just as popular and just as fallacious as the belief that the Enlightenment fathered nineteenth-century freedom is the belief that the American Revolution was based on the same principles as the French Revolution, and that it was actually its forerunner. Every history book in the United States or in Europe says so; and not a few of the chief actors both in the American and French Revolutions shared the belief. Yet it is a complete distortion of all facts.

The American Revolution was based on principles completely contrary to those of the Enlightenment and the French Revolution. In intention and effect it was a successful countermovement against the very rationalist despotism of the Enlightenment which provided the political foundation for the French Revolution. Though the French Revolution happened later in time, it had politically and philosophically been anticipated by the American Revolution. The conservatives of 1777 and 1787 fought and overcame the spirit of the French Revolution so that the American development actually represents a more advanced stage in history than the *Etats Généraux*, the Terror, and Napoleon. Far from being a revolt against the old tyranny of feudalism, the American Revolution was a conservative counterrevolution in the name of freedom against the new tyranny of rationalist liberalism and Enlightened Despotism.

The freedom of the Western world during the nineteenth century and up to this day has been based upon the ideas, principles, and institutions of the American conservative counterrevolution of 1776.

Actually, the American Revolution was as much a European as an American event. The Thirteen Colonies would sooner or later have become independent as one nation in the normal course of events. The best minds in England—especially Edmund Burke—fully realized that the Colonists had outgrown the old dependence. The American Revolution was only the concrete point at which the foreseeable and foreseen event of independence took place. Though in actual form it was as unique as any historical happening, the Revolution was a natural and logical development. There is a straight line from George Washington, the militia officer with his independent command in the French and Indian War, to George Washington, the Commander-in-Chief of the forces of the United States.

But as a European event the American Revolution was not foreseeable and foreseen. It reversed—first in England and then in the rest of Europe—a trend which had appeared to be inevitable, natural, and unchangeable. It defeated the rationalist liberals and their pupils, the Enlightened Despots, who had seemingly been irresistible and within an inch of complete and final victory. The American Revolution brought victory and power to a group which in Europe had been almost completely defeated and which was apparently dying out rapidly: the anticentralist, antitotalitarian conservatives with their hostility to absolute and centralized government and their distrust of any ruler claiming perfection.

It saved the autonomous common law from submersion under perfect law codes; and it re-established independent law courts. Above all, it reasserted the belief in the imperfection of man as the basis of freedom.

Had America not revolted against Enlightened Despotism there would hardly have been any freedom in the Europe of the nineteenth century. And the same would have been true if she had gone down before the armies of a rationalist and centralizing English king. There would hardly have been any effective English resistance against the French Revolution, and probably no national determination to fight it out with the aggressive totalitarianism of Napoleon. Above all, the justly celebrated English Constitution would not have survived to become for nineteenth-century Europe the symbol of freedom and of successful resistance against absolute tyranny.

That the thinly populated and remote American Colonies became independent was in itself of no great importance to the Western world of the late eighteenth and early nineteenth century. But in its effect upon Europe—as the defeat of the Enlightenment in the person of George III, as the basis of the emergence in England of the unenlightened but free conservatism of Burke against all apparent ratio, predictability, or probability—the American Revolution was the decisive historical event of the nineteenth century. It was the fountainhead and origin of the free society of the nineteenth century.

It is not a new assertion that the basis for all nineteenth-century freedom lay in the conservative movement which overcame the French Revolution. Nor is it a new discovery that, as far as Europe is concerned, this conservative movement was located in England. Before 1850 it was a commonplace of European political thought that England had found "the way out"—just as it had become a commonplace later on to trace all nineteenth-century freedom to the French Revolution. But how did England overcome the French Revolution? What enabled her to withstand it and, at the same time, to develop without civil war and social collapse a free, mercantile society as alternative to the despotism of the French Revolution and of Napoleon? The stock answers to these questions attribute the English achievement to the British racial genius, the English Channel, or the English Constitution. But none of the three is an adequate answer.

In 1770 everything in England was moving increasingly fast toward Enlightened Despotism. In 1780 the antitotalitarian forces were in the saddle. The King had lost—never to regain the chance for absolute power. And the revolutionary competitors of the King, the Rousseauan totalitarians, who wanted to establish their tyranny, their absolutism, their centralized government in the place of royal tyranny and royal centralized government had lost out too. Neither the absolutism of the King nor that of the masses survived.

Every single one of the free institutions of England's nineteenth-century political system actually traces back to the short tenure of office of the "Old Whigs" who came to power because they had opposed the war with the Thirteen Colonies. They introduced ministerial responsibility to Parliament, and the cabinet system. They founded the modern party system and the civil service. And they defined the relationship between Crown and Parliament. The England of 1790 was not a very healthy and certainly not an ideal society. But it had found the basic frame for a new free society. And that frame was the principles of the "Old Whigs" who had been practically destroyed before the American Revolution, and who were not only revived but put into power by the successful resistance of the Colonists.

The principles of the conservative counterrevolution resulted in a free society in the United States and in England although these two countries were dissimilar to start with. Though the American of 1776 was of the same racial stock as his contemporary in England, although he spoke the same language, had the same laws and, by and large, the same political tradition, he was sufficiently far removed from the mother country to rule out the attempt to explain the nineteenth-century free society in these two countries by the "racial genius" or the "political wisdom" of one race or nation.

It is not only true that the actual social and physical reality, the patterns of thought and of behavior, the concrete problems and the concrete answers given in these two countries during the nineteenth century were completely different. The United States also moved away from England and from Europe during the entire century at an increasing pace as a result of the Revolution and of the westward movement which started soon afterward. The America of 1917, that came in to decide the greatest European war since Napoleon, was further away from Europe than the America of the colonial towns, of Jefferson, Dr. Franklin, George Washington, and John Adams. Steamboats, transatlantic cables, and wireless by their very facility only tended to make contacts more superficial and passing than they had been in the days of the sailing vessel.

Every succeeding generation of Americans since the Revolution has been further away from England—or for that matter, from Europe—than its predecessors. Jackson and Clay were living at greater social and mental distance from Europe than John Quincy Adams or Daniel Webster—both of whom can be imagined as Englishmen though as Englishmen of the eighteenth century. Lincoln, Grant, Andrew Johnson, the railroad builders were even further away from Europe than Jackson and Clay. And with the next generation—that of Theodore Roosevelt and Woodrow Wilson, of Rockefeller, Morgan and Carnegie, Henry Adams and Lincoln Steffens—the United States was producing a type of leader and a mental and social climate which, for better or worse, was simply not imaginable in any European society—least of all in the England of 1900. There is a good deal of truth in the aphorism current among English newspaper correspondents that the United States had traveled so far away from Europe in mentality, customs, and institutions as to have become almost incomprehensible to a European. And it is a commonplace among writers and journalists who have to report on American developments for English readers (as I did for several years) that the common written language is more a handicap than a help, as it creates the illusion—fatal to a real understanding—that words and sentences have the same emotional and intellectual significance, the same associations and overtones, on either side of the Atlantic.

But the difference between these two countries only emphasizes the universality of the principles which both adopted. Starting from a different basis, wrestling with completely different realities, working in different social and emotional climates, both countries succeeded in developing a free mercantile society. However much they differed, they both took as their starting point that no man or group of men is perfect or in possession of Absolute Truth and Absolute Reason. And both the American Founding Fathers and the radical Conservatives in England believed in mixed government; in the consent of the governed as one, and in individual property rights as the other, limitation of government; in the separation of government in the political sphere from rule in the social sphere.

The American and English conservatives of 1776 and 1787 shared not only the principles; they also had in common the method which they used to develop a functioning society on a free basis. They both used it the same way and gave it the same consideration and the same importance.

The method of the conservative counterrevolution is just as important for us today as its principles—perhaps even more so. A good many political writers and thinkers today believe that principles are everything and that no such thing as method is required. This is a basic misunderstanding of the nature of politics and of political action which the generation of 1776 never would have made. They knew that principles without institutional realization are just as ineffective politically—and as vicious for the social order—as institutions without principles. Accordingly, method was as important to them as principles. And their success was just as much due to their method as to their principles.

Their method consisted in the last analysis of three parts:

In the first place, while conservative, they did not restore nor intend to restore. They never did idealize the past; and they had no illusions about the present in which they lived. They knew that the social reality had changed. They would never have conceived their task as anything but the integration of the new society on the basis of the old principles; never would they have countenanced any attempt to undo what had happened.

It is their unconditional refusal to restore which has made the Founding Fathers appear radical, and which has obscured the essentially conservative character of their work. Their social analysis was indeed radical—extremely radical. They never accepted the polite social conventions or the wishful restoration dreams which were based on the assumption that the old society was still functioning whereas in effect it had disappeared. The generation of 1776 and 1787 saw the essence of their conservatism in the fact that they did not intend to restore. For restoration is just as violent and absolutist as revolution.

The Founding Fathers in America and the radical conservatives in England were thus conservatives of the present and future, rather than conservatives of the past. They knew that their social reality was that of a mercantile system, while their social institutions were pre-mercantile. Their method was to start with this fact and to develop a free and functioning mercantile society. They wanted to solve the future, not the past, to overcome the next and not the last revolution.

The second basic characteristic of their method was that they did not believe in blueprints or panaceas. They believed in a broad frame of general principles; and there they admitted of no compromise. But they knew that an institutional solution is acceptable only if it works; that is, if it solves an actual social problem. They also knew that practically every concrete institutional tool can be made to serve practically every ideal aim. They were doctrinaire in their dogmas, but extremely pragmatic in their day-to-day politics. They did not try to erect an ideal or a complete structure; they were even willing to contradict themselves in the details of actual solutions. All they wanted was a solution that would do the job in hand—provided it could be fitted into the broad frame of principles.

For the United States it may be argued that the Founding Fathers did indeed set up a blueprint: the Constitution. But the wisdom of the Constitution lies not in the extent to which it lays down rules, but in its restraint. It contains a few basic principles, sets up a few basic institutions and lays down a few simple procedural rules. The members of the Philadelphia Convention opposed the inclusion of the Bill of Rights in the Constitution not so much out of hostility to its provision as from an aversion against mortgaging the future. Yet the provisions of the Bill of Rights are largely negative in character and lay down only what ought not, rather than what ought, to be done.

The final point in the method of the conservative counterrevolution is what Burke called "prescription." That has nothing to do with the "sacredness of tradition." Burke himself ruthlessly discarded traditions and precedents when they did not work. Prescription is the expression in the field of political method of the principle of human imperfection. It simply says that man cannot foresee the future. He does not know where he goes. The only thing he can possibly know and understand is the actual society which has grown historically. Hence he must take existing social and political reality, rather than an ideal society, as the basis for his political and social activities. Man can never invent perfect institutional tools. Hence he had better rely upon old tools than try to invent new ones to do an ideal job. We know how an old tool works, what it can do and what it cannot do, how to use it and how far to trust it. And not only do we not know anything about the new tools; if they are hawked about as perfect tools we can be reasonably certain that they will work less well than the old ones which nobody expected or claimed to be perfect.

Prescription is not only the expression of the belief in human imperfection. It is not only the expression of that awareness that all society is the result of long historical growth which distinguishes the statesman from the mere politician. It is also a principle of economy; it teaches one to prefer the simple, cheap and common to the complicated, costly, and shiny innovation. It is common sense pitted against Absolute Reason, experience and conscientiousness against superficial brilliance. It is plodding, pedestrian and not spectacular—but dependable.

The great practitioners of this principle were not so much the English as the American Founding Fathers. A vast amount of research has been done to show how completely they depended upon the institutions that had proved workable and dependable in colonial government and administration, upon past experience and tried tools. A good deal of this research has been done in a "debunking" mood with the object of showing that the Constitution makers were too dull and narrow to invent anything. This is, of course, as untenable as the proud belief of past generations that the America of 1788 had sprung fully armed out of the brains of the members of the Constitutional Convention. Actually, the caution with which the Founding

Fathers avoided new and untried institutional constructions at a time of great stress and crisis is one of their greatest claims to wisdom and to our gratitude. They knew that they could use only what they had; and they also knew that the future has always started in the past and that it is the job of the statesman to decide which part of an imperfect past to stretch into a better future rather than to try to find the secret of perpetual political motion—or of perpetual political standstill.

The society which the generation of 1776 built has largely broken down, and we must develop a new industrial society today. But both, the principles and the method of the conservative counterrevolution, still stand. If we want a free society, we can reach it only by adopting the same basic principles. The concrete social institutions of the future will be as different from those founded in 1776 and 1787 as they in turn were different from the institutions of the seventeenth or the eighteenth century. But if they are to be institutions of a free and a functioning society, the way to develop them is to use the same method as the generation of 1776: awareness that we cannot restore and that we have to accept the new industrial reality rather than try to go back to the old pre-industrial mercantile system: willingness to forego blueprints and panaceas and to be content with the humble and less brilliant task of finding workable solutions—piecemeal and imperfect—for immediate problems; and knowledge that we can use only what we have, and that we have to start where we are, not where we want to go.

The conservative counterrevolution of 1776 and 1787 achieved what had never been achieved before in Western history: the development of a new society with new values, new beliefs, new powers and a new social integration without social revolution, without decades of civil war, without totalitarian tyranny. It not only overcame the totalitarian revolution by offering a free and functioning social and political alternative; it developed this alternative without itself becoming entangled in totalitarianism and absolutism.

Our task today may seem bigger and more difficult than that of the generation of 1776—though we probably tend to underestimate their difficulties since we know the answers, and to overestimate our difficulties since we do not know what is to happen. But it is certain that we can hope to achieve our task only if we base ourselves on the principles and depend upon the methods which the generation of 1776 bequeathed to us.

3

A Conservative Approach

(from *The Future of Industrial Man*, 1942)

If the free industrial society is to be developed in a free, nonrevolutionary, nontotalitarian way, there is only one country that can do it today: the United States.

That the twentieth century is to be the "American Century" has recently become a popular catchphrase in the United States. It is certainly true that the United States can never again afford not to engage in power politics, not to develop lasting strategic concepts, not to determine where her strategic and military borders lie and which territories cannot be allowed to fall under the control of a potential enemy. It is also certain that both traditional American attitudes toward foreign affairs are obsolete, if not defunct. Both isolationism and interventionism assumed implicitly that the United States can decide whether she wants to be a participant in international affairs or not. Now that the United States has become the central power of the Western world, if not of the whole globe, there is no longer such a decision. America will have to take a stand whenever a power tries to assume hegemony on any continent—even when there is nothing more than a change in international power relations.

The United States as a world power—perhaps as *the* world power— will certainly have to use her power politically; that is, as power. But if the American century means nothing except the material predominance of the United States, it will be a wasted century. Some people today seem to think that it is the destiny of the United States to out-Nazi the Nazis in world conquest and to substitute the Yankee as the master race for Hitler's Nordics; some even call that "fighting for democracy." But this way would not lead to America's strength and greatness but only to her downfall. It would also not lead to a solution of the basic social crisis of which this war is but an effect. If the twentieth century is to have a free and functioning industrial society, the United States will have to solve the great problems of principles and institutions which today demand a solution. Then indeed the twentieth century will become an American century.

The totalitarian powers were absolutely correct in their conviction—ever since they started on the road to world conquest—that the United States is their ultimate, their real enemy. It is true in a material sense; it is even truer in a political and social sense. For only the United States of America can find the nontotalitarian, nonrevolutionary way to a free industrial society which is the absolutely certain—and at the same time the only—way to overcome totalitarianism.

Such a society must center on industry. It must be an attempt to develop something we have never had before: social institutions in industry. The fact that in total war the individual in industry has an important social function and a clear and unambiguous social status must be used to build a permanent functioning social organization. The fact that the outcome of the war depends above all on industrial production must be used to develop a legitimate power in industry on the basis of responsible self-government. In other words, the plant must be made into a functioning self-governing social community.

The central fact in the social crisis of our time is that the industrial plant has become the basic social unit, but that it is not yet a social institution. Industrial society can function only if the plant gives social status and function to its members. And only if the power in the plant is based on the responsibility and decision of the members can industrial society be free. The answer today is neither total planning nor the restoration of nineteenth-century laissez faire, but the organization of industry on the basis of local and decentralize self-government. And the time to start this is now when workers and management, producers and consumers are united in the one purpose of winning the war.

Part 2

The Rise of Totalitarianism

Introduction to Part 2

The End of Economic Man was the first of my books to be published—in the U.K. in late 1938—and, a few weeks later, in early
1939, in the U.S. It was the first book on the origins of totalitarianism. And it was—and still is—the only book that treats the emergence of totalitarianism as a *European* phenomenon, that is, as the
result of the collapse of nineteenth-century European society and its
creeds, whether bourgeois capitalism or Marxism.

It was also the first—and so far the only book—that treats the rise
of totalitarianism as a *social* phenomenon. There have been many,
many books since on the rise of Nazism—the best known, perhaps,
Hannah Arendt's classic *The Rise of Totalitarianism* (1951). But all
these books were written after Hitler had been defeated; all of them
are written from hindsight. *The End of Economic Man* is the only
book that looked at totalitarianism, and especially at Nazism, with
foresight. To this it owed its predictive power. It predicted—totally unimaginable to decent people then anywhere—Hitler's "Final Solution,"
that is, the attempted killing of *all* European Jews, and the Hitler-Stalin
pact (a full year before it happened). It predicted—only a few short
months after Munich—that Hitler could not be "appeased." And it
predicted that there would be no resistance in Western Europe to the
Nazis until *after* a country had been occupied by the German Army.

Every one of these conclusions—though inescapable to any one
who had read Hitler and took him seriously—was totally unaccept-
able at the time. Yet the book was a tremendous success, if only as a
succès de scandale. It owed this in large measure to Winston
Churchill. Churchill wrote a glowing review of the book in the (London) *Times Literary Supplement* and kept on discussing it in his widely
read weekly columns. And when, some fifteen months later, after
Dunkirk, he became British Prime Minister, he ordered that every
British officer candidate be issued a copy of the book.

On the collapse of Europe into totalitarianism *The End of Economic Man* is probably still the best—if not the only—book. But it

was dead wrong in its final conclusion: that there could be no return of Europe to bourgeois capitalism and liberal democracy—the "Demons" had destroyed both. Very few, if any, people would have disagreed with this conclusion in 1938 or 1939—or even six or seven years later after Hitler and Mussolini had been defeated and their regimes destroyed. Yet, by 1955 both bourgeois capitalism and liberal democracy had been restored in all Europe, west of the Iron Curtain. I myself in those years did a good deal of work for the Marshall Plan and the World Bank, that is, for the attempts to restore Europe—or, at least, to prevent its falling under Stalin's rule. We endlessly discussed what explained the resurgence of a Europe that, in many ways was closer to the pre-1913 Europe than even to the Europe of the 1920s—for instance in the acceptance of a market-based capitalism by most of the Left.

The Marshall Plan was clearly the trigger that released tremendous latent energies. But it was invented—and in a desperate hurry—because there were absolutely no signs of any such energies on a continent that was mired in lethargy and despair—even in the victorious U.K. there were not many signs of economic energy and recovery. Where then did the energy come from?

We never found a satisfactory answer. I myself have tried several times to answer the question—but gave up every time. Nor has any one else, to the best of my knowledge, even tried, let alone succeeded. It is the great mystery of twentieth-century history.

4

The Return of the Demons

(From *The End of Economic Man*, 1969 Preface)

When this book first came out, in early 1939—thirty long years ago—it was shockingly unconventional and heretical. It was, of course, by no means alone in its uncompromising rejection of the totalitarian creeds, or even in its firm conviction that Nazism was pure evil *sans* qualification or extenuation. But the other books—and there were hundreds of them—all explained away Hitler in those years before World War II. They either came up with some pseudo-history of Nazism as a "manifestation of German national character," or they depicted Nazism (and Fascism) as the "dying gasp of capitalism," with Marxist socialism as the coming savior. In this book, however, the "national-character" explanation is dismissed as intellectually shoddy; national character or national history may explain how a people does things, but not what things it does. This book rather diagnosed Nazism—and Fascism—as a pervasive sickness of the European body politic. And instead of proclaiming Marxism as the coming savior, I asserted that the total failure of Marxism had been a main reason for the flight of Europe's masses into the fervency of totalitarian despair.

These views, and the conclusions to which they led, were so heretical in the 1930s that I myself hesitated a long time before publishing them. The first draft of this book containing its main theses was actually done when Hitler was coming to power in 1933; I was, however, so perturbed by my own findings, inescapable though they seemed, that I decided to hold the manuscript until I could test its conclusions against actual events. But even after my predictions had been proven correct by the developments of the thirties, no publisher was willing for a long time to bring out the book. It was far too "extreme" in its conclusions: that Hitler's anti-Semitism would be propelled by its inner logic towards the "ultimate solution" of killing all Jews; that the huge armies of Western Europe would not offer effective resistance to the Germans; or that Stalin would end up signing a pact with Hitler.

Only after Munich, in the fall of 1938, did the late Richard J. Walsh, Sr., then head of John Day, the publishers, accept this book. He tried even then to make me tone down these "extreme" conclusions and imply them rather than come straight out with them. Yet Richard Walsh who was both a publisher and a leading liberal journalist of the times, was singularly well informed. He was also a courageous man who took quite a risk in publishing this book, and was, indeed, sharply attacked by "liberal" reviewers, most of whom in those days deluded themselves with dreams of Marxist utopia.

Six months after this book had first come out, in the spring of 1939, Stalin did, however, (as I had predicted) ally himself with Hitler. Another twelve or eighteen months later, in the bleak winter of 1940-41, after Dunkirk and the fall of France, the British selected *The End of Economic Man* as the one political book to distribute to the young men preparing to be officers of the first nation that chose to fight the Nazi evil.

The world "alienation" was not in the political vocabulary of the 1930s and cannot be found in the pages of *The End of Economic Man*. Still, that Western man had become alienated from Western society and Western political creeds is a central thesis of this book. In some ways, *The End of Economic Man* anticipated by more than a decade the existentialism that came to dominate the European political mood in the late 1940s and early 1950s. Two key chapters of the book are respectively entitled, "The Despair of the Masses," and "The Return of the Demons," terms that, though quite familiar today, were rudely foreign to the political rhetoric of the thirties or indeed of any earlier period since the French Revolution. *The End of Economic Man* was also, as far as I know, the first political book which treated Kierkegaard as a modern thinker relevant to modern politics. Yet, in sharp contrast to the massive literature on existentialism and alienation since World War II *The End of Economic Man* is a social and political rather than a philosophical, let alone a theological, book. Its first sentence reads: *"This is a political book."* To be sure, it considers doctrines, philosophies, political creeds. But it treats them as data in a concrete analysis of political dynamics. Its theme is the rise of a power rather than the rise of a belief. It is not concerned much with the nature of man and indeed not even with the nature of society. It treats one specific historical event: the breakdown of the social and political structure of Europe which culminated in the rise of Nazi totalitarianism to mastery over Europe. Politics, society, economics, rather than spiritual agonies, form the plot of this book.

Yet, unlike every other book of this period, *The End of Economic Man* explained the tragedy of Europe as the result of a loss of political faith, as a result of the political alienation of the European masses. In particular, it traces the headlong rush into totalitarian despair to the disillusionment with the political creeds that had dominated the "Modern Age" which had begun three hundred years earlier. The last of these creeds had been Marxism. And the final, the ultimate, cause of the rise of totalitarianism was the total failure of Marxism to make sense out of political reality and social experience. As a result, the European masses were overwhelmed by a "return of the demons." Central to the Modern Age had been the belief that society could be made rational, could be ordered, controlled, understood. With the collapse of Marxism as a secular creed, society became again irrational, threatening, incomprehensible, menaced by sinister powers against which the individual had no defense. Unemployment and war were the specific "demons" which obsessed the society of the inter-war years. The secular creeds of Liberal Europe—and Marxism was their logical and ultimate formulation and their dead end—could neither banish nor control these forces. Nor could any existing economic or political theory explain them. Though human and social in origin and within society, they proved as irrational, as unmanageable, as senseless and capricious as had been the demonic forces of a hostile nature before which earlier men had groveled in impotent despair. Yet twentieth-century men could not return to the rationality of the religious faiths that had given spiritual certainty to their forebears.

The End of Economic Man was perhaps least fashionable for its time in its respect for religion and in the attention it paid to the Christian churches. Insofar as contemporary *political* analysis paid attention at all, it considered religion an outmoded relic and the churches ineffectual reactionaries. Stalin's famous outburst: "How many divisions has the Pope?" shocked only the way a four-letter word shocks in the Victorian drawing room; it said bluntly what most people knew very well but covered up by polite circumlocution. My book, however, has a chapter, *"The Failure of the Christian Churches,"* which argues that the churches could have been expected to succeed, could have been expected to provide the new foundation. In this chapter, the Christian churches are seen as the one potential counterforce and the one available political sanctuary. The contemporaries, thirty years ago, still children of eighteenth-century Enlightenment and nineteenth-century anti-clericalism, tended to ignore the Christian dissenters—from Kierkegaard to the worker-priests of France—as isolated romantics, hopelessly out of touch with reality. *The End of Economic Man* was, to my knowledge, the first book that perceived them the way we tend to perceive them now, that is, as hard-headed realists addressing themselves to the true problems of modern society. This enabled the book to foreshadow both the emergence of Christian-Democratic parties that have been so prominent a feature of post-war Europe, and the *"aggiornamento"* of the Catholic Church under Pope John.

But *The End of Economic Man* also reached the conclusion that the churches could not, after all, furnish the basis for European society and European politics. They had to fail, though not for the reasons for which the contemporaries tended to ignore them. Religion could indeed offer an answer to the despair of the individual and to his existential agony. But it could not offer an answer to the despair of the masses. I am afraid that this conclusion still holds today. Western Man—indeed today Man altogether—is not ready to renounce this world. Indeed he still looks for secular salvation, if he expects salvation at all. Churches, especially Christian churches, can (and should) preach a "social gospel." But they cannot (and should not) substitute politics for Grace, and social science for Redemption. Religion, the critic of any society, cannot accept any society or even any social program, without abandoning its true Kingdom, that of a Soul alone with its God. Therein lies both the strength of the churches as the conscience of society and their incurable weakness as political and social forces in society.

There was much talk of "revolution" in those years. What was meant by the term was, however, a game of musical chairs, that is, the replacement of the "capitalist bosses" by the Marxist "Dictatorship of the Proletariat." This book can claim to have been the first to realize that this would simply be exchanging King Stork for King Log, and that indeed the new rulers would be forced to freeze the existing patterns of power and institutions. This is commonplace today after Orwell's 1984, Milovan Djilas' *The New Class*, or the Russian invasion of Czechoslovakia in the fall of 1968. But it was quite new thirty years ago when even the "anti-Communists" (indeed particularly the "anti-Communists") were absolutely sure that communism would indeed revolutionize society rather than replace one rulership group by another, an infinitely more rigid and autocratic one.

One result of my findings that what was called "revolution" then—and is, of course, still called "revolution" in Moscow today—was a power grab and very little else, and my conclusion that the specific social and economic institutions of the system of production and distribution, that was known as "capitalism," would survive and would, in all likelihood, prove itself capable of economic performance. Marxism, however, because of its millennial nature, I concluded, could not survive the first doubt in its infallibility. When I reached this conclusion thirty years ago, nothing was more "obvious" to anyone than that the traditional economy could not possibly outlast the war. The actual experience we have had since would have been unimaginable then: the resurgence of an economically "affluent" Europe and of an expanding world economy based on economic entrepreneurship organized in privately owned and privately managed world-wide corporations.

But while I realized that what to the contemporaries appeared as "inevitable revolution" was not likely to happen, I also realized that the new totalitarianisms, especially Nazism in Germany, were indeed a genuine revolution, aiming at the overthrow of something much more fundamental than economic organization: values, beliefs, and basic morality. It was a revolution which replaced hope by despair, reason by magic, and belief by the frenzied, bloodthirsty violence of the terror-stricken.

The End of Economic Man was meant to be a concrete social and political analysis of a profound crisis. It was not conceived as "history," and is not written as such. But it also does not "report" events. It tries to understand them.

It might, therefore, be read today as a portrait, perhaps a self-portrait, of the period and as a perception of those nightmare years between the two world wars. What comes through perhaps most strongly are the pervasive realities of these years which to us today, thirty years later, are almost inconceivable.

The most surprising of these realities of 1939 to the reader of 1969 will probably be that Europe was then the stage of world affairs. This book was written by a man living in the United States, at home there, and deeply enmeshed in its politics and economics. Indeed by the time this book came out, I was actually teaching American History and American Economics.

And yet the book takes for granted that what happens in Europe is what matters and decides. Franklin D. Roosevelt's America is, of course, mentioned many times in *The End of Economic Man*. And it is clear, right from the beginning, that its author hoped that America would prove immune to the infection that was destroying Europe and would overcome it in her own system and society. But otherwise the United States is clearly relegated to the rank of spectator. The fate of the world was at stake in Europe and would be decided there.

Today such a view would be almost unthinkable. Thirty years ago, however, Europe *was* indeed the center.

The second feature of the time portrayed in this book—and hard to imagine today—is the star role of Marxism in the constellation of movements, philosophies and emotions. This book proclaimed—and tried to prove—that Marxism had failed and had indeed lost all relevance for the industrially developed countries. Yet Marxism—to paraphrase the title of a book that appeared almost twenty years after *The End of Economic Man*—was "the God that failed." The creative era of Marxism had come to an end with World War I. In the decades before it had been the inspiration to all creative thinking in politics, society, and economics on the European scene. Even the anti-Marxists of those days had to define themselves in terms of their position towards Marx; and "non-Marxists" did not exist in Europe during the decades before World War I. After the failure of the Socialist International to avert or to settle World War I, followed by the failure of communism to come to power in any single developed European country despite the collapse and chaos which 1918 left behind on the Continent among victors and vanquished alike, Marxism rapidly lost its vigor and became a ritualized but meaningless chant.

But while Marxism rapidly lost credence and creativity for the intellectual elite, it became popularized. The vocabulary everywhere became Marxist, very much the way the American popular vocabulary suddenly became psychoanalytical in the mid-fifties. Marxism, no longer the solid gold of the "highbrows," became the small change of the "middlebrows." Marxism itself could no longer organize effectively for gaining power or even for gaining adherents, whether by the ballot box or by revolution. But demagogues could, with impunity, use Marxist rhetoric and could, as Mussolini did, cover up their intellectual nakedness by an "anti-Marxism" itself composed of Marxist tatters. This happened even in the United States. During its creative period, Marxism had not had impact on America. There is not one American thinker or American politician, not even of the second rank, who was influenced by Marxism to the slightest degree. But in its decay in the late thirties and early forties, Marxism suddenly began to supply the rhetoric of the pseudo-intellectuals and to serve them, for a decade, as a substitute for thinking and analysis.

In other words, Marxism, "the God that failed," dominated the European political scene more pervasively after it had become a corpse than it had done in its prime as a secular religion. And this comes out clearly in *The End of Economic Man*, where the failure of Marxism rather than its threat or its promise is shown to be the central factor in the rise of totalitarianism and a main reason of the flight of the masses into totalitarian despair.

The last reality of the thirties which *The End of Economic Man* clearly conveys is the total absence of leadership. The political stage was full of characters. Never before, it seems, had there been so many politicians, working so frenziedly. Quite a few of these politicians were decent men, some even very able ones. But excepting the twin Princes of Darkness, Hitler and Stalin, they were all pathetically small men; even mediocrities were conspicuous by their absence. The very villains, a Papen, a Laval, a Quisling, were pygmies whose foul treason was largely boneheaded miscalculation.

"But," today's reader will protest, "there was Churchill." To be sure, Churchill's emergence as the leader in Europe's fight against the evil forces of totalitarianism was the crucial event. It was, to use a Churchillan phrase, "the hinge of fate." Today's reader is indeed likely to underrate Churchill's importance. Until Churchill took over as leader of free peoples everywhere, after Dunkirk and the fall of France, Hitler had moved with apparent infallibility. After Churchill, Hitler was "off" for good, never regaining his sense of timing or his uncanny ability to anticipate every opponent's slightest move. The shrewd calculator of the thirties became the wild, uncontrolled plunger of the forties. It is hard to realize today, thirty years after the event, that without Churchill the United States might well have resigned itself to Nazi domination of Europe and of the still largely intact colonial empires of Europe. Indeed, even Russia might well not have resisted the Nazi invaders had not Churchill, a year earlier, broken the Nazi spell. What Churchill gave was precisely what Europe needed: moral authority, belief in values, and faith in the rightness of rational action.

But this is hindsight. Churchill appears in *The End of Economic Man* and is treated with great respect. Indeed, reading now what I then wrote, I suspect that I secretly hoped that Winston Churchill would indeed emerge into leadership. I also never fell for the *ersatz* leaders such as Marshal Pétain to whom a good many well-informed contemporaries—a good many members of Roosevelt's entourage in Washington, for instance—looked for deliverance. Yet, in 1939, Churchill was a might-have-been: a powerless old man rapidly approaching seventy; a Cassandra who bored his listeners in spite (or perhaps because) of his impassioned rhetoric; a two-time loser who, however magnificent in opposition, had proven himself inadequate to the demands of office. I know that it is hard to believe today that even in 1940 Churchill was by no means the inevitable successor when the "Men of Munich" were swept out of office by the fall of France and the retreat at Dunkirk. But we do know now that several other men were considered as prime ministers and that one or two of them actually had the "inside track" and almost got the appointment.

Churchill's emergence in 1940, more than a year after this book was first published, was the reassertion of the basic moral and political values for which *The End of Economic Man* had prayed and hoped. But all one could do in 1939 was pray and hope. The reality was the absence of leadership, the absence of affirmation, the absence of men of values and principle.

5

The Failure of Marxism

(Excerpts *From The End of Economic Man,* 1938-39)

Fascism is the result of the collapse of Europe's spiritual and social order. The last, decisive step leading to this collapse was the disintegration of the belief in Marxist socialism, which proved unable to overcome capitalism and to establish a new order.

Marxism stands and falls by the promise to overcome the unequal and unfree society of capitalism and to realize freedom and equality in the classless society. And it is because it has been proved that it cannot attain the classless society but must necessarily lead to an even more rigid and unfree pattern of classes that Marxist socialism has ceased to be a creed.

The one fundamental socialist dogma without which belief in the order of Marxism is impossible, is that capitalism in its trend toward larger and larger producing units must by necessity develop a social structure in which all are equal as proletarians except a few expropriators. The expropriation of those few would then usher in the classless society. In other words, while the producing unit will become necessarily larger, the number of privileged unequals will become necessarily smaller, and finally the conversion of the whole productive machinery into one unit, owned and operated by and for the community of workers, will be inevitable and will eliminate inequality and privilege altogether. Actually, however, the number of privileged unequals increases in almost geometrical proportion to the size of the producing unit. The number of independent "bosses" decreases, of course, especially if the individual small stockholder in a large company is not regarded as independent, since he has no control. But the larger the unit becomes, the larger is the number of intermediate privileged positions, the holders of which are not independent entrepreneurs but even less unequal members of the proletariat. Between the overpaid president of a large company and the worst-paid ledger clerk, from the chief designer to the semi-skilled foreman on an assembly line, there has come into existence a veritable army of dependent bourgeois classes. None of them has that interest in the "expropriated profit" which characterizes the "bourgeois" in Marxism. But all have a vested interest in the maintenance of an unequal society. With the complete socialization of productive capacity, the number, size, and rigidity of these privileged though employed intermediate layers and classes would increase so tremendously as to crowd out the unskilled laborer at the bottom, in whose name and for whose nominal benefit the rapidly multiplying bureaucracy would be planning, designing, directing, and administrating the social and economic fabric. Economically the system might perform miracles of efficiency and productivity. But, far from being classless, it would be a society with the most rigid and most complicated pattern of naturally antagonistic classes which the world has ever seen. Instead of establishing the true freedom, the socialist state would produce a genuinely feudal society, though the serf would be proclaimed the beneficiary. In the heyday of feudalism in the twelfth and early thirteenth centuries the social pyramid was rationalized by the creed on which society was based. But social stratification in the socialist state cannot be justified. It cannot even be explained. It is as senseless as a hierarchy without God. That such a society is the inevitable consequence of the realization of socialism invalidated, therefore, all basis of belief in the Marxist creed as the harbinger of the future order.

The failure of the socialist revolution in the precapitalist countries—the only ones where it is still possible and can still appeal to the masses—was admitted by the Russians themselves when they "postponed indefinitely" the day when the true socialist state of freedom would be realized. This—translated from Marxist into ordinary terms—means that the time will never come when the minority which has seized the power in the name of the proletariat will hand this power over to the proletarian masses. The dictatorship can no longer be justified as one of the proletariat over the bourgeois enemies, with those enemies completely destroyed. It is a dictatorship over an unequal and unfree proletariat itself.

These matters take up an unwarranted amount of space in our contemporary intellectual discussion. In reality they have no influence at all upon developments in the industrialized countries of Central and Western Europe and even less upon the United States. In industrialized Europe the belief in socialism as a creed and as the future order had ceased to exist long before it was put to the test in Russia. The process of disintegration was slow and gradual. If there is any specific date at which it can be supposed to have been completed, it was the day on which the World War started. On that day it was shown that the solidarity of interests and of beliefs between the masses and the capitalist society of each country is stronger than the international solidarity of the working class. From that day onward the class struggle became meaningless and destructive. Socialism had withdrawn its claim to establish the classless society and to be a new order.

That capitalism is doomed seems to be a commonplace. However, the arguments usually put forth in support of this statement—namely, that capitalism has failed as an economic system—not only betray profound ignorance of the nature of this system, but are provably wrong. As an economic system that produces ever-increasing quantities of goods at ever-decreasing prices and with steadily shorter hours of work, capitalism has not only not failed, it has succeeded beyond the wildest dreams. There is no economic reason why its greatest successes should not be just ahead in the industrialization of the colonial countries and in the industrialization of agriculture.

But capitalism as a social order and as a creed is the expression of the belief in economic progress as leading toward the freedom and equality of the individual in the free and equal society. Marxism expects this society to result from the abolition of private property and profit. Capitalism expects the free and equal society to result from the enthronement of private property and profit as supreme rules of social behavior. Capitalism did not, of course, invent the "profit motive"; nor is it sufficient evidence for the Marxist assertion that all past societies were fundamentally capitalist to show that the lust for profits was always a strong motive of individual action. Profit has always been one of the main motivating forces of the individual and will always be—regardless of the social order in which he lives. But the capitalist creed was the first and only social creed which valued the profit motive positively as the means by which the ideal free and equal society would be automatically realized. All previous creeds had regarded the private profit motive as socially destructive, or at least neutral. Capitalism has therefore to endow the economic sphere with independence and autonomy, which means that economic activities must not be subjected to noneconomic considerations, but must rank higher. All social energies have to be concentrated upon the promotion of economic ends, because economic progress carries the promise of the social millennium. This is capitalism; and without this social end it has neither sense nor justification nor possibility of existence.

But the failure to establish equality by economic freedom destroyed in early-twentieth-century Europe the belief in capitalism as a social system in spite of material blessings, not only for the proletariat but among the very middle classes who have benefited most economically and socially.

Capitalism came to be seen in Europe as a false god because it led to class war among rigidly defined classes. Socialism proved false because it was demonstrated that it cannot abolish these classes. The class society of the capitalist reality is irreconcilable with the capitalist ideology, which therefore ceased to make sense. The Marxist class war, on the other hand, while it recognizes and explains the actual reality, ceased to have any meaning because it leads nowhere. Both creeds and orders failed because their concept of the automatic consequences of the exercise of economic freedom on the individual was false.

Every organized society is built upon a concept of the nature of man and of his function and place in society. Whatever its truth as a picture of human nature, this concept always gives a true picture of the nature of the society which recognizes and identifies itself with it. It symbolizes the fundamental tenets and beliefs of society by showing the sphere of human activity which it regards as socially decisive and supreme. The concept of man as "Economic Man" is the true symbol of the societies of bourgeois capitalism and of Marxist socialism, which see in the free exercise of man's economic activity the means toward the realization of their aims. Economic satisfactions alone appear socially important and relevant. Economic positions, economic privileges, and economic rights are those for which man works. For these he wages war, and for these he is prepared to die. All others seem mere hypocrisy, snobbism, or romantic nonsense.

The collapse of the society of Economic Man was inevitable as soon as Marxism had proved itself unable to realize the free and equal society. Beyond Marxism there is no possibility of reconciling the supremacy of the economic sphere with the belief in freedom and equality as the true aims of society. And the only justification, the only basis for Economic Man or for any society based thereon, is the promise of the realization of freedom and equality.

With Christianity, freedom and equality became he two basic concepts of Europe; they are themselves Europe. For two thousand years all orders and creeds of Europe developed out of the Christian order and had freedom and equality as their goal and the promise of the eventual attainment of freedom and equality as their justification. European history is the history of the projection of these concepts into the reality of social existence.

Realization of freedom and equality was first sought in the spiritual sphere. The creed that all men are equal in the world beyond and free to decide their fate in the other world by their actions and thoughts in this one, which, accordingly, is but a preparation for the real life, may have been only an attempt to keep the masses down as the eighteenth century and the Marxists assert. But to the people in the eleventh or in the thirteenth century the promise was real. That every Last Judgment at a church door shows popes, bishops, and kings in damnation was not just the romantic fancy of a rebellious stonemason. It was a real and truthful expression of that epoch of our history which projected freedom and equality into the spiritual sphere. It saw and understood man as Spiritual Man, and his place in the world and in society as a place in a spiritual order.

And it made theology an "exact science."

When this order collapsed, freedom and equality became projected into the intellectual sphere. The Lutheran creed, which made man decide his fate by the use of his free and equal intellect in interpreting the Scriptures, is the supreme—though neither the only nor the last—metamorphosis of the order of Intellectual Man. After its breakdown freedom and equality became projected into the social sphere: man became first Political and then Economic Man. Freedom and equality became social and economic freedom and social and economic equality. Man's nature became a function of his place in the social and economic order in which his existence found its explanation and its reason.

Marxism, like bourgeois capitalism, sees in the establishment of true freedom the final aim of society. The Marxist opposition to capitalist society stems from this emphasis on freedom. But in order to prove that man will be free in the socialist state, Marx had to deny not only that he is actually free under capitalism, but even that he has the faculty of being free. The promise of socialism lies in the "automatism" of economic laws which deprive the individual of his freedom of will and make him subject to his class situation, i.e., unfree. It is as bold and daring a piece of speculative theology as the antinomy between actual freedom and complete predestination in Calvinism, to which Marxism bears a striking resemblance intellectually and ideologically and in its historical function.

To the subordination of freedom to class status Marxism owes its tremendous religious force. It gave the creed its inevitability, its certainty of final success, and its entrancing intellectual finality. Without it the demand to believe that the classless society would come because society had always been a society of class wars, or that the greatest inequality would bring real equality, would have appeared nonsensical—and not only in a "rational" age. But Marxism owes to it also its dogmatic and inflexible nature. Its intellectual tension is so severe that the whole edifice threatens to collapse if one stone is touched. Nothing can be changed in Marxism without abandoning freedom as a goal or the promise of its attainment. This explains the extreme vulnerability of the belief in Marxism and the rapidity with which it disintegrated, once the first doubts of the attainability of the free and equal socialist society had appeared.

With the collapse of Marxism as a creed, any society based upon the sovereignty and autonomy of the economic sphere becomes invalid and irrational, because freedom and equality cannot be realized in it and through it. But while the old orders of capitalism and socialism disintegrated, no new order arose. It is the characteristic feature of our times that no new concept of the nature of man lies ready under the surface to take the place of Economic Man. No new sphere of human activity offers itself for the projection of freedom and equality. While Europe becomes, therefore, unable to explain and to justify its old social orders with and from its old concepts, it has not as yet acquired or developed a new concept from which new valid social values, a new reason for a new order, and an explanation of man's place in it could be derived.

Through the collapse of Economic Man the individual is deprived of his social order, and his world of its rational existence. He can no longer explain or understand his existence as rationally correlated and coordinated to the world in which he lives; nor can he coordinate the world and the social reality to his existence. The function of the individual in society has become irrational and senseless. Man is isolated within a tremendous machine, the purpose and meaning of which he does not accept and cannot translate into terms of his experience. Society ceases to be a community of individuals bound together by a common purpose, and becomes a chaotic hubbub of purposeless isolated nomads.

The collapse of the belief in the capitalist and socialist creeds was translated into terms of individual experience by the World War and the Great Depression. These catastrophes broke through the everyday routine which makes men accept existing forms, institutions, and tenets as unalterable natural laws. They suddenly exposed the vacuum behind the façade of society. The European masses realized for the first time that existence in this society is governed not by rational and sensible, but by blind, irrational, and demonic forces. The World War and the Great Depression brought about *The Return of the Demons*.

In terms of human experience the war showed the individual suddenly as an isolated, helpless, powerless atom in a world of irrational monsters. The concept of society in which man is an equal and free member and in which his fate depends mainly upon his own merits and his own efforts, proved an illusion.

The Great Depression proved that irrational and incalculable forces also rule peacetime society: the threats of sudden permanent unemployment, of being thrown on the industrial scrap heap in one's prime or even before one has started to work. Against these forces the individual finds himself as helpless, isolated, and atomized as against the forces of machine war. He cannot determine when unemployment is going to hit and why; he cannot fight it, he cannot even dodge it. The great depression made society appear totally irrational. It no longer appeared to be ruled by "forces." It appeared to be ruled by demons.

But we cannot endure a world governed by demonic forces. Everywhere in Europe the beliefs and tenets of the society of Economic Man have therefore come to be judged only by whether they threaten to provoke the demons or promise to avert and to banish them. The tendency to subordinate everything to this new all-important and supreme goal has reversed our whole attitude toward the desirability of economic progress.

From such rejections of economic progress in limited fields we have proceeded during the last years to reject progress altogether. Not even lip service is paid any more to the god of progress. Instead, security—security from depressions, security from unemployment, security from progress—has become the supreme goal. If progress impedes security, then progress has to be abandoned. And in the event of a new depression no country in Europe will hesitate to introduce measures which, while forbidding progress and spelling economic retreat and lasting impoverishment, might perhaps banish the demons or at least mitigate their onslaught.

The same subordination of the old beliefs and institutions has been taking place with respect to democracy. The old aims and accomplishments of democracy: protection of dissenting minorities, clarification of issues through free discussion, compromise between equals, do not help in the new task of banishing the demons. The institutions devised to realize these aims have, therefore, become meaningless and unreal. They are no longer good, they are not bad; they are just entirely unimportant and unintelligible to the common man. He is unable to understand that the general franchise and suffrage for women were political issues of the first order only twenty years ago. Optimists might deceive themselves into believing that this apathy is due to "technical mistakes." Proportional representation is advertised as a panacea in England, just as the abolition of proportional representation was preached in pre-Hitler Germany. But the dwindling substance of democracy cannot be salvaged by a mechanical formula. Wherever it is deeply rooted in tradition and in the historical conscience of the people as something for which they have fought and suffered, democracy can still have a strong sentimental attraction. But this appeal collapses as soon as it is confronted with a reality which demands abandonment of democracy as the price for the banishing of the demons.

Finally, the concept of freedom itself has been debased and devalued.

It has been proved that economic freedom does not lead to equality. To act according to one's greatest economic advantage—the essence of economic freedom—has lost the social value that was placed upon it. Regardless of whether it is man's true nature to put his economic interests first, the masses have ceased to regard economic behavior as socially beneficial in itself, since it cannot promote equality. Hence, curtailment or abandonment of economic freedom are accepted or even welcomed if thereby the threat of unemployment, the danger of depression, or the risks of economic sacrifices promise to become less imminent.

The masses, then, have become prepared to abandon freedom if this promises to re-establish the rationality of the world. If freedom is incompatible with equality, they will give up freedom. If it is incompatible with security, they will decide for security. To be free or not has become a secondary question, since the freedom available does not help to banish the demons. Since the "free" society is the one which is threatened by demons, it seems more than plausible to blame freedom and to expect delivery from despair through the abandonment of freedom.

Throughout European history freedom was always the right of the individual. Freedom to choose between good and evil, freedom of conscience, freedom of religious worship, political freedom, and economic freedom—they all have no meaning except as freedom of the individual against the majority and against organized society.

The new freedom which is preached in Europe is, however, the right of the majority against the individual. It was internationally accepted in the Munich agreement which handed over to Germany all territory with a bare German majority. The Czech minority in these districts, even if it amounted to 49.9 percent of the population, were deprived of all rights and of all freedom. But the unlimited right of the majority is not freedom: it is license.

Yet the forms of formal democracy—the fiction of the popular opinion and of the popular will by vote, the formal equality of every voter—are being maintained. Hitler and Mussolini both proclaim that they have realized the only "true democracy," as their governments express the wishes of 99 percent of the people. Yet by making it a criminal offense to vote against them, both have openly given up the pretense that anybody has freedom to vote. Anyhow, both proclaim that they rule not by popular but by divine mandate.

This is a most important and unprecedented characteristic of our time. The mere façade of slogans and forms is being maintained as an empty shell while the whole structure has to be abandoned. The more intolerable the substance of the industrial order becomes for the masses, the more necessary does it become to retain its outward forms.

In this contradiction lies the true cause of fascism. It stems from the basic experience of the epoch in which we live: the absence of a

new creed and a new order. The old order has ceased to have valid-
ity and reality, and its world has therefore become irrational and
demonic. But there has emerged no new order which would have
brought a new basis of belief, and from which we could develop
new forms and new institutions to organize social reality so as to
enable us to attain a new supreme goal. We cannot maintain the
substance of our old order, since it brings spiritual chaos, which the
masses cannot bear. But neither can we abandon the old forms and
institutions, as this would bring social and economic chaos, which is
equally unbearable. To find a way out which gives a new substance,
which carries a new rationality, and which makes possible at the
same time the maintenance of the old outward forms is the demand
of the masses in their despair. And it is this task which fascism sets
out to accomplish.

The very nature of this task explains the stress laid upon "legal-
ity" and "legal continuity" which has been puzzling so many observers and which has been responsible for the failure to recognize
the revolutionary character of the movement. According to all historical experience, a revolution glories in breaking the old façades
and in producing new forms, new institutions, and new slogans. But—
as discerning observers always noticed even while the revolution
was still in progress—the social substance changes only slowly and
often not at all. In fascism the substance of the old order has been
ruthlessly destroyed. But the most superficial old form is carefully
preserved. No previous revolution would have retained Hindenburg
as president of the German Republic while abolishing the republic
of which he was the president. This perversion of all historical rule
is inevitable in fascism, which has to maintain the forms while destroying the substance.

That fascism opposes and abolishes all freedom, stems by equal
necessity from its assignment. Since it is caused by the absence of a
new sphere of human activity into which freedom could be projected, the new substance which it attempts to give to society, must
by necessity be an unfree substance of an unfree society. By equal
necessity all freedom must appear hostile to the unfree new goal, the
attainment of which depends upon complete compulsion and complete submission. Therefore fascism by its nature must deny all tenets, all concepts, all articles of the faith of Europe, because all of
them were built on the concept of freedom. Its own creed must be-

come all the more negative as it becomes the more difficult to save the forms, catchwords, and ornaments of the empty façade of Europe's past.

Finally, the nature of fascism explains why it has to turn against reason and why it is believed against belief. It can accomplish its task through a miracle only. To maintain the very outward forms which provoke the demons and to give a new substance which banishes or rationalizes the same demons, is a contradiction which reason cannot resolve. But it must be solved because the masses can bear the despair of complete senselessness as little as they can bear that of social chaos. They must turn their hopes toward a miracle. In the depths of their despair reason cannot be believed, truth must be false, and lies must be truth. I once, in 1932, heard Hitler say in a public speech: "We don't want higher bread prices; we don't want lower bread prices; we want national-socialist bread prices." And 5,000 people in the audience cheered wildly. "Higher bread prices," "lower bread prices," have both failed. The only hope lies in a kind of bread price which is none of these, which nobody has ever seen before, and which belies the evidence of one's reason.

It is not in spite of its being contrary to reason and in spite of its rejecting everything of the past without exception, but because of it, that the masses flocked to fascism and Nazism and that they abandoned themselves to Mussolini and Hitler. The sorcerer is a sorcerer because he does supernatural things in a supernatural way unknown to all reasonable tradition and contrary to all laws of logic. And it is a sorcerer able to work powerful miracles that the masses in Europe demand and need to allay their intolerable terror of a world which the demons have reconquered.

The most fundamental, though least publicized, feature of totalitarianism in Italy and Germany is the attempt to substitute noneconomic for economic satisfactions, rewards, and considerations as the basis for the rank, function, and position of the individual in industrial society.

The noneconomic industrial society constitutes fascism's social miracle, which makes possible and sensible the maintenance of the industrial, and therefore necessarily economically unequal, system of production.

It is a moot question whether totalitarianism is capitalist or socialist. It is neither. Having found both invalid, fascism seeks a society beyond socialism and capitalism that is not based upon economic considerations. Its only economic interest is to keep the machinery of industrial production in good working order. At whose expense and for whose benefit is a subsidiary question; for economic consequences are entirely incidental to the main social task.

The apparent contradiction of simultaneous hostility to the capitalist supremacy of private profit as well as to socialism, is, though muddleheaded, a consistent expression of fascism's genuine intentions. Fascism and Nazism are social revolutions but not socialist; they maintain the industrial system but they are not capitalist.

Mussolini and Hitler, like so many revolutionary leaders before them, probably did not understand the nature of their revolutions. Social necessity forced them to invent new noneconomic satisfactions and distinctions and, finally, to embark upon a social policy which aims at constructing a comprehensive noneconomic society side by side with, and within, an industrial system of production.

The first step in this direction was to offer the underprivileged lower classes some of the noneconomic paraphernalia of economic privilege. These attempts are largely organized in the fascist organizations of the leisure hours of the workers: *"Dopo Lavoro"* ("after work") in Italy, *"Kraft durch Freude"* ("strength through joy") in Germany. Of course, these compulsory organizations are primarily designed as means of political control of a potentially dangerous and hostile class. They are honeycombed with police spies and propagandists, whose duty it is to prevent any meeting of workers except under proper supervision. The attractions offered by these organizations are intended as bribes for the workers. But—and this is their important feature—they do not attempt to offer economic rewards as bribes, although this is the traditional form which has proved effective, from the Romans to the communist regime in Russia. Though economic bribes would probably have been cheaper financially, the fascist organizations of the workers' leisure offer, besides propaganda and the usual program of political and technical education, satisfactions in the form of theater, opera, and concert tickets, holiday trips to the Alps and to foreign countries, Mediterranean and African cruises in winter, cruises to the North Cape in summer, etc. In other words, they offer the typical noneconomic "conspicuous consumption" of a leisure class of economic wealth and privilege. These satisfactions have in themselves no economic value at all, but they are powerful symbols of social position. They are intended to suggest a measure of social equality as compensation for continued economic inequality. They are accepted as such by a large part of the working class, especially in Germany where even the most confirmed Marxists regarded cultural satisfactions as something higher, more important, and more valuable than many economic rewards. The leisure-time organizations fulfill, therefore, a definite and highly important function in the solution of the fascist task. They make the existing economic inequality appear far less intolerable than before.

Similarly, attempts are made to sever the connection between the social and economic status of the other classes and to found their social position upon considerations outside the realm of economics. The social prominence, indispensability, and equality of the working class is given symbolic expression in the conversion of the socialist May Day into a festival of labor and in its elevation to the most important holiday of Nazism. The worker is proclaimed in Nazism to be the "spiritual center" of the nation. He determines the new human concept which fascism strives to develop—the Heroic Man, with his preparedness to sacrifice himself, his self-discipline, his self-abnegation, and his "inner equality"—all independent of his economic status.

The middle class has been distinguished by still another noneconomic claim to equal and indispensable social position. It has been declared the "standard-bearer of national culture." The "Fuehrer Prinzip," the heroic principle of personal leadership, confirms the class of industrialist entrepreneurs in their social position. This principle also claims to be based upon entirely noneconomic distinctions. The leader does not owe his social function and position to his economic function and wealth. The spurious thesis that a leader must prove his qualifications in the spiritual field and that he must be deprived of his economic position if he fails on this score, is taken seriously by its inventors—and by many others.

The semi-military formations, the Fascist Militia, the Storm Troops, and the Elite Guards, the Hitler Youth, and the women's organizations serve the same noneconomic ends. The military value of these formations and organizations is extremely dubious. In Germany the idea of using them as auxiliary army corps was given up a long time ago. But to the extent to which the military value of these organizations decreased, their social importance increased. Their purpose is to give the underprivileged classes an important sphere of life in which they command while the economically privileged classes obey. In the Nazi Storm Troops as well as the Fascist Militia the greatest care is taken to make promotion entirely independent of class distinction. Units are socially mixed. The son of the "boss" or the boss himself is intentionally put under one of the unskilled laborers who has been longer in the party. The same principle is applied in the organizations of children and adolescents. It is rumored in Germany that no rich man's son will be admitted to the "Ordensburgen," the Nazi academies in which the future elite is to be trained, although officially the selection is made according to fitness and reliability alone.

Yet at best these attempts are a poor substitute for the real thing. They compensate for economic inequality but do not remove it as a factor of social distinction. They are effective in the same way in which an insurance payment may be considered adequate compensation by a man who has lost a leg in an automobile accident; yet no insurance payment will ever give him a new leg. Even the complete success of these attempts would therefore not be enough. They might theoretically give all classes an equality in social fundamentals, sufficient to compensate them for their inevitable rigid economic inequality.

But they cannot provide a clear-cut, constructive principle of social organization which would give the individual rank and function in a noneconomic society under a noneconomic order of values.

It is therefore quite certain that totalitarianism cannot survive. It is a cover-up for the absence of a social order rather than a new social order itself.

Part 3

The Sickness of Government

Introduction to Part 3

Nothing I have ever written has had greater political impact than the chapter "The Sickness of Government" in my 1969 book *The Age of Discontinuity* (excerpted in chapter 7 below).

As Mrs. Thatcher said publicly many times, she derived her policies largely from this chapter—(it did, for instance, invent and advocate "privatization"—I originally called it *re*-privatization). And it gave her her key argument: that to be effective a government had to stop "doing" and concentrate on setting policy and making decisions, on establishing standards and on giving vision, that is, on governing. But the chapter "The Sickness of Government" (and the book *The Age of Discontinuity* of which it was a part) also provided the basic concepts for the policy that, between 1970 and 1980 made Japan's the world's second economic world power—or so Japan's then prime minister asserted. In fact, he devoted most of his 1970 New Year's Message to the book (and especially to this chapter).

These political responses were, to a large extent, accidents of timing. I had said many of the same things earlier—for example, in my 1949 book *The New Society*—without anyone's paying attention to them. In fact, if they were noticed at all they were usually misunderstood as arguments for a *weak* government rather than as arguments for an *effective* one. For more than fifty years—from the end of World War I until Mrs. Thatcher around 1970—it was believed all but universally that a government is the more effective the bigger it is and the more it *does*. During these fifty years the entire world—and especially the developed countries—were mesmerized by government and believed that any social task is already *accomplished* the moment it is handed over to government. This belief was just as pervasive in the democracies as it was in the totalitarian regimes—their differences were in their beliefs in the rights of the Individual rather than in their beliefs in the competence of government and of the state. But by the end of the 1960s enough evidence of the incompetence of government as a doer had accumulated to create receptivity

53

for a discussion of the limits of government—the subject of the chapter on "The Sickness of Government." A few years later—in my 1989 book *The New Realities* (excerpted in chapter 8 below: "No More Salvation by Society")—a book that for instance foretold the collapse of the Soviet Union—it could be shown that the nearly three hundred years had come to an end in which most people in developed countries—and equally in the developing ones—expected a social creed, for example, capitalism or Marxism, to take care of *all* problems of community, society, and polity. The first chapter of this part—"From Nation State to Mega-State" (published in *Post-Capitalist Society* in 1993) presents the basic historical development which led to the Mega-State but also to "The Sickness of Government."

6

From Nation-State to Megastate
(from *Post-Capitalist Society*, 1993)

Everybody knows—and every history book teaches—that the last four hundred years of world history were the centuries of the Western nation-state. And for once, what everybody knows is true; but it is a paradoxical truth.

For the great political thrusts in these four centuries were all attempts to transcend the nation-state and to replace it with a transnational political system, whether a colonial empire or a European (or Asian) super state. These were the centuries in which the great colonial empires rose and fell: the Spanish and Portuguese empires emerging in the sixteenth and collapsing in the early nineteenth century; then, beginning in the seventeenth and continuing into the twentieth century, the English, Dutch, French, and Russian empires. As soon as a new major player emerged on the stage of world history during these four centuries, that player immediately set about transcending the nation-state and transforming it into an empire—Germany and Italy, barely unified, went in for colonial expansion between 1880 and World War I, with Italy trying again as late as the 1930s. Even the United States became a colonial power in the early twentieth century. And so did the one non-Western country to become a nation-state, Japan.

In Europe itself, the home of the nation-state, these four centuries were dominated by one attempt after another to establish a transnational super state.

Six times in this period, a European nation-state attempted to become the ruler of Europe and to transform the continent into a European super state under its control and domination. The first such attempt was made by Spain, beginning in the middle of the sixteenth century, when Spain itself was just emerging as a unified nation out of a congeries of squabbling kingdoms, duchies, counties, and free cities, precariously held together in the person of the Prince. Spain did not give up the dream of being master of Europe until a hundred years later, when it had all but ruined itself economically and militarily. Almost immediately, France, first under Richelieu, then under Louis XIV, took off where Spain had ended—again, to give up seventy-five years later, financially and spiritually exhausted. This did not deter another French ruler, Napoleon, only seventy-five years later, from trying again and subjecting all of Europe to twenty years of war and turmoil in his bid to become the ruler of Europe and build a French-dominated European super state. Then, in this century, came the two German wars for mastery of Europe; and, after Hitler's defeat, Stalin's attempt to create, by force of arms and by subversion, a Soviet-ruled Europe. And just as Japan had tried to build a Western-style colonial empire as soon as it had become a nation-state, it too followed the Western example and tried, in this century, to create a Japanese-ruled Asian super state.

In fact, it was not the nation-state that begat the empires. The nation-state itself arose as a response to transnational drives. The Spanish Empire in the Americas produced so much gold and silver that Spain, under Philip II, Charles V's son and successor, could finance the first standing army since the Roman legions, the Spanish Infantry—arguably the first "modern" organization. Thus equipped, Spain launched the first campaign for the mastery of Europe, the first attempt to unify Europe under Spanish rule. Countering Spain's threat became the motivation and avowed aim of the inventor of the nation-state, the French lawyer-politician Jean Bodin, in his book *Six Livres de la République* (1576).

It was the Spanish threat that made Bodin's nation-state the "progressive" cause throughout Europe. And it was only because the threat was so great and so real that Bodin's recommendations were accepted. In the late sixteenth century, Bodin's model of the nation-state looked like pure fantasy. What Bodin prescribed was a centrally controlled civil service, answerable only to the sovereign; central control of the military, and a standing army officered by professional soldiers appointed by and accountable to central government; central control of coinage, taxes, customs; a centrally appointed professional judiciary rather than courts staffed by local magnates. All of these recommendations were the opposite of what had existed for a thousand years, that is, since the collapse of the Roman Empire.

All of them threatened powerfully entrenched "special interests": an autonomous Church and exempt bishoprics and abbeys; local lords of all sizes, each with his own armed retainers owing fealty only to him, and each with his own jurisdiction and his own taxing powers; free cities and self-governing trade guilds; and scores of others.

But the Spanish bid for mastery of Europe left no alternative: the choice was subjection to the national sovereign or conquest by a foreign sovereign.

From then on, practically every change in the political structure of the European nation-state was caused—or at least triggered—by similar attempts to gain the mastery of Europe and to replace the nation-state with a super state, dominated in turn by France, Germany, or Russia.

One might therefore expect political scientists to have studied the colonial empire and to have developed a political theory for it. They have done neither. Instead, they have focused on the political theory and institutions of the nation-state. One might have expected historians similarly to have studied the European super states. But in every university the prestigious chairs of history are chairs of *national* history. The famous history books all deal with the nation-state—whether England or France, the United States or Spain, Germany, Italy, Russia. Even in Great Britain, ruler of the biggest and, for many years, the most successful colonial empire, the study and teaching of history still centers on the nation-state.

The modern empires lacked integrative power. The nation-state alone could integrate, could form a polity—a political society—could create citizenship.

All modern empires and all super states have foundered because of their inability to transcend the nation-state, let alone to become its successor.

But while the nation-state thus was the sole political reality in the centuries of empires and super states, it has transformed itself profoundly in the last hundred years. *It mutated into the Megastate.*

By 1870, the nation-state had triumphed everywhere; even Austria had become Austria-Hungary, a federation of two nation-states. And the nation-states of 1870 still looked and acted like the sovereign nation-state Bodin had invented three hundred years earlier.

But the nation-state of 1970, a century later, bore little resemblance to Bodin's state or, indeed, to the nation-state of 1870. It had mutated into the *Megastate*—the same species perhaps as its 1870 progenitor, but as different from it as the panther is from the pussycat.

The national state was designed to be the guardian of civil society.

The Megastate became its master. And in its extreme, totalitarian form, it replaced civil society completely. In totalitarianism, all society became political society.

The national state was designed to protect both the citizen's life and liberty and the citizen's property against arbitrary acts of the sovereign. The Megastate, even in its least extreme, Anglo-American form, considers a citizen's property to be held only at the discretion of the tax collector. As Joseph Schumpeter first pointed out in his essay *Der Steuerstaat* (*The Fiscal State*, 1918), the Megastate asserts that citizens hold only what the state, expressly or tacitly, allows them to keep.

Bodin's national state had as its first function the maintenance of civil society, especially in times of war. This is in effect what "defense" meant.

The Megastate has increasingly blurred the distinction between peacetime and wartime. Instead of peace, there is "Cold War."

The shift from the national state to the Megastate began in the last decades of the nineteenth century. The first small step toward the Megastate was Bismarck's invention in the 1880s of the Welfare State. Bismarck's goal was to combat the rapidly rising socialist tide. It was a response to the threat of class war. Government had previously been perceived exclusively as a political agency. Bismarck made government into a social agency. His own welfare measures— health insurance, insurance against industrial accidents, old-age pensions (followed thirty years later, after World War I, by the British invention of unemployment insurance)—were modest enough. But the principle was radical; and it is the principle that has had far greater effect than the individual actions taken in its name.

In the 1920s and 1930s, communists, fascists, and Nazis took over social institutions. But in the democracies, government still only insured or, at most, offered payments. By and large it still stayed out of doing actual social work or forcing citizens into proper social behavior.

This changed rapidly after World War II. From being a provider, the state now became a *manager*. The last of the traditional Welfare

State measures—and arguably the most successful one—was the U.S. G.I. Bill of Rights, enacted right after World War II. It gave every returning American veteran the means to attend a college and to acquire higher education.

The government did not, however, attempt to dictate which college a veteran should attend. It did not attempt to run any college. It offered money if the veteran chose to go to college; the veteran then decided where to go and what to study. And no college had to accept any applicant.

The other major social program of the immediate postwar period, the British National Health Service, was the first one (outside of the totalitarian countries) to take government beyond the role of insurer or provider. But only in part. For standard medical care, government in the National Health Service is an insurance carrier: it reimburses the physician who takes care of a patient.

But the physician does not become a government employee; nor is the patient in any way limited as to which physician he or she chooses. On the other hand, hospitals and hospital care under the National Health Service *were* taken over by government. The people working in hospitals became government employees; and government actually manages the hospitals. This was the first step toward a changed role for government in the social sphere. Government ceased to be the rule setter, the facilitator, the insurer, the disbursement agent. It became the doer and the manager.

By 1960, it had become accepted doctrine in all developed Western countries that government is the appropriate agent for *all* social problems and *all* social tasks. In fact, nongovernmental, private activity in the social sphere became suspect; so-called liberals considered it "reactionary" or "discriminatory." In the United States, government became the actual doer in the social sphere, especially in the attempt to change human behavior in a multi-racial society by government action or government order. So far, the United States is the only country (outside of totalitarian ones) where government has attempted to command changes in social values and individual behavior in order to stamp out discrimination by race, age, or gender.

By the late nineteenth century, the nation-state was being made over into an economic agency. The first steps were taken in the United States, which invented both governmental regulation of business and governmental ownership of the new businesses of a capitalist economy. Beginning in the 1870s, regulation of business—banking, railways, electric power, telephones—was gradually established in the United States. Such government regulation—one of the most original political inventions of the nineteenth century, and initially a hugely successful one—was clearly seen from the beginning as a "third way" between "unfettered" capitalism and socialism, and as a response to the tensions and problem created by the rapid spread of capitalism and technology.

A few years later, the United States began to take businesses into government ownership—first in the 1880s in the state of Nebraska under the leadership of William Jennings Bryan. Another few years later, between 1897–1900, Karl Lueger (1844-1910), mayor of Vienna, expropriated and took into municipal ownership the streetcar companies and the electric power and gas companies of the Austrian capital. Like Bismarck, who had acted to combat socialism, neither Bryan nor Lueger were socialists as such; both were what the United States calls "populists." Both saw in government ownership primarily a means of assuaging a rapidly escalating class war between "capital" and "labor."

Still, few people in the nineteenth century—indeed, few people before 1929—believed that government could or should manage the economy, let alone that government could or should control recessions and depressions. Most economists believed that a market economy is "self-regulating." Even Socialists believed that the economy would regulate itself once private property had been abolished. The job of the nation-state and of its government was seen as maintaining the "climate" for economic growth and prosperity—by keeping the currency stable, taxes low, and by encouraging thrift and savings. Economic "weather," that is, economic fluctuations, was beyond anyone's control, if only because the events causing these fluctuations were likely to be world market events rather than events within the nation-state itself.

The Great Depression gave rise to the belief that the national government is—and should be—in control of the economic weather. The English economist John Maynard Keynes (1883-1946) first asserted that the national economy is insulated from the world economy, at least in mid-sized and large countries.

Then he claimed that this insulated national economy is totally determined by governmental policy, to whit, by government spending. However much today's economists otherwise differ from each other, all of them: Friedmanites, supply-siders, and the other post-Keynesians all follow Keynes in these two tenets. They all consider the nation-state and its government the master of the national economy and the controller of its economic weather.

The two world wars of this century transformed the nation-state into a "fiscal state."

Until World War I, no government in history was ever able—even in wartime—to obtain from its people more than a very small fraction of the country's national income, perhaps 5 or 6 percent. But in World War I every belligerent, even the poorest, found that there was practically no limit to what government can squeeze out of the population. By the outbreak of World War I, the economies of all the belligerent countries were fully monetized. As a result, the two poorest countries, Austria-Hungary and Russia, in several war years could actually tax and borrow more than the total annual income of their respective populations. They managed to liquidate capital accumulated over long decades and turn it into war materiel.

Joseph Schumpeter, who was then still living in Austria, understood immediately what had happened. But the rest of the economists and most governments needed a second lesson: World War II. Since then, however, all developed and many developing countries have become "fiscal states."

They have all come to believe that there are no *economic* limits to what government can tax or borrow and, therefore, no economic limits to what government can spend.

What Schumpeter pointed out was that as long as governments have been around, the budget process has begun with an assessment of the available revenues. Expenditures then had to be fitted to these revenues. And since the supply of "good causes" is inexhaustible, and the demand for spending therefore infinite, the budgeting process mostly consisted of deciding where to say no.

As long as revenues were known to be limited, governments, whether democracies or absolute monarchies like Russian tsars, operated under extreme restraints. These restraints made it impossible for the government to act as either a social or an economic agency.

But since World War I—and even more noticeably since World War II—the budgeting process has meant, in effect, saying yes to everything.

Traditionally, government, the political society, had available to it only such means as were granted by the civil society, and then only within the very narrow limits of a few percentage points of national income, which was all that could be monetized. Only that amount could be converted into taxes and loans, and hence into government revenues. Under the new dispensation, which assumes that there are no economic limits to the revenues it can obtain, government becomes the master of civil society, able to mold and shape it. Above all, by using taxes and expenditures, government can redistribute society's income. Through the power of the purse, it can shape society in the politician's image.

The Welfare State, government as the master of the economy, and the fiscal state, each arose out of social and economic problems, and social and economic theories. The last of the mutations that created the megastate, the Cold War State, was a response to technology.

Its origin was the German decision, in the 1890s, to build in peacetime a massive naval deterrent. This started the armaments race. The Germans knew that they were taking an enormous political risk; in fact, most politicians resisted the decision. But the German admirals were convinced that technology left them no choice. A modern navy meant steel-clad ships, and such ships had to be built in peacetime. To wait for the outbreak of war, as traditional policy dictated, would have meant waiting too long.

Since 1500 or so, when the knight had become obsolete, warfare increasingly was waged with weapons produced in ordinary peacetime facilities with the minimum of delay or adaptation. In the American Civil War, cannons were still being produced in peacetime workshops and factories hastily adapted after hostilities had broken out. Textile mills switched production practically overnight from civilian clothing to uniforms. Indeed, the two major wars fought during the second half of the nineteenth century, the American Civil War (1861-65) and the Franco-Prussian War (1870-71), were still largely fought by civilians who had put on their uniforms only a few weeks before engaging in combat.

Modern technology—the German admirals of 1890 argued—had changed all this. The wartime economy could no longer be an adaptation of the peacetime economy. The two had to be separate. Both weapons and fighting men had to be made available, in large quantities, *before* the outbreak of hostilities. To produce either required increasingly long lead times.

Defense, it was implicit in the German argument, no longer means keeping the warfare away from civilian society and civilian economy. Under conditions of modern technology, defense means a permanent wartime society and a permanent wartime economy. It means the "Cold War State."

The most astute political observer around the turn of the century, the French socialist leader Jean Jaurés (1859-1914), understood this even before World War I. President Woodrow Wilson (1859-1924) learned it from World War I; it underlay his proposal for a League of Nations, that is, for a permanent organization monitoring national armaments. The first attempt to use military buildups as a means for arms control was the abortive Washington Naval Armaments Conference of 1923.

But even after World War II, the United States for a few short years tried to revert to a "normal" peacetime state. It tried to disarm as fast as possible, and as completely as possible. The coming of the Cold War in the Truman and Eisenhower years changed all this. Since then, the Cold War State has been the dominant organization of international politics.

By 1960, the Megastate had become a political reality in developed countries in all its aspects: as social agency; as master of the economy; as fiscal state; and in most countries as Cold War State.

The one exception is Japan. Whatever the truth about "Japan Inc."—and there is little truth to what is commonly understood in the West by this term—the Japanese after World War II did not adopt the Cold War State. Their government did not try to become master of the economy. It did not try to become master of society. Rather, it rebuilt itself after its shattering defeat on what in effect were traditional nineteenth-century lines. Militarily, of course, Japan had no choice. But Japan instituted almost no social programs. In effect, Japan was the only developed country—until Mrs. Thatcher's Britain began to privatize industry in the 1980s—in which industries that had earlier become nationalized (such as the steel industry) were returned to private ownership.

Viewed through the lens of traditional political theory of the eighteenth and early nineteenth centuries, Japan is clearly a "statist" country. But it is statist in the way in which Germany or France in 1880 or 1890 were "statist" compared to Great Britain or the United States. It has a large civil service (though no larger proportionately than the civil services of the English-speaking countries). Government service enjoys tremendous prestige and respect, the way government service in 1890 Germany, 1890 Austria-Hungary, or 1890 France enjoyed such respect. Government in Japan works closely with big business—again, no different from the way government in Continental Europe worked with economic interests during the late nineteenth century, and in fact not too different from the way American government worked with business or the farm interest around the turn of the century.

If the Megastate is taken as the norm—if reality rather than theory is the basis for judging political systems—Japan since World War II has been the country in which government has played the most restrictive and in fact the most restrained role. It is exceedingly powerful in traditional nineteenth-century terms. It is least prominent in the spheres into which twentieth-century government has moved in the rest of the world. Government in Japan still functions primarily as a guardian.

But except for Japan, the movement toward the Megastate has been universal throughout the developed world; and the developing countries rapidly followed suit. No sooner was a new nation-state formed out of the dissolution of an empire than it adopted the new military policy, building in peacetime a wartime military establishment, and manufacturing or at least procuring the advanced arms needed in case of war. It immediately attempted to get control of society.

It immediately tried to use the tax mechanism to redistribute income. And finally, almost without exception, it tried to become the manager and , in large part, the owner of the economy.

In terms of political, intellectual, and religious freedom, the totalitarian countries (especially the Stalinist ones) and the democracies (which for a good many years meant primarily the English-speaking countries) were total antitheses. But in terms of the underlying theory of government, these systems differed more in degree than they did in kind. The democracies differed in how to do things; they differed far less in respect to *what* things should be done. They all saw government as the master of society and the master of the economy. And they all defined peace as equating with "Cold War."

Has the Megastate worked? In its most extreme manifestation, totalitarianism, whether of the Nazi or the communist variety, it has surely been a total failure—without a single redeeming feature. It may be argued that the Cold War State worked militarily for the USSR. For forty years, it was a military superpower. But the economic and social burden of the military establishment was so great as to become unbearable. It certainly contributed, and heavily, to the collapse of communism and of the entire Soviet Empire.

But has the Megastate worked in its much more moderate form? Has it worked in the developed countries of Western Europe and in the United States? The answer is: Hardly any better. By and large it has been almost as great a fiasco there as in Hitler's Germany or in Stalin's Soviet Union.

The Megastate has been least successful as fiscal state. Nowhere has it succeeded in bringing about a meaningful redistribution of income. In fact, the past forty years have amply confirmed Pareto's Law, according to which income distribution between major classes in society is determined by the level of productivity within the economy. The more productive an economy, the greater the equality of income; the less productive, the greater the inequality of income. Taxes, so Pareto's Law asserts, cannot change this. But the advocates of the fiscal state based their case in large measure on the assertion that taxation could effectively and permanently change income distribution. All our experience of the last forty years disproves this claim.

The clearest case is the Soviet Union. Officially dedicated to equality, it established a very large *nomenklatura* of privileged functionaries who enjoyed income levels way beyond anything even the rich enjoyed under the tsars.

The more Soviet productivity stagnated, the greater income inequality became in the Soviet Union. But the United States is also a good example. As long as American productivity increased, until the late 1960s or early 1970s, equality of income distribution increased steadily. While the rich were still getting richer, the poor were getting richer much faster, and the middle class got richer faster still. As soon as the productivity increases dropped or disappeared—that is, beginning with the Vietnam War—income inequality began to increase steadily, regardless of taxation. It made little difference that in the Nixon and Carter years the rich were taxed heavily or that in the Reagan years they were taxed much more lightly. Similarly, in the United Kingdom, despite a professed commitment to egalitarianism and a tax system designed to minimize income inequality, income distribution has become steadily less equal in the last thirty years as productivity stopped growing.

Despite all its corruptions and scandals, the most egalitarian country is now Japan—the country of the fastest productivity increases and the fewest attempts to redistribute income through taxation.

The other economic claim of the Megastate and of modern economic theory, that the economy can be successfully managed if government controls substantial parts of the gross national income, has equally been disproven.

The Anglo-American countries fully embraced this theory. Yet there has been no decline in the number, the severity, or the length of their recessions. Recessions have been as numerous and have lasted just as long as they did in the nineteenth century. In the countries that did not embrace modern economic theory (Japan and Germany), recessions have been less frequent, less severe, and of shorter duration than in the countries that believe that the size of the government surplus or the government deficit (i.e., government spending) effectively manages the economy and can as effectively smooth out cyclical fluctuations.

The sole result of the fiscal state has been the opposite of what it aims at: governments in all developed countries—and in most developing ones as well—have become such heavy spenders that they cannot increase their expenditures in a recession. But that, of course, is the time when, according to economic theory, they should do so in order to create purchasing power and thus revive the economy. In every single developed country, governments have reached the limits of their ability to tax and their ability to borrow. They have reached these limits during the boom times when, according to modern economic theory, they should have built up sizable surpluses. The fiscal state has spent itself into impotence.

Worst of all, the fiscal state has become a "pork-barrel state." If budget making starts with expenditures, there is no fiscal discipline; government spending becomes the means for politicians to buy votes. The strongest argument against the *ancien régime*, in the eighteenth-century absolute monarchy, was that the king used the public purse to enrich his favorite courtiers. Fiscal accountability, and especially budget accountability to an elected legislature, was established to build accountability into government and to prevent courtiers from looting the commonwealth. In the fiscal state, the looting is done by politicians to ensure their own election.

Democratic government rests on the belief that the first job of elected representatives is to defend their constituents against rapacious government. The pork-barrel state thus increasingly undermines the foundations of a free society. The elected representatives fleece their constituents to enrich special-interest groups and thereby to buy their votes. This is a denial of the concept of citizenship— and is beginning to be seen as such. The fact that it is undermining the very foundations of representative government is shown by the steady decline in voting participation. It is shown also by the steady decline in all countries of interest in the function of government, in issues, in policy.

Instead, voters increasingly vote on the basis of "what's in it for me."

Joseph Schumpeter warned in 1918 that the fiscal state would in the end undermine government's ability to govern. Fifteen years later, Keynes hailed the fiscal state as the great liberator; no longer limited by restraints on spending, government in the fiscal state could govern effectively, Keynes maintained.

We now know that Schumpeter was right.

The Megastate has been somewhat more successful in the social sphere than in the economic one. Still, it has not even earned a passing grade.

Or rather, the social actions and policies that have worked well are those that by and large do not fit the doctrine of the Megastate. They are the social policies that follow earlier rules and earlier concepts. They are the social policies that *regulate* or the social policies that *provide*. They are not the social policies in which government becomes the doer. Those, with few exceptions, have not been successful.

In the British National Health Service, the part that pays physicians for patients on their lists, works extremely well. But in the other part—where government manages hospitals and dispenses health care—there has been problem after problem. Costs are high and are going up as fast as health-care costs go up in any other country. Patients have to wait months and sometimes years for elective surgery to correct conditions that are serious but not life-threatening, whether a hip replacement, a prolapsed uterus, or a cataract in the eye.

That during these months or years the patient is in pain and often disabled is irrelevant. As a doer, government has become so incompetent that the National Health Service is now encouraging hospitals to "contract out." Government will pay hospitals as it does physicians, but it will no longer manage them.

Equally instructive are the American policies of the War on Poverty which President Lyndon B. Johnson started with such good intentions in the 1960s. One of these programs has worked. It is Headstart, which pays independent and locally managed organizations to teach disadvantaged preschool children. None of the programs government itself runs has had results.

The Cold War State did not guarantee "peace": during the post-World War II years, there were as many "minor" conflicts as in any period of history, all over the world. But the Cold War State made possible the avoidance of major global war, not despite the tremendous military arsenal, but because of it.

The arms race made possible arms control. This resulted in the longest period without great power war in modern history. Fifty years have now gone by without military conflict between great powers. The peace settlement of the Congress of Vienna after the Napoleonic Wars—so celebrated by present-day *"real-politicians"* like Henry Kissinger—maintained great power peace for thirty-eight years, from 1815 until the outbreak of the Crimean War in 1853. Then, after almost twenty years of major conflicts—the American Civil War, the war between Prussia and Austria, the war between France and Germany—there were forty-three years, from 1871 to 1914, in which no great power fought another (except for the war between Japan and Russia in 1905; but Japan was not considered a great power until after that war). Only twenty-one years elapsed between World War I and World War II. The near-fifty years following 1945 in which no great power fought another great power is thus a record. Precisely because they had become Cold War states, the major powers could control armaments and thereby make sure that there was no such preponderance of military might as would tempt one of them to risk major conflict.

The fifty years since the end of World War II have fully proven the basic assumptions on which the Cold War State was based. The weapons of modern warfare can no longer be produced in facilities that also produce the goods needed for peacetime. They cannot be produced by converting civilian facilities to wartime production as was still largely done in World War II. In turn, the facilities that produce the weapons of modern warfare—whether an aircraft carrier, a "smart bomb," or a guided missile—have to be built long before there is a war or even the threat of one.

If any proof of these assumptions had been needed, the 1991 war against Iraq provided it. None of the weapons which paralyzed what was one of the world's largest military forces, and which decided a war in the shortest time in which any war had ever been decided before, could have been produced in any peacetime facility. Each weapons system had required at least ten and in most cases fifteen years of work before it could become effective on the battlefield.

There is no going back, in other words, to the assumption on which the traditional nation-state was founded: that a small military force, augmented by reservists, is all that is needed to hold the field while civilian economic facilities are being converted to wartime production.

But the fifty years during which the Cold War State worked are also over. We need arms control now more than ever. There can be no return to "peace" if it is defined as the absence of military might. Innocence, once lost, can never be recovered. But the so-called Cold War State is no longer tenable. It no longer works.

The Cold War State has become economically self-destructive. The Soviet Union, as we have seen, succeeded in building an exceedingly powerful military force. But the burden this military force imposed became so intolerably heavy that it played a major part in the collapse of Soviet economy and Soviet society.

But even militarily, the Cold War State no longer works. In fact, the Cold War State can no longer guarantee arms control. Even small nations can no longer be prevented from building total-war capacity—whether nuclear, chemical, or biological. The worry over how to control the Soviet Union's nuclear arsenal as the empire disintegrates into individual nation-states is just one indication of this. So is the fact that any number of countries that are otherwise quite insignificant in terms of population or economic strength are rapidly acquiring nuclear, chemical, and biological warfare capacities; Iraq was one example, Libya is another, and so are Iran, North Korea, and Pakistan. These small countries could not, of course, win a war against a great power—as Iraq's Saddam Hussein still believed. But they can become international blackmailers and terrorists. With such countries as their base, small bands of adventurers (land-based pirates, in effect) could hold the world to ransom.

Arms control can thus no longer be exercised through the Cold War State as it was exercised for the half-century after World War II. Unless arms control becomes transnational, it cannot be exercised at all—which would make global conflict practically inevitable, even if the major powers still manage to avoid a Hot War between themselves.

Unlike the fiscal state and the Nanny State, the Cold War State has not been a total failure. In fact, if the aim of the national policy in the age of the absolute weapons can be said to be the avoidance of World War III, then it must be considered a success—the only success of the Megastate. But in the end this success has turned to failure, both economically and militarily.

The Megastate has thus reached a dead end.

7

The Sickness of Government

(from *The Age of Discontinuity*, 1969)

Government surely has never been more prominent than today. The most despotic government of 1900 would not have dared probe into the private affairs of its citizens as income tax collectors now do routinely in the freest society. Even the tsar's secret police did not go in for the security investigations we now take for granted. Nor could any bureaucrat of 1900 have imagined the questionnaires that governments now expect businesses, universities, or citizens to fill out in ever-mounting number and ever-increasing detail. At the same time, government has everywhere become the largest employer.

Government is certainly all-pervasive. But is it truly strong? Or is it only big?

There is mounting evidence that government is big rather than strong; that it is fat and flabby rather than powerful; that it costs a great deal but does not achieve much. There is mounting evidence also that the citizen less and less believes in government and is increasingly disenchanted with it. Indeed, government is sick—and just at the time when we need a strong, healthy, and vigorous government.

There is certainly little respect for government among the young—and even less love. But, the adults, the taxpayers, are also increasingly disenchanted. They still want more services from government. But they are everywhere approaching the point where they balk at paying for a bigger government, even though they may still want what government promises to give.

The disenchantment with government cuts across national boundaries and ideological lines. It is as prevalent in communist as in democratic societies, as common in white as in nonwhite countries. This disenchantment may well be the most profound discontinuity in the world around us. It marks a sharp change in mood and attitude between this generation and its predecessors. In the seventy years or so from the 1890s to the 1960s, mankind, especially in the developed countries, was hypnotized by government. We were in love with it and saw no limits to its abilities, or to its good intentions. Rarely has there been a more torrid political love affair than that between government and the generations that reached manhood between 1918 and 1960. Anything anyone felt needed doing during this period was to be turned over to government—and this, everyone seemed to believe, made sure that the job was already done.

But now our attitudes are in transition. We are rapidly moving to doubt and distrust of government and, in the case of the young, even to rebellion against it. We still, if only out of habit, turn social tasks over to the government. We still revise unsuccessful programs over and over again, and assert that nothing is wrong with them that a change in procedures or "competent administration" will not cure. But we no longer believe these promises when we reform a bungled program for the third time. Who, for instance, believes any more that administrative changes in the foreign aid program of the United States (or of the United Nations) will really produce rapid worldwide development?

Who really believes that the War on Poverty will vanquish poverty in the cities? Or who, in Russia, really believes that a new program of incentives will make the collective farm productive?

We still repeat the slogans of yesteryear. Indeed, we still act on them. But we no longer believe in them. We no longer expect results from government. What was a torrid romance between the people and government for so very long has now become a tired, middle-aged liaison that we do not quite know how to break off, but that only becomes exacerbated by being dragged out.

What explains this disenchantment with government?

We expected miracles—and that always produces disillusionment. Government, it was widely believed (though only subconsciously), would produce a great many things for nothing. Cost was thought a function of who did something rather than of what was being attempted.

This belief was, in effect, only one facet of a much more general illusion from which the educated and the intellectuals in particular suffered: that by turning tasks over to government, conflict and decision would be made to go away. Once the "wicked private interests" had been eliminated, the right course of action would emerge from the "facts," and decision would be rational and automatic. There would be neither selfishness nor political passion. Belief in government was thus largely a romantic escape from politics and responsibility.

That motives other than the desire for monetary gain could underlie self-interests and that values other than financial values could underlie conflict, did not occur to the generation of the thirties. Theirs was a world in which economics seemed to be the one obstacle to the millennium. Power did not appear in their vision, though this blindness in the decade of Hitler and Stalin is hard to imagine, let alone to understand.

One need not be in favor of free enterprise—let alone a friend of wealth—to see the fallacy in this argument. But reason had little to do with the belief in government ownership as the panacea. The argument was simply: "private business and profits are bad—*ergo* government ownership must be good." We may still believe in the premise; but we no longer accept the *ergo* of government ownership.

No one, least of all the young, believes any more that the conflicts, the decisions, the problems will be eliminated by turning things over to government. Government, on the contrary, has itself become one of the wicked "vested interests" for the young. And few even of the older generation expect any more than the political millennium will result from government control.

In fact, most of us today realize that to turn an area over to government creates conflict, creates vested and selfish interests, and complicates decisions. We realize that to turn something over to government makes it political instead of abolishing politics. We realize, in other ways, that government is no alternative to decision. It does not replace conflict of interests by rational decision making.

But the greatest factor in the disenchantment with government is that government has not performed. The record over these last thirty or forty years has been dismal. Government has proved itself capable of doing only two things with great effectiveness. It can wage war. And it can inflate the currency.

Other things it can promise but only rarely accomplish. Its record as an industrial manager, in the satellite countries of Eastern Europe as well as in the nationalized industries of Great Britain, has been depressing. Whether private enterprise would have done worse is not even relevant. For we expected perfection from government as industrial manager. Instead we only rarely obtained even below-average mediocrity.

Government as a planner has hardly done much better (whether in Communist Czechoslovakia or in de Gaulle's capitalist France).

But the greatest disappointment, the great letdown, is the fiasco of the welfare state. Not many people would want to do without the social services and welfare benefits of an affluent modern industrial society. But the welfare state promised a great deal more than to provide social services. It promised to release creative energies. It promised to do away with ugliness and envy and strife. No matter how well it is doing its jobs—and in some areas in some countries some jobs are being done very well—the welfare state turns out at best to be just another big insurance company, as exciting, as creative, and as inspiring as insurance companies tend to be. No one has ever laid down his life for an insurance policy.

The best we get from government in the welfare state is competent mediocrity. More often we do not even get that; we get incompetence such as we would not tolerate in an insurance company. In every country there are big areas of government administration where there is no performance whatever—only costs. This is true not only of the mess of the big cities, which no government—United States, British, Japanese, or Russian—has been able to handle. It is true in education . It is true in transportation. And the more we expand the welfare state the less capable even of routine mediocrity does it seem to become.

The great achievement of the modern state, as it emerged in the seventeenth and eighteenth centuries, was unified policy control. The great constitutional struggles of the last three hundred years were over the control powers of the central government in a united and unified nation. But this political organ, no matter how it is selected, no longer exercises such control,

Not so long ago policy control by the political organs of government could be taken for granted. Of course there were "strong" and "weak" presidents as there were "strong" and "weak" prime ministers. A Franklin Roosevelt or a Winston Churchill could get things done that weaker men could not have accomplished. But this was not, people generally believed, because they knew how to make the bureaucracy do their bidding. It was because they had the courage of strong convictions, the willingness to lay down bold and effective policies, the ability to mobilize public vision.

Today a "strong" president or a "strong" prime minister is not a man of strong policies; he is the man who knows how to make the lions of the bureaucracy do his bidding. John Kennedy had all the strength of conviction and all the boldness of a "strong" president; this is why he captured the imagination, especially of the young. He had, however, no impact whatever on the bureaucracy. He was a "strong" president in the traditional sense. But he was a singularly ineffectual one.

His contemporary, Mr. Khrushchev in Russia, similarly failed to be effective despite his apparent boldness and his popular appeal. By contrast, bureaucratic men who have no policies and no leadership qualities emerge as effective; they somehow know how to make red tape do their bidding. But then, of course, they use it for the one thing red tape is good for, i.e., to bundle up yesterday in neat packages.

This growing disparity between apparent power and actual lack of control is perhaps the greatest crisis of government. We are very good at creating administrative agencies. But no sooner are they called into being than they become ends in themselves, acquire a "vested right" to grants from the Treasury and to continuing support by the taxpayer, and achieve immunity to political direction. No sooner, in other words, are they born than they defy public will and public policy.

In 1900 there were fewer than fifty sovereignties in the whole world—twenty in Europe and twenty in the Americas, with the rest of the world having fewer than a dozen. World War I increased the number to about sixty. Now we have more than one hundred and sixty, with new "ministates" joining the ranks almost every month. Only on the American continents has there been no splintering of sovereignties. There the twenty-odd sovereignties of 1900 are still, by and large, the political reality of today (except in the rapidly fragmenting Caribbean area). Some of the new sovereignties are very large countries: India, Pakistan, Indonesia. But most of them are smaller than the Central American countries an earlier generation contemptuously dismissed as "banana republics," and much too small to discharge the minimum responsibilities of sovereignty. Today we have scores of "independent nations" whose population is well below a million people. Indeed we have some whose population is hardly as large as a good-sized village.

At the other end of the scale we have the "superpowers" whose very size and power debar them from having a national policy. They are concerned with everything, engaged everywhere, affected by every single political event no matter how remote or petty. But policy is choice and selection. If one cannot choose not to be engaged, one cannot have a policy—and neither the United States nor Russia can, in effect, say: "We are not interested." The "superpowers" are the international version of the welfare state, and, like the welfare state, incapable of priorities or of accomplishments.

The might of the superpowers is much too great to be used. If all one has at hand to swat flies is a hundred-ton drop hammer, one is defenseless. The superpowers, therefore, invariably overreact—as Russia has done in the satellite countries and as the United States has done in the Congo, in Santo Domingo, and perhaps in Vietnam. Yet they underachieve. Their might, while great enough to annihilate each other—and the rest of us into the bargain—is inappropriate to the political task. They are too powerful to have allies; they can only have dependents. And one is always the prisoner of one's dependents, while being hated by them. Only a government totally bereft of moral authority and self-confidence would act the way the Russian government, in August 1968, reacted to the developments in Czechoslovakia.

This means that decisions in the international sphere can no longer be made in an orderly and systematic fashion. It is no longer possible for any decision to be arrived at by negotiation, consultation, agreement. It can only be arrived at by dictation or by exhaustion. While force has, therefore, become infinitely more important in the international system, it has become infinitely less decisive—unless it be the ultimate force of a nuclear war that might destroy mankind.

Yet never has strong, effective, truly performing government been needed more than in this dangerous world of ours. Never has it been needed more than in this pluralist society of organizations. Never has it been needed more than in the present world economy.

We need government as the central institution in the society of organizations. We need an organ that expresses the common will and the common vision and enables each organization to make its own best contribution to society and citizen and yet to express common beliefs and common values. We need strong, effective governments in the international sphere so that we can make the sacrifices of sovereignty needed to give us working supranational institutions for world society and world economy.

The answer to diversity is not uniformity. The answer is unity. We cannot hope to suppress the diversity of our society. Each of the pluralist institutions is needed. Each discharges a necessary economic task. We cannot suppress the autonomy of these institutions. Their task makes them autonomous whether this is admitted by political rhetoric or not. We therefore have to create a focus of unity. This can only be provided by strong and effective government.

Certain things are inherently difficult for government. Being by design a protective institution, it is not good at innovation. It cannot really abandon anything. The moment government undertakes anything, it becomes entrenched and permanent. Better administration will not alter this. Its inability to innovate is grounded in government's legitimate and necessary function as society's protective and conserving organ.

A government activity, a government installation, and government employment become immediately built into the political process itself. This holds true whether we talk of a declining industry such as the nationalized British coal mines or the government-owned railroads of Europe and Japan. It holds equally true in Communist countries. No matter how bankrupt, for instance, the Stalinist economic policies have become in Czechoslovakia, Hungary, or Poland, any attempt to change them immediately runs into concern for the least productive industries which, of course, always have the most, the lowest paid, and the least skilled—and, therefore, the most "deserving"—workers.

This is not to say that all government programs are wrong, ineffectual or destructive—far from it. But even the best government program eventually outlives its usefulness. And then the response of government is likely to be: "Let's spend more on it and do more of it."

Government is a poor manager. It is, of necessity, concerned with procedure, for it is also, of necessity, large and cumbersome. Government is also properly conscious of the fact that it administers public funds and must account for every penny. It has no choice but to be "bureaucratic"—in the common usage of the term.

Whether government is a "government of laws" or a "government of men" is debatable. But every government is, by definition, a "government of forms." This means, inevitably, high cost. For "control" of the last 10 percent of phenomena always costs more than control of the first 90 percent. If control tries to account for everything it becomes prohibitively expensive. Yet this is what government is always expected to do.

The reason is not just "bureaucracy" and red tape; it is a much sounder one. A "little dishonesty" in government is a corrosive disease. It rapidly spreads to infect the whole body politic. Yet the temptation to dishonesty is always great. People of modest means and dependent on a salary handle very large public sums. People of modest position dispose of power and award contracts and privileges of tremendous importance to other people—construction jobs, radio channels, air routes, zoning laws, building codes, and so on. To fear corruption in government is not irrational.

This means, however, that government "bureaucracy"—and its consequent high costs—cannot be eliminated. Any government that is not a "government of forms" degenerates rapidly into a mutual looting society.

The purpose of government is to make fundamental decisions, and to make them effectively. The purpose of government is to focus the political energies of society. It is to dramatize issues. It is to present fundamental choices.

The purpose of government, in other words, is to govern.

This, as we have learned in other institutions, is incompatible with "doing." Any attempt to combine governing with "doing" on a large scale, paralyzes the decision-making capacity. Any attempt to have decision-making organs actually "do," also means very poor "doing." They are not focused on "doing." They are not equipped for it. They are not fundamentally concerned with it.

There is good reason today why soldiers, civil servants, and hospital administrators look to business management for concepts, principles, and practices. For business, during the last thirty years, has had to face, on a much smaller scale, the problem which modern government now faces: the incompatibility between "governing" and "doing." Business management learned that the two have to be separated, and that the top organ, the decision-maker, has to be detached from "doing." Otherwise he does not make decisions, and the "doing" does not get done either.

In business this goes by the name of "decentralization." The term is misleading. It implies a weakening of the central organ, the top management of a business. The purpose of decentralization as a principle of structure and constitutional order is, however, to make the center, the top management, strong and capable of performing the central, the top-management, task. The purpose is to make it possible for top management to concentrate on decision making and direction by sloughing off the "doing" to operating managements, each with its own mission and goals, and with its own sphere of action and autonomy.

If this lesson were applied to government, the other institutions of society would then rightly become the "doers." "Decentralization" applied to government would not just be another form of "federalism" in which local rather than central government discharges the "doing" tasks. It would rather be a systematic policy of using the other, the nongovernmental institutions of the society of organizations, for the actual "doing," i.e., for performance, operations, execution. Such a policy might be called "*reprivatization*." The tasks which flowed to government in the last century because the original private institution of society, the family, could not discharge them, would be turned over to the new, nongovernmental institutions that have sprung up and grown these last sixty to seventy years.

Government would start out by asking the question: "How do these institutions work and what can they do? It would then ask: "How can political and social objectives be formulated and organized in such a manner as to become opportunities for performance for these institutions?" It would also ask: "And what opportunities for accomplishment of political objectives do the abilities and capacities of these institutions offer to government?"

This would be a very different role for government from that it plays in traditional political theory. In all our theories government is *the* institution.

If "reprivatization" were to be applied, however, government would become *one* institution albeit the central, the top, institution.

Reprivatization would give us a different society from any our social theories now assume. In these theories government does not exist. It is outside of society. Under reprivatization government would become the central social institution.

Political theory and social theory, for the last two hundred and fifty years, have been separate. If we applied to government and to society what we have learned about organization these last fifty years, the two would again come together. The nongovernmental institutions—university, business, and hospital, for instance—would be seen as organs for the accomplishment of results. Government would be seen as society's resource for the determination of major objectives, and as the "conductor" of social diversity.

We do not face a "withering away of the state." On the contrary, we need a vigorous, a strong, and a very active government. But we do face a choice between big but impotent government and a government that is strong because it confines itself to decision and direction and leaves the "doing" to others.

We do not face a "return of laissez-faire" in which the economy is left alone. The economic sphere cannot and will not be considered to lie outside the public domain. But the choices for the economy—as well as for all other sectors—are no longer *either* complete governmental indifference or complete governmental control.

Ultimately we will need a new political theory and probably new constitutional law. We will need new concepts and new social theory. Whether we will get these and what they will look like, we cannot know today. But we can know that we are disenchanted with government, primarily because it does not perform. We can say that we need, in pluralist society, a government that can and does govern. This is not a government that "does"; it is not a government that "administers"; it is a government that governs.

8

No More Salvation by Society
(from *The New Realities*, 1989)

"As long as it does not threaten the Communist Party's monopoly of power, it's socialism." This is the new "party line" preached by Mikhail Gorbachev in Russia and by Xiaoping Deng in China. But this is not a new pragmatism, as the Western press calls it. It is the ideology of naked power (and very old). It totally abjures everything that communism of any kind—or socialism for that matter— ever stood for. It is as if the Pope declared that as long as Catholics pay the Peter's Pence to Rome, it does not matter whether they believe in Christ or not. Yet no one except a small handful of superannuated party hacks was surprised by Gorbachev's ideology of power. Everybody else—and especially in the Communist countries—had much earlier lost all faith in *salvation by society*. Everybody else had become not a pragmatist but a cynic.

Mr. Gorbachev in Russia, and Mr. Deng and his successors in China, may succeed in maintaining their party's monopoly of power or even in reviving the economy. But one thing they cannot restore is the belief in salvation by society, whether through communism or by any other ism. It is gone for good. The belief in salvation by society is equally gone in non-Communist countries. No one—except perhaps the "liberation theologians" in South America—believes any more in the power of social action to create a perfect society, or even to bring society closer to such an ideal, or in fundamentally changing the individual to produce the "new Adam."

Fifty years ago, such beliefs were commonplace. Not only Socialists but the great majority of political thinkers all over the world believed that social action—and especially the abolition of private property—would fundamentally change the human being. There would be Socialist Man, Nazi Man, Communist Man, and so on. The differences were not over the basic creed itself but over the speed of advance, over which particular action would be most productive. The main argument was over means. Should it be the role of politics and government to remove obstacles to social perfectibility—what today would be called "neoconservative" and sixty years ago was called "Liberal?" Or should government actively create new institutions and new conditions?

The belief in salvation by *faith* dominated medieval Europe. Revived in the Protestant Reformation of the sixteenth century, it had waned by the middle of the seventeenth century. To be sure, each religious denomination proclaimed—and still proclaims—its way as "the only right way." But by the middle of the seventeenth century it had become widely accepted that faith was a personal matter. This did not mean that religious persecutions stopped; there were still some even in the nineteenth-century West. And not until the middle of the nineteenth century did political disabilities based on religion totally disappear even in Western countries. But the belief that religious faith could create the City of God on earth had disappeared— or become irrelevant—a hundred years earlier.

The void created by the disappearance of the belief in salvation through faith was filled in the mid-1700s by the emergence of the belief in salvation by society, that is, by a temporal social order, embodied in an equally temporal government. This belief was first enunciated by Jean-Jacques Rosseau in France. Thirty years later, Jeremy Bentham in England worked it up into a political system. It was cast in its permanent form, into a "scientific" absolutism, by the "father of sociology," Auguste Comte, in France, and by G. W. F. Hegel in Germany. Those two then "begat" Marx. Lenin, Hitler, and Mao were all Marx's children.

In the rise of the West to world dominance, superiority in machines, money, and guns was probably less important than the promise of salvation by society. *And now it is gone.*

The vision was revived after the failure of the 1848 revolutions in continental Europe. It became central to Marx and Marxism when the Paris Commune of 1871 ended in bloody massacre and military suppression. It still sustained Mao's followers in the "Great Cultural Revolution" in China only fifteen years ago. But even the terrorists who kill and burn in the name of The Revolution—the small band of

Maoists, for instance, who terrorize the Peruvian Andes—no longer believe in the messianic promise. They destroy not because they hope but because they despair.

There may well be new messianic movements. The disappearance of the belief in salvation by society and in the second coming of a secular revolution may call forth new prophets and new messiahs. But these new messianic movements are likely to be anti-society and based on the assertion that there can be salvation only outside society, only in and the through the person, perhaps even only in and through withdrawal from society.

Part 4

The New Pluralism

Introduction to Part 4

I cannot claim to have discovered the New Organization. Walter Rathenau (1867-1922) —philosopher, industrialist, statesman,and early victim of right-wing terrorism—first pointed out in his 1918 book *Die Neue Wirtschaft*, (*The New Economy*), that the business corporation was new and unprecedented and an "organization," that is, an autonomous center of power with its own governance, its own goals, its own values. Fifteen years later—and quite independently— so did the American economist, John R. Commons (1862-1945), in his 1934 book *Institutional Economics*. But I can claim that I was the first to realize that the business corporation was only the earliest of these new institutions and that ours had become a society of organizations—and with it a society of a New Pluralism.

For six hundred years—from the middle of the thirteenth century on—political history in the West was largely the history of the dismantling of pluralism. By the mid-nineteenth century that task had been accomplished. There was then only one power center in society—the Government. Except in the U.S. (and to a lesser degree in the U.K.) all earlier power centers had either been suppressed; or they had become organs of the state and government servants such as the clergy in all European Continental countries. But just when Pluralism seemed to have been abolished, the business corporation arose as a new and autonomous power center within society. Small wonder that for a long time only the business corporation was seen as an "organization." In fact this was still the position taken by John Kenneth Galbraith (b. 1908), in the most influential of his books, the 1967 *The New Industrial State*.

I too held at first the same position—for example, in my 1942 book *The Future of Industrial Man*. But then, in the mid- and late1940s I began to work with other institutions—hospitals, for instance, unions, universities. And I began to realize that they were different indeed from the institutions whose names they had inherited. They were fast becoming something quite new, that is, organizations. I also gradually began to realize that they, rather than the business corporation, were the growth sectors of a modern society. In fact, the business corporation as *the* organization probably peaked around the time of World War I—and no later than the 1930s. *The* growth organization—both in size and in power—of the second half of the twentieth century was surely the university.

We are moving—and rapidly—into a New Pluralism. But the organizations of this new pluralism are quite different from any earlier organization. First, they are single-purpose institutions—the only mission and purpose of the hospital is to take care of the sick. This singleness of purpose is both the secret of their effectiveness and their limitation. Secondly, they are not "communities"; their mission, purpose and results are totally *outside* of them. Finally, while they exist, of necessity, in a place (thought the Internet may change this) they are not and cannot be "members" of that geographic and local community. They have their own separate mission, goals, values.

I came to realize this fairly early—in the last years of the 1940s. And from the late 1940s on, more and more of my own work has been with organizations other than businesses—hospitals, universities, community organizations, unions (and government agencies as well). But I did not write about the Society of Organizations until my 1959 book *The Landmarks of Tomorrow* and then, especially, until my 1969 book *The Age of Discontinuity* from which two of the three chapters of this part on the New Pluralism are chosen.

9

The New Pluralism

(from *The Age of Discontinuity*, 1969)

Historians two hundred years hence may see as central to the twentieth century what we ourselves have been paying almost no attention to: the emergence of a society of organizations in which every single social task of importance is entrusted to a large institution. To us, the contemporaries, one of these institutions—government or big business, the university or the union—often looks like *the* institution. To the future historian, however, the most impressive fact may be the emergence of a new and distinct pluralism, that is, of a society of institutional diversity and diffusion of power.

Sixty years ago, before World War I, the social scene everywhere looked much like the Kansas prairie: the largest thing on the horizon was the individual. Most social tasks were accomplished in and through family-sized units. Even government, no matter how formidable it looked, was really small and cozy. The government of Imperial Germany looked like a colossus to its contemporaries; but an official in the middle ranks could still know personally everyone of importance in every single ministry and department.

The scaling-up in size since then is striking. There is no country in the world today where the entire government establishment of 1910 could not comfortably be housed in the smallest of the new government buildings now going up, with room to spare for a grand-opera house and a skating rink.

In the days before World War I, the one "large" organization around was business. But the "big business" of 1910 would strike us today as a veritable minnow. The "octopus" that gave our grandparents nightmares, John D. Rockefeller's Standard Oil Trust, was cut into fourteen pieces by the Supreme Court in 1911. Less than thirty years later, by 1940, every one of these successor companies was larger than Rockefeller's Standard Oil Trust had been—by every measurement: employees, sales, capital invested, and so on. Yet only three of these fourteen Standard Oil daughter companies (Jersey Standard, Socony Mobil, and Standard of California) were "major" international oil companies. The rest ranked from "small" to "middling" by 1940 yardsticks and would be "small business" today, another thirty years later.

We cannot hope to understand this society of ours unless we accept that *all* institutions have become giants. Businesses today are a good deal bigger than the biggest company was in John D. Rockefeller's time. But universities are relatively a good deal bigger still than Rockefeller's other creation: the University of Chicago, which he founded, around the turn of the century, as perhaps the first modern university in America. Hospitals are relatively bigger still and a great deal more complex than any of the other institutions.

The problem of the "concentration" of power is no longer peculiar to the economy. Business concentration has not increased in the last sixty years or so, and "small" business (which is also a good deal bigger than it used to be) is holding its own, apparently without difficulty. But the three or four largest unions hold relatively much more industrial power than the ten or twenty or thirty largest businesses. And we have a "concentration of brain power" in a few large universities such as has never been seen in any other area of social life—and such as would not have been tolerated earlier. The great majority of all doctorates in the United States are given by some twenty universities—one-tenth of one percent of all institutions of higher learning in the country. And nothing resembling the concentration of military might in the arsenals of the "superpowers," the United States and Russia, has been known in international society since the Roman Empire at the peak of its power in the first century A.D.

But the scaling-up in size and budget is not the most important change. What makes the real difference is that all our major social functions are today being discharged in and through these large, organized institutions. Every single social task of major impact—defense and education, government and the production and distribution of goods, health care and the search for knowledge—is increasingly entrusted to institutions which are organized for perpetuity and which are managed by professionals, whether they are called "managers," "administrators," or "executives."

Government looks like the most powerful of these institutions—it is certainly the one that spends the most. But each of the others discharges a function that is essential to society and has to be discharged in its own right. Each has its own autonomous management. Each has its own job to do and therefore its own objectives, its own values, and its own rationale. If government is still the "lord," it can no longer be the "master." Increasingly, whatever the theory of a government or its constitutional law, government functions as a "coordinator," a "chairman," or at most a "leader." Yet, paradoxically, government suffers from doing too much and too many things. Government, to be effective and strong, may have to learn to "decentralize" to the other institutions, to *do* less in order to *achieve* more.

What has emerged in this half-century is *a new pluralism*. There is little left of the structure that our seventeenth-century political theory still preaches, a structure in which government is the only organized power center. It is totally inadequate, however, to see just one of these new institutions—business, for instance, or the union, or the university—and proclaim it *the* new institution. Social theory, to be meaningful at all, must start out with the reality of a pluralism of institutions—a galaxy of suns rather than one big center surrounded by moons that shine only by reflected light.

Pluralist power centers of yesterday—the duke, the count, the abbot, even the yeoman—differed from each other only in titles and revenues. One was the superior and overlord of the other. Each center was limited in territory, but each was a total community and embraced whatever organized social activity and political life there was. Each center was concerned with the same basic activity, above all, wresting a livelihood from the land. The federalism of the American system still assumes this traditional pluralism. The federal government, state governments, and municipalities all have their own distinct geographic limitations and stand to each other in a position of higher and lower. But each has essentially the same function. Each is a territorial government with police powers and tax powers, charged with traditional government tasks, whether defense or justice or public order.

This is simply not true of the new institutions. Each of them is a special-purpose institution. The hospital exists for the sake of health care, the business to produce economic goods and services, the university for the advancement and teaching of knowledge, each government agency for its own specific purpose, the armed services for defense, and so on. Not one of them can be considered "superior" or "inferior" to the other, for only a fool would consider the advancement of knowledge superior to health care or to the provision of economic goods and services. But at the same time, not one of them can be defined territorially. Each, in other words, is "universal" in a way that none of the old institutions (excepting only the medieval church) ever claimed to be. And yet each of them is limited to a small fragment of human existence, to a single facet of human community.

The problems of this new pluralism are quite different from the problems of both the pluralisms of our past and the unitary society of our political theory and constitutional law. In earlier pluralisms every member of the system, from the yeoman up to the most powerful king, understood exactly the positions of the other members of the hierarchy, their tasks and their problems. Indeed, everyone had exactly the same tasks and the same problems; only the scale varied. In the new pluralism each institution has different tasks. It takes different things for granted. It considers different things to be important. While the vice president of a big business, the division chief in the government agency, and the department chairman in the university may operate on a very similar scale and have managerial problems of comparable magnitude, they do not easily understand each other's roles, tasks, and decisions. The members of earlier pluralisms were forever worried about their "precedence" and their place in the hierarchy relative to each other. This is not a major concern in today's pluralism. The hospital administrator is not particularly concerned as to whether he ranks the corporation president or the union leader or the air force general. But they all worry about "communications." It takes a great deal of experience—or, at the least, a great deal of imagination—for one of the executives in today's pluralism to have any idea what the other ones are up to and why.

These organizations have to live together and to work together. They are interdependent. Not one of them could exist by itself. Not one of them is by itself viable, let alone a total community, as were the components of earlier pluralist society.

A theory of the society of organizations would have to be built on organizational interdependence. The "interdependence" of organizations is different from anything we ever meant before by this term. It is not a new observation, of course, that no man in society is an island. It is not new that all of us, including the hermit, can only live our way because we can take it for granted that a host of other people will do their jobs for us.

This physical interdependence is what people usually have in mind when they think about "interdependence" at all. And of course this traditional kind of interdependence has become much more pronounced. The megalopolis, above all, is a universe of interacting, interdependent services, each absolutely essential for the functioning of the whole and the very existence of each member of the community.

But the new interdependence among organizations is not primarily physical. Increasingly, major organizations farm out to each other the very performance of their own functions. Increasingly each organization is using the others as agents for the accomplishment of its own tasks. There is an intertwining of functions such as we have never known before. The roles are subject to rapid change; what one organization is expected to do today, another one may take on tomorrow.

It no longer shocks anyone to hear that the hospital of tomorrow or the school of tomorrow may be designed, built, and largely run by businesses—for trustees or the school board, or course. It no longer shocks anyone to hear the mayor of New York City propose that the city hospitals be turned over to the private hospitals—just at the time when the private hospitals increasingly talk about turning over their administration to large companies with "systems" experience. And what many hail as the first promising attacks on the horrible mess of urban housing are the proposals of a few large companies, e.g., General Electric, to develop whole planned cities within reasonable commuting distance of the major metropolitan areas.

What used to be simple relationships in which major institutions rarely met each other, and even more rarely had much to do with each other, is becoming an increasingly complex, confused, diffuse and crowded living-together. It is a chaotic, a developing, and by no means a clear, let alone clean, relationship. Political scientists are wont to talk of the "web" of government. But what we now have could only be described as a "felt" in which strands of the most diverse kinds are tangled together in no order at all.

These are truly *liaisons dangereuses* and difficult relationships. Indeed the more results they produce, the more friction they also entail. If government, for instance in the defense programs, insists that its private contractors adapt to the logic and rationale of a government service, they smother the contractor in red tape, in regulations, and in bureaucratic restrictions. And in the end, government is greatly irked because the contractor does not produce. But if government accepts the contractor's rationale and way of operating, that is, a business logic, the hard-won principles of accountability for public money all go by the board.

In public accounts it is assumed that results, as a rule, cannot be clearly measured. What matters, therefore, is that costs be scrupulously recorded. Costs exist—results are hypothetical. But in business logic, costs exist only in contemplation of results. As long as the results are there, the less spent on controlling costs the better. The government servant simply does not understand this. But the businessman equally does not understand the government man's logic. Each rubs the other raw trying to work together, each resents the attitude of the other and is deeply suspicious of it, and yet each is dependent on the other.

The same is true of yoking together government and the medical profession. Medical men see individuals. Indeed none of us would want to be treated by a physician who treats "averages." But no government can handle anything but large numbers or go by anything but averages. The relationship between university and business, between university and government, between university and the armed forces is similarly one of mutual failure to understand, of mutual suspicion and constant friction. And yet we will continue to see more of these relationships. They are necessary to produce the results that society wants.

The pluralist structure of modern society is independent, by and large, of political constitution and control, of social theory, or of economics. It requires a political and social theory of its own.

This is true of each individual organization as well. It too is new. We have, of course, had large organizations for centuries. The pyramids were built by highly organized masses of people. Armies have often been large and highly organized. But these organizations of yesterday were fundamentally different from the institutions of today.

Today's organization is a knowledge organization. It exists to make productive hundreds, sometimes thousands, of specialized kinds of knowledge. This is true of the hospital where we now have some thirty-odd or more health-care professions—each with its own course of study, its own diploma, and its own professional code and standards. It is true of today's business, of today's government agency, and increasingly of today's army. In every one of them, the bulk of the workers are hired not to do manual work but to do knowledge work. The Egyptian fellahin who pulled at the ropes when Cheops' supervisors barked out the order did not have to do any thinking and were not expected to have any initiative. The typical employee in today's large organization is expected to use his head to make decisions and to put knowledge responsibly to work.

But perhaps even more important: today's knowledge organization is designed as a permanent organization. All the large organizations of the past were short-lived. They were called into being for one specific task and disbanded when the task had been accomplished. They were temporary.

They were clearly the exception as well. The great majority of people in earlier society were unaffected by them. Today the great majority of people depend on organizations for their livelihood, their opportunities, and their work. The large organization is the environment of man in modern society.

It is the source also of the opportunities of today's society. It is only because we have these institutions that we have jobs for educated people. Without them we would be confined, as always in the past, to jobs for people without education, people who, whether skilled or unskilled, work with their hands. Knowledge jobs exist only because permanent knowledge organization has become the rule.

At the same time, modern organization creates new problems as well; above all, problems of authority over people. For authority is needed to get the job done. What should it be? What is legitimate? What are the limitations? There are also problems of the purpose, task, and effectiveness of each organization. There are problems of management. For the organization itself, like every collective, is a legal fiction. It is individuals in the organization who make the decisions and take the actions which are then ascribed to the institution, whether it be the "United States," the "General Electric Company," or "Misericordia Hospital." There are problems of order and problems of morality. There are problems of efficiency and problems of relationships. And for none of them does tradition offer us much guidance.

The permanent organization in which varieties of knowledge are brought together to achieve results is new. The organization as the rule rather than as the exception is new. And a society of organizations is the newest thing of all.

What is therefore urgently needed is a theory of organizations.

10

Toward a Theory of Organizations
(from *The Age of Discontinuity*, 1969)

In the spring of 1968, a witty book made headlines for a few weeks. Entitled *Management & Machiavelli*, it asserted that every business is a political organization and that, therefore, Machiavelli's rules for princes and rulers are fully applicable to the conduct of corporation executives.

The suburban ladies at whom the reviews of *Management & Machiavelli* were largely aimed are probably fully aware that the bridge club and the PTA have nothing to learn about politicking from big business, or indeed from Machiavelli. That every organization must organize power and must therefore have politics is neither new nor startling.

But during the last twenty years, nonbusinesses—government, the armed services, the university, the hospital—have begun to apply to themselves the concepts and methods of business management. And this is indeed new. This is indeed startling.

When the Canadian armed services were unified in the spring of 1968, the first meeting of general officers from all the services had as its theme "managing by objectives." Government after government has organized "administrative staff colleges" for its senior civil servants in which it tries to teach them "principles of management." And when 9,000 secondary school principals of the United States met in the crisis year of 1968, with its racial troubles and its challenges to established curricula, they chose for their keynote speech, "The Effective Executive," and invited an expert on business management to deliver it.

The British Civil Service, that citadel of the "arts degree" in the classics, now has a management division, a management institute, and management courses of all kinds. Demand from nonbusiness organizations for the services of "management consultants" is rising a great deal faster than the demand from business.

What is new is the realization that all our institutions are "organizations" and have, as a result, a common dimension of management. These organizations are complex and multidimensional. They require thinking and understanding in at least three areas—the functional or operational, the moral, and the political. The new general theory of a society of organizations will look very different from the social theories we are accustomed to. Neither Locke nor Rousseau has much relevance. Neither has John Stuart Mill nor Karl Marx.

How do organizations function and operate? How do they do their job? There is not much point in concerning ourselves with any other question about organizations unless we first know what they exist for.

The functional or operational area by itself has three major parts, each a large and diverse discipline in its own right. They have to do with goals, with management, and with individual performance.

1. Organizations do not exist for their own sake. They are means: each is society's organ for the discharge of one social task. Survival is not an adequate goal for an organization as it is for a biological species. The organization's goal is a specific contribution to individual and society. The test of its performance, unlike that of a biological organism, therefore, always lies outside of it.

The first area in which we need a theory of organizations is, therefore, that of the organization's goals. How does it decide what its objectives should be? How does it mobilize its energies for performance? How does it measure whether it performs?

It is not possible to be effective unless one first decides what one wants to accomplish. It is not possible to manage, in other words, unless one first has a goal. It is not even possible to design the structure of an organization unless one knows what it is supposed to be doing and how to measure whether it is doing it.

Anyone who has ever tried to answer the question, "What is our business?" has found it a difficult, controversial, and elusive task.

In fact, it is never possible to give a "final" answer to the question, "What is our business?" Any answer becomes obsolete within a short period. The question has to be thought through again and again.

But if no answer at all is forthcoming, if objectives are not clearly set, resources will be splintered and wasted. There will be no way to measure the results. If the organization has not determined what its objectives are, it cannot determine what effectiveness it has and whether it is obtaining results or not.

There is no "scientific" way to set objectives for an organization. They are rightly value judgments, that is, true political questions. One reason for this is that the decisions stand under incurable uncertainty. They are concerned with the future. And we have no "facts" regarding the future. In this area, therefore, there is always a clash of programs and a conflict of political values.

The twentieth-century political scientist was not entirely irresponsible when he abandoned concern with values, political programs, and ideologies and focused instead on the process of decision-making. The most difficult and most important decisions in respect to objectives are not what to do. They are, first, what to abandon as no longer worthwhile and, second, what to give priority to and what to concentrate on. These are not, as a rule, ideological decisions. They are judgments, of course; they are, and should be, informed judgments. Yet they should be based on a definition of alternatives rather than on opinion and emotion.

The decision about what to abandon is by far the most important and the most neglected.

Large organizations cannot be versatile. A large organization is effective through its mass rather than through its agility. Fleas can jump many times their own height, but not elephants. Mass enables the organization to put to work a great many more kinds of knowledge and skill than could possibly be combined in any one person or small group. But mass is also a limitation. An organization, no matter what it would like to do, can only do a small number of tasks at any one time. This is not something that better organization or "effective communications" can cure. *The law of organization is concentration.*

2. In their objectives the major organizations are all different. Each of them serves a different purpose of the community. In the managerial area, however, organizations are essentially similar.

Since all organizations require large numbers of people brought together for joint performance and integrated into a common undertaking, they all have the problem of balancing the objectives of the institution against the needs and desires of the individual. Each organization has the task of balancing the need for order against the need for flexibility and individual scope. Each requires a structure determined by the task and its demands. Each also requires a structure determined by generic "principles of organization," that is, in effect, by constitutional rules. Unless each recognizes the authority inherent in the "logic of the situation" and the knowledge of individuals, there will be no performance. Unless each also has a decision-making authority beyond which there is no appeal, there will be no decision. And the two different structures, each with a logic of its own, have to coexist in dynamic balance within the same organization.

It is in the field of management that we have done the most work during the last half-century. We had never before faced the task of organizing and leading large knowledge organizations. We had to learn rapidly. No one who knows the field would maintain that we yet know much. Indeed, if there is any agreement in this hotly contested area, it is that tomorrow's organization structures will look different from any we know today. Yet work in management is by now no longer pioneering. What is taught under this name in our universities may be 90 percent old wives' tales—and the rest may be procedures rather than management. Still the main challenges in the area are sufficiently well known.

We know, for instance, that we have to measure results. We also know that with the exception of business, we do not know how to measure results in most organizations.

It may sound plausible to measure the effectiveness of a mental hospital by how well its beds—a scarce and expensive commodity—are utilized. Yet a study of the mental hospitals of the Veterans' Administration brought out that this yardstick leads to mental patients' being kept in the hospital—which, therapeutically, is about the worst thing that can be done to them. Clearly, however, lack of utilization, that is, empty beds, would also not be the right yardstick. How then does one measure whether a mental hospital is doing a good job within the wretched limits of our knowledge of mental diseases?

And how does one measure whether a university is doing a good job?

By the jobs and salaries its students get twenty years after graduation? By that elusive myth, the "reputation" of this or that faculty which, only too often, is nothing but self-praise and good academic propaganda? By the number of Ph.D.s or scientific prizes the alumni have earned? Or by the donations they make to their alma mater? Each such yardstick bespeaks a value judgment regarding the purpose of the university.

3. The last field within the operational area is probably the one in which there is the least difference in organizations. This is the area of personal effectiveness within organizations.

Organizations are legal fictions. By themselves they do nothing, decide nothing, plan nothing. Individuals do decide and plan. Above all, organizations only "act" insofar as the people act whom we commonly call "executives," that is, the people who are expected to make decisions that affect the results and performance of the organization.

In the knowledge organization every knowledge worker is an "executive." The number of people who have to be effective for modern organization to perform is therefore very large and rapidly growing. The well-being of our entire society depends increasingly on the ability of these large numbers of knowledge workers to be effective in a true organization. And so, largely, do the achievement and satisfaction of the knowledge worker.

Executive effectiveness is not only something the organization needs. It is not the formula for the "organization man" of popular myth. It is, above all, something the individual needs. For the organization must be *his* tool, while at the same time it produces the results that are needed by society and community.

Executive effectiveness is not automatic. It is not "how to be successful without half trying." It is not even "how to be successful while trying." The organization is a new and different environment. It makes new and different demands on the executive. But it also gives him new and different opportunities. It does not require so much new behavior as it requires new understanding.

Ultimately, it requires that the individual be able to make decisions that get the right things done. This demand is not made on people in traditional environments. The peasant is told by tradition what to do and how to do it.

The craftsman had his guild practices that laid down the work, its sequence and its standards. But the executive in organization is not informed by his environment. He has to decide for himself. If he does not decide, he cannot achieve results. He is bound to be both unsuccessful and unfulfilled.

So far management theory has given little attention to this area. We have stressed the abilities of the executive, his training, and his knowledge, but not his specific attribute, which is effectiveness. This is what the executive is expected to be, yet we do not know, by and large, what it means. All anyone knows is that few executives attain one-tenth of the effectiveness their abilities, their knowledge, and their industry deserve.

Executive effectiveness will eventually occupy, in the theory of institutions, the place that, throughout the history of political theory, has been occupied by the discussion of the education of the ruler (to which tradition Machiavelli fully belonged, though his answers were different). The constitutional lawyers, the earlier exponents of what we now call "management," asked: "What structure does the polity require?" The thinkers and writers on the "education of the ruler" (of whom Plato, in the *Republic* and in the *Seventh Letter*, was the first great name) asked, "what kind of man does the ruler have to be, and what does he have to do?" It is this question that is now being asked again when we talk of the "effective executive." Only we no longer talk of the "Prince," that is, of one man in a high place. In the knowledge organization, almost everybody occupies a "high place" in the traditional meaning of the term.

These three areas: policy objectives and the measurement of performance against targets, management, and executive effectiveness are quite different. Yet they all belong to the same field and same dimension of organization. They all deal with the functioning of organization.

The "social responsibility of business" has become a favorite topic of journalists, of business leaders, of politicians, and of business schools. The ethics of organization is indeed a central concern of our times. But to speak of the "social responsibility of business" assumes that responsibility and irresponsibility are a problem for business alone. Clearly, however, they are central problems for all organizations. All institutions have power, and all of them exercise power. All of them need to take responsibility for their actions, therefore.

The least responsible of our major institutions today is not business; it is the university. Of all our institutions, it probably has the greatest social impact.

It has a monopoly position such as no other organization occupies. Once a young person has finished college, he has a multitude of career choices. But until then education controls him and controls his access to all the choices: the business corporation and the civil service, the professions and the hospital, and so on. Yet the university has not even realized that it has power. It has not even realized that it has impact and, therefore, a problem of responsibility.

In any case, the approach from "responsibility" is too limited and therefore a misdirection. There is, as every constitutional lawyer knows, no such word as "responsibility" in the dictionary of politics. The word is "responsibility *and* authority." Whoever assumes "responsibility" asserts "authority." Conversely, one is responsible for whatever one has authority over. To take responsibility where one has no authority is usurpation of power.

The question, therefore, is not what are the "social responsibilities" of organizations. The question is what is the proper authority. What impacts do the organizations have because of their function?

1. Any institution has to have impact on society in order to carry out its mission. Similarly, an institution has to be somewhere. This means impacts on the local community and the natural environment. Every institution, moreover, employs people, which implies a good deal of authority over them. These impacts are necessary; we could not otherwise obtain the goods and services from business, the education from the schools, the new knowledge from the research labs, or the traffic control from local government. But they are not the purpose of the organization. They are incidental to it.

These impacts then are a necessary evil in the fullest meaning of the phrase.

We would most certainly not permit authority over people if we knew how to obtain without it the performance for the sake of which we maintain the institution. Indeed every manager, if he had sense, would be happy to get the job done without people. They are a nuisance. He does not want to be a "government." It only gets in the way of his doing his job.

The first law of "social responsibility" is, therefore, to limit impacts on people as much as possible. And the same is true for all other impacts. The impacts on society and community are interferences. They can be tolerated only if narrowly defined and interpreted strictly. In particular, to claim "loyalty" from employees is impermissible and illegitimate. The relationship is based on the employment contract which should be interpreted more narrowly than any other contract in law. This does not rule out affection, gratitude, friendship, mutual respect, and confidence between the organization and the people in its employ. These are valuable. But they have to be earned.

The second law, perhaps even more important, is the duty to anticipate impact. It is the job of the organization to look ahead and to think through which of its impacts are likely to become social problems. And then it is the duty of the organization to try to prevent these undesirable side results.

This is in the self-interest of the organization. Whenever an undesirable impact is not prevented by the organization itself, it ultimately boomerangs. It leads to regulation, to punitive laws, and to outside interference. In the end, the annoying or damaging impact leads to a "scandal"; and laws that result from a "scandal" are invariably bad laws. They punish ninety-nine innocents to foil one miscreant. They penalize good practice, yet rarely prevent malpractice. They express emotion rather than reason.

Conversely, whenever the leaders of an institution anticipate an impact and think through what needs to be done to prevent it or to make it acceptable, they are given a respectful hearing by the public and the politicians. This is particularly true of business. Whenever business leaders have anticipated an impact of business and have thought through its prevention or treatment, their proposals have been accepted. Whenever they have waited until there was a "scandal," and a public outcry, they have been saddled with punitive regulation which, only too often, has aggravated the problem.

It is for instance not true that the American automobile industry has not been safety-conscious. On the contrary, it pioneered in safe-driving instruction and in the design of safe highways. It did a great deal to reduce the frequency of accidents—and with considerable success. What it is being penalized for today, however, is its failure to make an accident itself less dangerous. Yet when the manufacturers tried to introduce safety-engineered cars (as Ford did in the early fifties when it tried to introduce safety belts), the public refused to buy them. The automobile manufacturers bitterly resent as rank ingratitude that they are being blamed for unsafe cars, subjected to punitive legislation, and held up to public scorn. Yet, the automobile industry deserves the blame. It should have agitated for accident-prevention measures instead of waiting until Ralph Nader did.

Whatever can be done only if everybody does it requires law. "Voluntary effort" in which everyone has to do something that in the short run is risky and unpopular has never succeeded. There is generally, in every group, at least one member who is stupid, greedy, and shortsighted. If one waits for "voluntary action" on the part of everyone, no one acts. The individual organization that anticipates a problem has, therefore, the duty of doing the unpopular: to think the problem through, to formulate a solution, and to lobby for the right public policy despite open disapproval by other "members of the club." No one who has taken this responsibility has ever failed—or ever suffered. But whenever an institution shrinks back, pleading "the public won't let us," or "the industry won't let us" it pays a heavy price in the end. The public will forgive blindness. It will not forgive failure to act on one's own best knowledge. This is rightly considered cowardice.

2. Ideally an organization converts into opportunities for its own performance the satisfaction of social needs and wants, including those created by its own impacts. In pluralist society every organization is expected to be an entrepreneur in the traditional meaning of the term, that is, the agent of society which shifts resources from less productive to more productive employment. Each organization defines "productive" in terms of its own area of performance. Each, therefore, measures results differently. But all of them have the same task.

This means, in particular, that it is an ethical demand on business to convert into profitable business the satisfaction of social needs and wants.

This aspect of the "social responsibilities of organizations"—the anticipation of social needs and their conversion into opportunities for performance and results—may be particularly important in a period of discontinuity such as we are facing. For the last fifty years or so, these opportunities were not common. The major challenge to all institutions lay in doing better what was already being done. Opportunities for tackling new and different things, whether in business, in health care, or in education were scarce.

But this was not always so. A hundred years ago the great entrepreneurial opportunities lay, like those of today, in the satisfaction
of social needs and wants. To make education into a profitable large
business, or to make urban housing into such a business, may
strike people today—businessmen as well as their critics—as
rather outlandish. But these are not too different from the opportunities that led to the development of the modern electrical industry, the telephone, the big-city newspaper and the book publisher, the department store, or to urban transit. All those were community wants a hundred years ago. They all required vision and
entrepreneurial courage. They all required a considerable amount of
new technology and also a good deal of social innovation. They all
were needs of the individual which could only be satisfied on a mass
basis.

These needs were not satisfied because they were seen as "bur-
dens," that is, as "responsibilities." They were satisfied because they
were seen as opportunities. To seek opportunity, in other words, is
the ethics of organization.

Organizations, to sum up, do not act "socially responsible" when
they concern themselves with "social problems" outside of their own
sphere of competence and action. They act "socially responsible"
when they satisfy society's needs through concentration on their own
specific job. They act the most responsibly when they convert public need into their own achievements.

The great majority of people, and especially the overwhelming
majority of the educated people in our society, are employees of
large organizations. As such, the organization exercises, of necessity, considerable authority over them. It is, in fact, the one immediate authority for most of them. There are also the students of the
schools, colleges, and universities, and a great many other publics
who are inexorably subject to direction and control by one or more
of these institutions. The legitimacy of organizational power and of
organization-managements—whether of government agency, of
hospital, of university, or of business—is, therefore, a problem. It is
the political problem of the society of organizations.

However, the organizations of our pluralist society are not and
cannot be genuine communities. The aim of true community is always to fulfill itself. But within itself today organization has no aim,
just as within itself it has no results. All it has within itself are costs.

The comparison of management, whether in business, in the university, the government agency, or in the hospital, with a true "government," which is done so entertainingly in *Management & Machiavelli*, is, therefore, half-truth. The managements of modern social institutions (including the government agency that administers, e.g., a post office) are not "governments." Their job is functional rather than political. Such power and authority as they have, they exercise to satisfy one partial need of society. Unlike earlier pluralist powers, their sphere is not the totality of social and community needs or of social and community resources. Their sphere is one specific social demand and want. Their command is over resources allocated to a specific and limited, though vital, task. Whatever capacity to perform these institutions enjoy, they owe to their specialization, to their confinement to one limited task, and to their investment of their resources in a specific definable and limited purpose.

What this means, above all, is that their leaders, the heads of these organizations, cannot base their position, power, and authority on any traditional principle of legitimacy. They cannot, for instance, base their authority on the "consent of the governed." For the "governed" are not and cannot be, as in a true political society, the beneficiaries and the purpose of the "government."

The large business corporation does not exist for the sake of the employees. Its results lie outside and are only tangentially affected by employee approval, consent, and attitude. Similarly the hospital's "constituency" is not the people who work in the hospital, but the patients. And to the patient who needs a liver transplant, it is irrelevant whether the hospital's nurses are satisfied or not. All that matters to the patient is the hospital's survival rate on liver transplants.

Organization, *in its own interest*, needs to force the utmost responsibility on its members.

Yet in the areas that directly affect standards, performance, and results of the institution, the members cannot take over. There, the standards, the performance, and results must rule them. What is done, and how, is largely determined by what outsiders want and need. It is largely determined by "discipline," whether that of a science or of the marketplace. The vote of General Motors workers on a new automobile design would be totally irrelevant. What matters is whether the consumer buys it or not.

The old response of the Left to this is, of course, the demand that these institutions be "legitimized" by being taken over by the "political sovereign," the state. Their managers would then be appointed by legitimate political authority and derive their power from the true sovereign. Experience has shown this to be naive sophistry. All that really happens is that the same losses, which formerly were censured as horrible examples of mismanagement, now are seen as contributions to social welfare. Government ownership or government appointment of managers does not alter the function of institutions. The moment organizations begin to discharge their function they are outside of effective political control by government. Indeed they have to be outside of it to perform. They have to be controlled and measured by performance.

What applies to the "consent of the governed" applies to every other known principle of political legitimacy. Of course, an institution whose members reject it altogether cannot function. The institution must make it possible for its members to achieve their own ends. We have long known that modern organization must give its members status and function. But the members must also serve and accomplish the institution's purposes, which can never be their own. To satisfy their members is not and can never be the first task or the test of the pluralist organizations of our society. They must satisfy people outside, must serve a purpose outside, must achieve results outside. At best, they can integrate and harmonize the ends, values, and wants of their members with the demands of their mission. But the mission comes first. It is given. It is objective. It is impersonal. It is, at the same time, specific, limited, and aimed at only one of the many needs and wants of society, community, and individual.

It is this dedication to one limited purpose of larger society that makes our modern organization effective.

Clearly there is only one foundation for the authority which our organizations and the managements must have: performance. It is the only reason that we have them at all. It is the only reason why we can tolerate their exercise of power and their demand for authority.

Specifically, this means that we need to know what "performance" means for this or that institution. We need to be able to measure, or at least to judge, the discharge of its responsibility by an institution and the competence of its management. We need to insist that institutions and their managements confine themselves to the specific tasks whose performance justifies their existence and their power. Everything beyond is usurpation.

Concentration on the specific task emerges as the key to strength, performance, and legitimacy of organization in the pluralist society. Opinions can and should differ as to the specific task of a particular organization. The definition will change as circumstances, social needs, community values, and technologies change. Indeed different institutions of the same kind, e.g., different universities within a country, might define their objectives quite differently, as should different businesses within an industry, or even different hospitals. But each of them will be stronger the more clearly it defines its objectives. It will be more effective the more specific the yardsticks and measurements against which its performance can be appraised. It will be more legitimate the more strictly it bases its authority on justification by performance.

"By their fruits ye shall know them—" this might well be the fundamental constitutional principle of the new pluralist society.

11

The Society of Organizations
(first published in the *Harvard Business Review*, 1992)

The transformation of our time is not confined to Western society and Western history. Indeed, one of the fundamental changes is that there is no longer a "Western" history or a "Western" civilization. There is only world history and world civilization.

Whether this transformation began with the emergence of the first non-Western country, Japan, as a great economic power or with the first computer—that is, with information—is moot. My own candidate would be the GI Bill of Rights, which gave every American soldier returning from World War II the money to attend a university, something that would have made absolutely no sense only thirty years earlier at the end of World War I. The GI Bill of Rights and the enthusiastic response to it on the part of America's veterans signaled the shift to a knowledge society.

In this society, knowledge is *the* primary resource for individuals and for the economy overall. Land and capital—the economist's traditional factors of production—do not disappear, but they become secondary. They can be obtained, and obtained easily, provided there is specialized knowledge.

At the same time, however, specialized knowledge by itself produces nothing.

It can become productive only when it is integrated into a task. And that is why the knowledge society is also a society of organizations: the purpose and function of every organization, business and nonbusiness alike, is the integration of specialized knowledges into a common task.

This will raise new questions. But where the big issues will lie we can, I believe, already discover with a high degree of probability.

In particular, we already know the central tensions and issues that confront the society of organizations: the tension created by the community's need for stability and the organization's need to destabilize; the relationship between individual and organization and the responsibilities of each to the other, the tension that arises from the organization's need for autonomy and society's stake in the Common Good; the rising demand for socially responsible organizations; the tension between specialists with specialized knowledges and the organization's need for these specialists to perform as a team. All of these will be central concerns, especially in the developed world, for years to come. They will not be resolved by pronunciamento or philosophy or legislation.

They will be resolved where they originate: in the individual organization and in the individual executive's office.

Society, community, and family are all conserving institutions. They try to maintain stability and to prevent, or at least to slow, change. But the modern organization is a destabilizer. It must be organized for innovation, and innovation, as the great Austrian-American economist Joseph Schumpeter said, is "creative destruction." And it must be organized for the systematic abandonment of whatever is established, customary, familiar, and comfortable, whether that is a product, a service, or a process; a set of skills; human and social relationships; or the organization itself. In short, it must be organized for constant change. The organization's function is to put knowledge to work—on tools, products, and processes; on the design of work; on knowledge itself.

It is the nature of knowledge that it changes fast and that today's certainties always become tomorrow's absurdities.

This is doubly important because the changes that affect a body of knowledge most profoundly do not, as a rule, come out of its own domain.

After Gutenberg first used movable type, there was practically no change in the craft of printing for four hundred years—until the steam engine came in.

The greatest challenge to the railroad came not from changes in railroading but from the automobile, the truck, and the airplane. The pharmaceutical industry is being profoundly changed today by knowledge coming from genetics and microbiology, disciplines that few biologists had heard of forty years ago.

And it is by no means only science or technology that creates new knowledge and makes old knowledge obsolete. Social innovation is equally important and often more important than scientific innovation. Indeed, what triggered the present worldwide crisis in the proudest of nineteenth-century institutions, the commercial bank, was not the computer or any other technological change. It was the discovery by nonbankers that an old but hitherto rather obscure financial instrument, commercial paper, could be used to finance companies and would thus deprive the banks of the business on which they had held a monopoly for two hundred years and which gave them most of their income: the commercial loan. The greatest change of all is probably that in the last forty years, purposeful innovation—both technical and social—has itself become an organized discipline that is both teachable and learnable.

Nor is rapid knowledge-based change confined to business, as many still believe. No organization in the fifty years since World War II has changed more than the U.S. military. Uniforms have remained the same. Titles of rank have remained the same. But weapons have changed completely, as the Gulf War of 1991 dramatically demonstrated; military doctrines and concepts have changed even more drastically, as have the armed services' organizational structures, command structures, relationships, and responsibilities.

Similarly, it is a safe prediction that in the next fifty years, schools and universities will change more and more drastically than they have since they assumed their present form more than three hundred years ago, when they reorganized themselves around the printed book. What will force these changes is in part new technology, such as computers, videos, and telecasts via satellite; in part the demands of a knowledge-based society in which organized learning must become a lifelong process for knowledge workers; and in part new theory about how human beings learn.

For managers, the dynamics of knowledge impose one clear imperative: every organization has to build the management of change into its very structure.

On the one hand, this means every organization has to prepare for the abandonment of everything it does. Managers have to learn to ask every few years of every process, every product, every procedure, every policy: "If we did not do this already, would we go into it now knowing what we now know?" If the answer is no, the organization has to ask, "What do we *do* now?" And it has to *do* something, and not say, "Let's make another study." Indeed, organizations increasingly will have to *plan* abandonment rather than try to prolong the life of a successful product, policy, or practice.

On the other hand, every organization must devote itself to creating the new. Specifically, every management has to draw on three systematic practices. The first is continuing improvement of everything the organization does, the process the Japanese call *kaizen*. Every artist throughout history has practiced *kaizen*, or organized, continuous self-improvement. But so far only the Japanese—perhaps because of their Zen tradition—have embodied it in the daily life and work of their business organizations (although not in their singularly change-resistant universities). The aim of *kaizen* is to improve a product or service so that it becomes a truly different product or service in two or three years' time.

Second, every organization will have to learn to exploit its knowledge, that is, to develop the next generation of applications from its own successes.

Again, Japanese businesses have done the best with this endeavor so far, as demonstrated by the success of the consumer electronics manufacturers in developing one new product after another from the same American invention, the tape recorder. But successful exploitation of their successes is also one of the strengths of the fast-growing American pastoral churches.

Finally, every organization will have to learn to innovate—and innovation can now be organized—as a systematic process. And then, of course, one comes back to abandonment, and the process starts all over. Unless this is done, the knowledge-based organization will very soon find itself obsolescent, losing performance capacity and with it the ability to attract and hold the skilled and knowledgeable people on whom its performance depends.

The need to organize for change also requires a high degree of decentralization. That is because the organization must be structured to make decisions quickly. And those decisions must be based on closeness—to performance, to the market, to technology, and to all the many changes in society, the environment, demographics.

All this implies, however, that the organizations of the post-capitalist society must constantly upset, disorganize, and destabilize the community.

They must change the demand for skills and knowledges. Just when every technical university is geared up to teach physics, organizations need geneticists. Just when bank employees are most proficient in credit analysis, they will need to be investment counselors. But also, businesses must be free to close factories on which local communities depend for employment or to replace grizzled model makers who have spent years learning their craft with twenty-five-year-old whiz kids who know computer simulation.

Similarly, hospitals must be able to move the delivery of babies into a free-standing birthing center when the knowledge base and technology of obstetrics change. And we must be able to close a hospital altogether when changes in medical knowledge, technology, and practice make a hospital with fewer than two hundred beds both uneconomical and incapable of giving first-rate care.

For a hospital—or a school or any other community organization—to discharge its social function we must be able to close it down, no matter how deeply rooted in the local community it is and how much beloved, if changes in demographics, technology, or knowledge set new prerequisites for performance.

But every one of such changes upsets the community, disrupts it, deprives it of continuity. Every one is "unfair." Every one destabilizes.

Equally disruptive is another fact of organizational life: the modern organization must be *in* a community but cannot be *of* it. An organization's members live in a particular place, speak its language, send their children to its schools, vote, pay taxes, and need to feel at home there. Yet the organization cannot submerge itself in the community or subordinate itself to the community's ends. Its "culture" has to transcend community.

It is the nature of the task, not the community in which the task is being performed, that determines the culture of an organization. The American civil servant, though totally opposed to communism, will understand immediately what a Chinese colleague tells him about bureaucratic intrigues in Beijing. But he would be totally baffled in his own Washington, D.C., if he were to sit in on a discussion of the next week's advertising promotions by the managers of the local grocery chain.

To perform its task the organization has to be organized and managed the same way as others of its type. For example, we hear a great deal about the differences in management between Japanese and American companies. But a large Japanese company functions very much like a large American company; and both function very much like a large German or British company. Likewise, no only will every doubt that he or she is in a hospital, no matter where the hospital is located. The same holds true for schools and universities, for unions and research labs, for museums and opera houses, for astronomical observatories and large farms.

In addition, each organization has a value system that is determined by its task. In every hospital in the world, health care is considered the ultimate good. In every school in the world, learning is considered the ultimate good. In every business in the world, production and distribution of goods or services is considered the ultimate good. For the organization to perform to a high standard, its members must believe that what it is doing is, in the last analysis, the one contribution to community and society on which all others depend.

In its culture, therefore, the organization will always transcend the community. If an organization's culture and the values of its community clash, the organization must prevail—or else it will not make its social contribution. "Knowledge knows no boundaries," says an old proverb. There has been a "town and gown" conflict ever since the first university was established more than 750 years ago. But such a conflict—between the autonomy the organization needs in order to perform and the claims of the community, between the values of the organization and those of the community, between the decisions facing the organization and the interests of the community—is inherent in the society of organizations.

The issue of social responsibility is also inherent in the society of organizations. The modern organization has and must have social power—and a good deal of it. It needs power to make decisions about people: whom to hire, whom to fire, whom to promote. It needs power to establish the rules and disciplines required to produce results: for example, the assignment of jobs and tasks and the establishment of working hours. It needs power to decide which factories to build where and which factories to close. It needs power to set prices, and so on.

And nonbusinesses have the greatest social power—far more, in fact, than business enterprises. Few organizations in history were ever granted the power the university has today. Refusing to admit a student or to grant a student a diploma is tantamount to debarring that person from careers and opportunities. Similarly, the power of the American hospital to deny a physician admitting privileges is the power to exclude that physician from the practice of medicine. The union's power over admission to apprenticeship or its control of access to employment in a "closed shop," where only union members can be hired, gives the union tremendous social power.

The power of the organization can be restrained by political power. It can be made subject to due process and to review by the courts. But it must be exercised by individual organizations rather than by political authorities. This is why post-capitalist society talks so much about social responsibilities of the organization.

It is futile to argue, as Milton Friedman, the American economist and Nobel laureate does, that a business has only one responsibility: economic performance. Economic performance is the *first* responsibility of a business. Indeed, a business that does not show a profit at least equal to its cost of capital is irresponsible; it wastes society's resources. Economic performance is the base without which a business cannot discharge any other responsibilities, cannot be a good employee, a good citizen, a good neighbor. But economic performance is not the *only* responsibility of a business any more than educational performance is the only responsibility of a school or health care the only responsibility of a hospital.

Unless power is balanced by responsibility, it becomes tyranny. Furthermore, without responsibility, power always degenerates into nonperformance, and organizations must perform. So the demand for socially responsible organizations will not go away; rather, it will widen.

Fortunately, we also know, if only in rough outline, how to answer the problem of social responsibility. Every organization must assume full responsibility for its impact on employees, the environment, customers, and whomever and whatever it touches. That is its social responsibility. But we also know that society will increasingly look to major organizations, for-profit and nonprofit alike, to tackle major social ills. And there we had better be watchful, because good intentions are not always socially responsible. It is irresponsible for an organization to accept—let alone to pursue—responsibilities that would impede its capacity to perform its main task and mission or to act where it has no competence.

Organization has become an everyday term. Everybody gives a nod of understanding when somebody says, "In our organization, everything should revolve around the customer" or "In this organization, they never forget a mistake you made." And most, if not all, social tasks in every developed country are performed in and by an organization of one kind or another. Yet no one in the United States—or anyplace else—talked of "organizations" until after World War II. *The Concise Oxford Dictionary* did not even list the term in its current meaning in the 1950 edition. It is only the emergence of management since World War II that has allowed us to see the organization as discrete and distinct from society's other institutions.

Unlike communities, societies, or families, organizations are purposefully designed and always specialized. Communities and societies are defined by the bonds that hold their members together, whether they be language, culture, history, or locality. An organization is defined by its task. The symphony orchestra does not attempt to cure the sick; it plays music. The hospital takes care of the sick but does not attempt to play Beethoven.

Indeed, an organization is effective only if it concentrates on one task. Diversification destroys the performance capacity of an organization, whether it is a business, a union, a school, a hospital, a community service, or a house of worship. Society and community must be multidimensional; they are environments. An organization is a tool. And as with any other tool, the more specialized it is, the greater its capacity to perform its given task.

Because the modern organization is composed of specialists, each with his or her own narrow area of expertise, its mission must be crystal clear.

The organization must be single-minded, or its members will become confused. They will follow their own speciality rather than apply it to the common task. They will each define "results" in terms of their own specialty and impose its values on the organization. Only a focused and common mission will hold the organization together and enable it to produce. Without such a mission, the organization will soon lose credibility and consequently its ability to attract the very people it needs to perform.

All organizations now say routinely, "People are our greatest asset." Yet few practice what they preach, let alone truly believe it.

Most still believe, though perhaps not consciously, what nineteenth-century employers believed: people need us more than we need them. But in fact, organizations have to market membership as much as they market products and services—perhaps more. They have to attract people, hold people, recognize and reward people, motivate people, and serve and satisfy people.

The relationship between knowledge workers and their organizations is a distinctly new phenomenon, one for which we have no good term. For example, an employee, by definition, is someone who gets paid for working. Yet the largest single group of "employees" in the United States consists of the millions of men and women who work several hours a week without pay for one or another non-profit organization. They are clearly 'STAFF' and consider themselves as such, but they are unpaid volunteers. Similarly, many people who work as employees are not employed in any legal sense. Fifty or sixty years ago, we would have spoken of these people (many, if not most, of whom are educated professionals) as "independent;" today we speak of the "self-employed."

These discrepancies—and they exist in just about every language—remind us why new realities often demand new words. But until such a word emerges, this is probably the best definition of employees in the post-capitalist society: people whose ability to make a contribution depends on having access to an organization.

As far as the employees who work in subordinate and menial occupations are concerned—the salesclerk in the supermarket, the cleaning woman in the hospital, the delivery-truck driver—the consequences of this new definition are small. For all practical purposes, their position may not be too different from that of the wage earner, the "worker" of yesterday, whose direct descendants they are.

But the relationship between the organization and knowledge workers, who already number at least one-third and more likely two-fifths of all employees, is radically different, as is that between the organization and volunteers. They can work only because there is an organization, thus they too are dependent. But at the same time, they own the "means of production"—their knowledge. In this respect, they are independent and highly mobile.

Knowledge workers still need the *tools* of production. In fact, capital investment in the tools of the knowledge employee may al-

ready be higher than the capital investment in the tools of the manufacturing worker ever was.

(And the social investment, for example, the investment in a knowledge worker's education, is many times the investment in the manual
worker's education.) But this capital investment is unproductive unless the knowledge worker brings to bear on it the knowledge that
he or she owns and that cannot be taken away. Machine operators in
the factory did as they were told. The machine decided not only
what to do but how to do it. The knowledge employee may well
need a machine, whether it be a computer, an ultrasound analyzer,
or a microscope. But the machine will not tell the knowledge worker
what to do, let alone how to do it. And without this knowledge,
which belongs to the employee, the machine is unproductive.

Further, machine operators, like all workers throughout history,
could be told what to do, how to do it, and how fast to do it. Knowledge workers cannot be supervised effectively. Unless they know
more about their specialty than anybody else in the organization,
they are basically useless. The marketing manager may tell the market researcher what the company needs to know about the design of
a new product and the market segment in which it should be posi-
tioned. But it is the market researcher's job to tell the president of the
company what market research is needed, how to set it up, and what
the results mean.

During the traumatic restructuring of American business in the
1980s, thousands, if not hundreds of thousands, of knowledge employees lost their jobs. Their companies were acquired, merged, spun
off, or liquidated. Yet within a few months, most of them found new
jobs in which to put their knowledge to work. The transition period
was painful, and in about half the cases, the new job did not pay
quite as much as the old one did and may not have been as enjoy-
able.

But the laid-off technicians, professionals, and managers found
they had the "capital," the knowledge: they owned the means of
production. Somebody else, the organization, had the tools of production. The two needed each other.

One consequence of this new relationship—and it is another new
tension in modern society—is that loyalty can no longer be obtained
by the paycheck. The organization must earn loyalty by proving to
its knowledge employees that it offers them exceptional opportunities for putting their knowledge to work. Not so long ago, we talked

about "personnel." Increasingly we are talking about "human re-sources." This change reminds us that it is the individual, and espe-cially the skilled and knowledgeable employee, who decides in large measure what he or she will contribute to the organization and how great the yield from his or knowledge will be.

Because the modern organization consists of knowledge special-ists, it has to be an organization of equals, of colleagues and associ-ates. No knowledge ranks higher than another; each is judged by its contribution to the common task rather than by any inherent superi-ority or inferiority. Therefore, the modern organization cannot be an organization of boss and subordinate. It must be organized as a team.

There are only three kinds of teams. One is the sort of team that plays together in tennis doubles. In that team—and it has to be small—each member adapts himself or herself to the personality, the skills, the strengths, and the weaknesses of the other member or members. Then there is the team that plays soccer. Each player has a fixed position; but the whole team moves together (except for the goal-keeper) while individual members retain their relative positions. Fi-nally, there is the baseball team—or the orchestra—in which all the members have fixed positions.

At any given time, an organization can play only one kind of game. And it can use only one kind of team for any given task. Which team to use or game to play is one of the riskiest decisions in the life of an organization. Few things are as difficult in an organiza-tion as transforming from one kind of team to another. Changing a team demands the most difficulty learning imaginable: unlearning. It demands giving up hard-earned skills, habits of a lifetime, deeply cherished values of craftsmanship and professionalism, and—per-haps the most difficult of all—it demands giving up old and trea-sured human relationships. It means abandoning what people have always considered "our community" or "our family."

But if the organization is to perform, it must be organized as a team. When modern organizations first arose in the closing years of the nineteenth century, the only model was the military. The Prus-sian army was as much a marvel of organization for the world of 1870 as Henry Ford's assembly line was for the world of 1920. In the army of 1870, each member did much the same thing, and the number of people with any knowledge was infinitesimally small. The army was organized by command-and-control, and business enterprise as well as most other institutions copied that model. This is now rapidly changing. As more and more organizations become information-based, they are transforming themselves into soccer or tennis teams, that is, into responsibility-based organizations in which every member must act as a responsible decision-maker. All members, in other words, have to see themselves as "executives."

An organization must be managed. The management may be intermittent and perfunctory, as it is, for instance, in the Parent-Teacher Association at a U.S. suburban school. Or management may be a full-time and demanding job for a fairly large group of people, as it is in the military, the business enterprise, the union, and the university. But there have to be people who make decisions or nothing will ever get done. There have to be people who are accountable for the organization's mission, its spirit, its performance, its results. Society, community, and family may have "leaders," but only organizations know a "management." And while this management must have considerable authority, its job in the modern organization is not to command. It is to inspire.

The society of organizations is unprecedented in human history. It is unprecedented in its performance capacity both because each of its constituent organizations is a highly specialized tool designed for one specific task and because each bases itself on the organization and deployment of knowledge. It is unprecedented in its structure. But it is also unprecedented in its tensions and problems. Some of them we already know how to resolve—issues of social responsibility, for example. But there are other areas where we do not know the right answer and where we may not even be asking the right questions yet.

There is, for instance, the tension between the community's need for continuity and stability and the organization's need to be an innovator and destabilizer. There is the split between "literati" and "managers." Both are needed: the former to produce knowledge, the latter to apply knowledge and make it productive. But the former focus on words and ideas, the latter on people, work, and performance. There is the threat to the very basis of the society of organizations—the knowledge base—that arises from ever-greater specialization, from the shift from knowledge to *knowledges*. But the greatest and most difficult challenge is that presented by society's *new pluralism*.

For more than six hundred years, no society has had as many centers of power as the society in which we now live. The Middle Ages indeed knew pluralism. Society was composed of hundreds of competing and autonomous power centers: feudal lords and knights, exempt bishoprics, autonomous monasteries, "free" cities. In some places, the Austrian Tyrol, for example, there were even "free peasants," beholden to no one but the Emperor. There were also autonomous craft guilds and transnational trading leagues like the Hanseatic Merchants and the merchant bankers of Florence, toll and tax collectors, local "parliaments" with legislative and tax-raising powers, private armies available for hire, and myriads more.

Modern history in Europe—and equally in Japan—has been the history of the subjugation of all competing centers of power by one central authority, first called the "prince," then the "state." By the middle of the nineteenth century, the unitary state had triumphed in every developed country except the United States, which remained profoundly pluralistic in its religious and educational organizations. Indeed, the abolition of pluralism was the "progressive" cause for nearly six hundred years.

But just when the triumph of the state seemed assured, the first new organization arose—the large business enterprise. (This, of course, always happens when the "End of History" is announced.) Since then, one new organization after another has sprung up. And old organizations like the university, which in Europe seemed to have been brought safely under the control of central governments, have become autonomous again. Ironically, twentieth-century totalitarianism, especially communism, represented the last desperate attempt to save the old progressive creed in which there is only one center of power and one organization rather than a pluralism of competing and autonomous organizations.

That attempt failed, as we know. But the failure of central authority, in and of itself, does nothing to address the issues that follow from a pluralistic society. To illustrate, consider a story that many people have heard of or, more accurately, misheard.

During his lifetime, Charles E. Wilson was a prominent personality in the United States, first as president and chief executive officer of General Motors, at the time the world's largest and most successful manufacturer, then as secretary of defense in the Eisenhower administration. But if Wilson is remembered at all today it is for something he did *not* say: "What is good for General Motors is good for the United States." What Wilson actually said in his 1953 confirmation hearings for the Defense Department job was, "What is good for the United States is good for General Motors, and vice versa."

Wilson tried for the remainder of his life to correct the misquote. But no one listened to him. Everyone argued that "if he didn't say it, he surely believes it—in fact he *should* believe it." For as has been said, executives in an organization—whether business or university or hospital or the Boy Scouts—must believe that its mission and task are society's most important mission and task as well as the foundation for everything else. If they do not believe this, their organization will soon lose faith in itself, self-confidence, pride, and the ability to perform.

The diversity that is characteristic of a developed society and that provides its great strength is only possible because of the specialized, single-task organizations that we have developed since the Industrial Revolution and, especially, during the last fifty years. But the feature that gives them the capacity to perform is precisely that each is autonomous and specialized, informed only by its own narrow mission and vision, its own narrow values, and not by any consideration of society and community.

Therefore, we come back to the old—and never resolved—problem of the pluralistic society: Who takes care of the Common Good? Who defines it? Who balances the separate and often competing goals and values of society's institutions? Who makes the trade-off decisions and on what basis should they be made?

Medieval feudalism was replaced by the unitary sovereign state precisely because it could not answer these questions. But the unitary sovereign state has now itself been replaced by a new pluralism—a pluralism of function rather than one of political power—because it could neither satisfy the needs of society nor perform the necessary tasks of community. That, in the final analysis, is the most fundamental lesson to be learned from the failure of the belief in the all-embracing and all-powerful state. The challenge that faces us now, and especially in the developed, free-market democracies such as the United States, is to make the pluralism of autonomous, knowledge-based organizations redound both to specialized performance and to political and social cohesion.

Part 5

The Corporation as a Social Institution

Introduction to Part 5

The two main parts of my 1946 book, *Concept of the Corporation* (a study of General Motors—GM—then, as now, the world's largest manufacturing company), were titled respectively "The Corporation as Human Effort" and "The Corporation as a Social Institution." Fifty-five years ago these titles were shockers—meant to be as such and seen as such. Within GM the entire book was extremely controversial, was indeed considered by many GM executives to be ultra-critical if not downright hostile. But even the book's defenders within the company found it hard to accept these two titles and what they implied. And outside of GM they were almost universally rejected—by economists as much as by social and political scientists. Everybody "knew" that a business could be seen and analyzed *only* in terms of economics. That view has still by no means disappeared—it is strongly held, for instance, by America's premier economist, Milton Friedman. But no one today would be very much surprised—let alone shocked—by these two titles. They have become truisms.

For this reason, I have chosen for this volume only a very few examples of my writings on business enterprise as a community, a society, a polity. One of these excerpts (chapter 13 – "The Corporation as a Social Institution") dates back to the 1946 book. Of the other two, the first—chapter 12, was first written in 1990 as an epilogue to a reissue of my 1976 book *The Unseen Revolution* (reissued in 1996 under the title *The Pension Fund Revolution*). It first pointed out that the pension fund had made "the workers" into the only "capitalists" that mattered and the "employees" into the "owners"—and then discussed what that implied both, for society and for the corporation. The second (chapter 14 – "The Corporation as a Political Institution") is concerned with the corporation (and with the other autonomous institutions of a pluralist society) as power centers.

Logically, the discussion of the future of the corporation should probably have been included in this Part. It seemed to me however, to fit better into the last chapter of this book (chapter 19 – "The Next Society") for which it was originally written in 2001.

12

The Governance of Corporations

(first published in the *Harvard Business Review*, 1991)

Institutional investors—primarily pension funds—control close to 40 percent of the common stock of the country's large (and of many midsize) businesses. The largest and fastest-growing funds, those of public employees, are no longer content to be passive investors. Increasingly, they demand a voice in the companies in which they invest—for instance, a veto over board appointments, executive compensation, and critical corporate charter provisions.

Equally important, and still largely overlooked, pension funds also hold 40 percent or so of the medium-term and long-term debt of the country's bigger companies. Thus, these institutions have become corporate America's largest lenders as well as its largest owners. As the finance texts have stressed for years, the power of the lender is as great as the power of the owner—sometimes greater.

The rise of pension funds as dominant owners and lenders represents one of the most startling power shifts in economic history. The first modern pension fund was established in 1950 by General Motors. Four decades later, pension funds control total assets of $2.5 trillion, divided about equally between common stocks and fixed-income securities. Demographics guarantee that these assets will grow aggressively for at least another ten years. Barring a prolonged depression, pension funds will have to invest $100 billion to $200 billion in new resources every year throughout the 1990s.

America's failure, until quite recently, to recognize (let alone address) this power shift accounts in large measure for much of the financial turbulence of the 1980s—the hostile takeovers, the leveraged buyouts, and the general restructuring frenzy. Two problems in particular demand attention: For what should America's new owners, the pension funds, hold corporate management accountable?

And what is the appropriate institutional structure through which to exercise accountability?

Pension funds first emerged as the premier owners of the country's share capital in the early 1970s. But for fifteen or twenty years thereafter, the realities of pension fund ownership were ignored. In part this was because the pension funds themselves did not want to be "owners." They wanted to be passive "investors" and short-term investors at that. "We do not buy a company," they asserted. "We buy shares that we sell as soon as they no longer offer good prospects for capital gains over a fairly short time."

Finally, though, the fog has begun to lift. The trustees of pension funds, especially those representing public employees, are waking up to the fact that they are no longer investors in shares. An investor, by definition, can sell holdings. A small pension fund may still be able to do so. There are thousands of such small funds, but their total holdings represent no more than a quarter or so of all pension fund assets. The share holdings of even a midsize pension fund are already so large that they are not easily sold. Or more precisely, these holdings can, as a rule, be sold only if another pension fund buys them. They are much too large to be easily absorbed by the retail market and are thus permanently part of the circular trading among institutions.

Ownership in the United States is far less concentrated than in Germany, Japan, or Italy—and will remain far less concentrated. Hence, the U.S. pension fund still has more elbow room than the big bank in Germany, the keiretsu in Japan, or the industrial conglomerate in Italy. But some large U.S. pension funds each own as much as 1 percent or even 2 percent of a big company's total capital. All pension funds together may own 50 percent or more of the company's total capital. (For example, pension funds own 75 percent of the equity of the Chase Manhattan Bank.) The 1 percent holder cannot sell easily. And the 50 percent holder, that is, the pension fund community at large, cannot sell at all. It is almost as committed as the German *hausbank* to a client company or the Japanese *keiretsu* to a member company. Thus, the large funds are beginning to learn what Georg Siemens, founder of the Deutsche Bank and inventor of the *hausbank* system, said a hundred years ago, when he was criticized for spending so much of his and bank's time on a troubled client company: "If one can't sell, one must care."

Pension funds cannot be managers as were so many nineteenth-century owners. Yet a business, even a small one, needs strong, autonomous management with the authority, continuity, and competence to build and run the organization. Thus, pension funds, as America's new owners, will increasingly have to make sure that a company has the management it needs. As we have learned over the last forty years, this means that management must be clearly accountable to somebody and that accountability must be institutionally anchored. It means that management must be accountable for *performance* and *results* rather than for good intentions, however beautifully quantified. It means that accountability must involve financial accountability, even though everyone knows that performance and results go way beyond the financial "bottom line."

Surely, most people will say, we know what performance and results mean for business enterprise. We should, of course, because clearly defining these terms is a prerequisite both for effective management and for successful and profitable ownership. In fact, there have been two definitions offered in the forty years since World War II. Neither has stood the test of time.

The first definition was formulated around 1950, at about the same time at which the modern pension fund was invented. The most prominent of the period's "professional managers," Ralph Cordiner, CEO of the General Electric Company, asserted that top management in the large, publicly owned corporation was a "trustee." Cordiner argued that senior executives were responsible for managing the enterprise "in the best-balanced interest of shareholders, customers, employees, suppliers, and plant community cities." That is, what we now call "stakeholders."

Cordiner's answer, as some of us pointed out right away, still required a clear definition of results and of the meaning of "best" with respect to "balance." It also required a clear structure of accountability with an independent and powerful organ of supervision and control to hold management accountable for performance and results. Otherwise, professional management becomes an enlightened despot—and enlightened despots, whether platonic philosopher kings or CEOs, neither perform nor last.

But Cordiner's generation and its executive successors did not define what performance and results produce the best balance, nor did they develop any kind of accountability. As a result, professional management, 1950s-style, has neither performed nor lasted.

The single most powerful blow to Cordiner-style management was the rise of the hostile takeover in the late 1970s. One after the other of such managements has been toppled. The survivors have been forced to change drastically how they manage or at least to change their rhetoric. No top management I know now claims to run its business as a "trustee" for the "best-balanced interests" of "stakeholders."

Pension funds have been the driving force behind this change. Without the concentration of voting power in a few pension funds and the funds' willingness to endorse hostile transactions, most of the raiders' attacks would never have been launched. A raider who has to get support from millions of dispersed individual stockholders soon runs out of time and money.

To be sure, pension fund managers had serious doubts about many buyouts and takeovers, about their impact on the companies in play, and about their value to the economy. Pension fund managers—especially the moderately paid civil servants running the funds of public employees—also had serious aesthetic and moral misgivings about such things as "greenmail" and the huge fortunes earned by corporate raiders, lawyers, and investment bankers. Yet they felt they had no choice but to provide money for takeovers and buyouts and to tender their shares into them. They did so in droves.

One reason for their support was that these transactions kept alive the illusion that pension funds could in fact sell their shares—that is, that they were "investors" still. Takeovers and LBOs also offered immediate capital gains. And since pension fund portfolios have by and large done quite poorly, such gains were most welcome—though, as will be discussed shortly, they too were more illusion than reality.

What made takeovers and buyouts inevitable (or at least created the opportunity for them) was the mediocre performance of enlightened-despot management, the management without clear definitions of performance and results and with no clear accountability to somebody. It may be argued that the mediocre performance of so many of America's large corporations in the last thirty years was not management's fault, that it resulted instead from wrong-headed public policies that have kept American savings rates low and capital costs high. But captains are responsible for what happens on their watches. And whatever the reasons or excuses, the large U.S. company has not done particularly well on professional management's watch—whether measured by competitiveness, market standing, or innovative performance. As for financial performance, it has, by and large, not even earned the minimum acceptable result, a return on equity equal to its cost of capital.

The raiders thus performed a needed function. As an old proverb has it, "If there are no grave diggers, one needs vultures." But takeovers and buyouts are very radical surgery. And even if radical surgery is not life-threatening, it inflicts profound shock. Takeovers and buyouts deeply disturb and indeed alienate middle managers and professionals, the very people on whose motivation, effort, and loyalty a business depends. For these people, the takeover or dismantling of a company to which they have given years of service is nothing short of betrayal. It is a denial of all they must believe in to work productively and with devotion. As a result, few of the companies that were taken over or sold in a buyout performed any better a few years later than they had performed under the old dispensation.

Today nearly all CEOs of large U.S. companies proclaim that they run their enterprises "in the interest of the shareholders" and "to maximize shareholder value." This is the *second definition* of performance and results developed over the past forty years. It sounds much less noble than Cordiner's assertion of the "best-balanced interest," but it also sounds much more realistic. Yet its life span will be even shorter than yesterday's professional management. For most people, "maximizing shareholder value" means a higher share price within six months or a year—certainly not much longer. Such short-term capital gains are the wrong objective for both the enterprise and its dominant shareholders. As a theory of corporate performance, then, "maximizing shareholder value" has little staying power.

We no longer need to theorize about how to define performance and results in the large enterprise. We have successful examples. Both the Germans and the Japanese have highly concentrated institutional ownership. In neither country can the owners actually manage. In both countries industry has done extremely well in the forty years since its near destruction in World War II. It has done well in terms of the overall economy of its country. It has also done exceedingly well for its shareholders. Whether invested in 1950, 1960, 1970, or 1980, $100,000 put into something like an index fund in the stock exchanges of Tokyo or Frankfurt would today be worth a good deal more than a similar investment in a New York Stock Exchange index fund.

How, then, do the institutional owners of German or Japanese industry define performance and results? Though they manage quite differently, they define them in the same way. Unlike Cordiner, they do not "balance" anything. They maximize. But they do not attempt to maximize shareholder value or the short-term interest of any one of the enterprise's "stakeholders." Rather, they *maximize the wealth-producing capacity of the enterprise*. It is this objective that integrates short-term and long-term results and that ties the operational dimensions of business performance—market standing, innovation, productivity, and people and their development—with financial needs and financial results.

It is also this objective on which all constituencies depend for the satisfaction of their expectations and objectives, whether shareholders, customers, or employees.

To define performance and results as "maximizing the wealth-producing capacity of the enterprise" may be criticized as vague. To be sure, one doesn't get the answers by filling out forms. Decisions need to be made, and economic decisions that commit scarce resources to an uncertain future are always risky and controversial. When Ralph Cordiner first attempted to define performance and results—no one had tried to do so earlier—maximizing the wealth-producing capacity of the enterprise would indeed have been pretty fuzzy. By now, after four decades of work by many people, it has become crisp. All the elements that go into the process can be quantified with considerable rigor and are indeed quantified by those arch quantifiers, the planning departments of large Japanese companies, and by many of the German companies as well.

The one thing that we in the United States have yet to work out is how to build the new definition of management accountability into an institutional structure. We need what a political scientist would call a constitution—provisions that spell out (as does the German company law), the duties and responsibilities of management and clarify the respective rights of other groups, especially the shareholders.

I suspect that in the end we shall develop a formal business-audit practice, analogous perhaps to the financial-audit practice of independent professional accounting firms. For while the business audit need not be conducted every year—every three years may be enough in most cases—it needs to be based on predetermined standards and go through a systematic evaluation of business performance: starting with mission and strategy, through marketing, innovation, productivity, people development, community relations, all the way to profitability. The elements for such a business audit are known and available. But they need to be pulled together into systematic procedures. And that is best done, in all likelihood, by an organization that specializes in audits, whether an independent firm or a new and separate division of an accounting practice.

Thus, it may not be too fanciful to expect that in ten years a major pension fund will not invest in a company's shares or fixed-income securities unless that company submits itself to a business audit by an outside professional firm. Managements will resist, of course. But only sixty years ago, managements equally resisted—in fact, resented—demands that they submit themselves to a financial audit by outside public accountants and even more to publication of the audit's findings.

Still, the question remains: Who is going to use this tool? In the American context, there is only one possible answer: a revitalized board of directors.

The need for an effective board has been stressed by every student of the publicly owned corporation in the last forty years. To run a business enterprise, especially a large and complex enterprise, management needs considerable power. But power without accountability always becomes flabby or tyrannical and usually both. Surely, we know how to make boards effective as an organ of corporate governance. Having better people is not the key; ordinary people will do. Making a board effective requires spelling out its work, setting specific objectives for its performance and contribution, and regularly appraising the board's performance against these objectives.

We have known this for a long time. But American boards have on the whole become less, rather than more, effective. Boards are not effective if they represent good intentions. Boards are not effective if they represent "investors." Boards of business enterprises are effective if they represent strong owners, committed to enterprise.

Almost sixty years ago, in 1933, Adolph A. Berle, Jr. and Gardner C. Means published *The Modern Corporation and Private Property*, arguably the most influential book in U.S. business history. They showed that the traditional "owners," the nineteenth-century capitalists, had disappeared, with the title of ownership shifting rapidly to faceless multitudes of investors without interest in or commitment to the company and concerned with only short-term gains. As a result, they argued, ownership was becoming divorced from control and a mere legal fiction, with management becoming accountable to no one and for nothing. Then, twenty years later, Ralph Cordiner's *Professional Management* accepted this divorce of ownership from control and tried to make a virtue out of it.

By now, the wheel has come full circle. The pension funds are very different owners from nineteenth-century tycoons. They are not owners because they want to be owners but because they have no choice. They cannot sell. They also cannot become owner-managers. But they are owners nonetheless. As such, they have more than mere power. They have the responsibility to ensure performance and results in America's largest and most important companies.

13

The Corporation as a Social Institution
(from *Concept of the Corporation*, 1946)

Since the big-business corporation has become America's representative social institution it must realize the basic beliefs of American society—at least enough to satisfy minimum requirements. It must give status and function to the individual, and it must give him the justice of equal opportunities. This does not mean that the economic purpose of the corporation, efficient production, is to be subordinated to its social function, or that the fulfillment of society's basic belief is to be subordinated to the profit and survival-interest of the individual business. The corporation can only function as the representative social institution of our society if it can fulfill its social functions in a manner which strengthens it as an efficient producer, and vice versa. But as the representative social institution of our society the corporation in addition to being an economic tool is a political and social body; its social function as a community is as important as its economic function as an efficient producer.

The demand for status and function as an individual means that in the modern industrial society the citizen must obtain both standing in his society and individual satisfaction through his membership in the plant, that is, through being an employee. This is not a demand for "industrial democracy" if by that is meant a structure of industry in which everybody is equal in rank, income or function. On the contrary it is basically a hierarchical concept in which positions of widely divergent rank, power and income are each seen as equally important to the success of the whole because of the subordination of one man under the other. To attack industrial society, as would the sentimental equalitarian, because it is based on subordination instead of on formal equality, is a misunderstanding of the nature of both industry and society. Like every other institution which co-ordinates human efforts to a social end, the corporation must be organized on hierarchical lines. But also everybody from the boss to the sweeper must be seen as equally necessary to the success of the common enterprise.

At the same time the large corporation must offer equal opportunities for advancement. This is simply the traditional demand for justice, a consequence of the Christian concept of human dignity. What is new is only that we today look for the realization of justice in this life and in and through the industrial sphere. The demand for equal opportunities is not, as is often mistakenly assumed, a demand for equality of rewards. For the very concept of justice implies rewards graduated according to unequal performance and unequal responsibilities.

Equal opportunity means obviously that advancement not be based on external, on hereditary or on other fortuitous factors. But it also means that advancement be given according to rational and reasonable criteria.

This question of criteria for advancement constitutes the real problem the modern corporation has to solve in this area.

There is nothing new in these beliefs and demands. But never before have we looked to the industrial sphere for their realization. In spite of a century of industrialization the American, in common with all Westerners, has been pre-industrial in his mentality and consciousness until the most recent years.

He has looked for the realization of his promises and beliefs to farm and small town regardless of the reality of big industrial plant and big city. Only now have we realized that the large mass-production plant is our social reality, our representative institution, which has to carry the burden of our dreams.

The survival of our basic beliefs and promises—the survival of the very meaning of our society—depends on the ability of the large corporation to give substantial realization of the American creed in an industrial society.

The popular conviction that modern industrial society fails to realize equality of opportunities and justice of economic rewards to a substantial degree is therefore in politics conclusive evidence that the modern industrial corporation does not perform adequately its social job. It may well give more men more opportunities than the small business society which it succeeded. But it certainly does not yet do it in a way and through methods which appear rational and meaningful to the individual in our society.

14

The Corporation as a Political Institution
(from *Managing in Turbulent Times*, 1980)

The modern state that emerged from the inflations and religious wars of the sixteenth century rested on the premise that there is only one political institution in society, namely, the central government. There are no other legitimate institutions. Modern political doctrine asserted that there are no legitimate power centers elsewhere, inside or outside the state. The modern state began by taking away the political functions of existing institutions. Aristocrats became land-owners, rich commoners rather than local rulers. Churches became administrative units registering births, marriages, and deaths. Free cities lost their self-governments and became units in the administrative structure. A great English social scientist, Henry Maine, proclaimed in the nineteenth century that the trend of history had been from "status to contract," and that outside of the central government no one had political or social power. The only organized unit in society that was accepted was the family—a social molecule in a field of forces created by the powers that radiated from a central government.

In that respect, there was no difference between conservatives and liberals. They differed only in respect to the institutional structure of central government itself. In this respect, there was also no difference between classical economists and Karl Marx. Both envisaged the same basic structure of society. Marx even shared the delusion of his most liberal contemporaries in believing that central government itself was fast becoming an anachronism and would "wither away." He only wanted central government controlled by different people, by "our gang" rather than "their gang."

Our textbooks still pay lip service to the political and social theory of the "modern state." But in this century the reality has changed drastically. In this century, and especially in the thirty years since the end of World War II, society has become a society of institutions. A hundred and fifty years ago, every single social task was either discharged in and through the family or it was not discharged at all. The care of the sick and the care of the old; the upbringing of children and the distribution of income; even getting a job; all were done by the family if they were done at all. Any one of these tasks the family did poorly.

The shift to institutional performance thus meant a very great advance in the level of performance. But it also meant that society became pluralist. Today, every single task is being carried out in and through an institution, organized for perpetuity and dependent on leadership and direction given by managers in a formal structure. In the United States, the business enterprise is usually seen as the prototype of these institutions; but it was only the first to become visible.

On the continent of Europe, the civil service or the university were at least as visible. This explains why "management," that is, the study of formal modern organization, focused in the United States on the business enterprise, whereas on the continent of Europe it focused on public administration and, with Max Weber, on "bureaucracy." But the phenomenon is worldwide and the institutionalization is complete in every developed country.

The institutions of modern society were each created for a single specific purpose. Business exists to produce goods and services; it is an economic institution. Hospitals exist to take care of the sick; universities exist to train tomorrow's educated leaders and professionals; and so on. Every one of these institutions, while expected to provide a service of high quality, was also expected to concentrate on one service. It had "public relations." It was, in other words, expected to look upon other social concerns as restraints. But it did its job by producing the contribution for the sake of which it existed, and it justified itself in terms of one specific area of contribution and performance.

With the emergence of the society of institutions, all this has changed. Central government has become the more impotent the bigger it has grown.

The special-purpose institutions have progressively become carriers of social purpose, social values, social effectiveness. Therefore they have become politicized. They cannot justify themselves any longer in terms of their own contribution areas alone; all of them have to justify themselves now in terms of the impacts they have on society overall. All of them have outside "constituencies" they have to satisfy, where formerly they had only restraints that created "problems" for them when disregarded. The university still would like to define itself in terms of its own values. But in all developed countries, demands are today being made on higher education that are clearly not the demands of scholarship or of teaching, but are based on different social needs and social values: demands that the university, in the composition of its student body, reflect society and furthermore, in effect, the society deemed to be desirable for tomorrow rather than the society of today. Such expectations underlie the increasing interference with the American or the German university in respect to admissions, to faculty, and even to curriculum. The hospital, which could define its mission as remedying health damage that had already been incurred, is increasingly seen in developed countries as the center of a very different kind of health care, one of social action that enables people to prevent ill health or, as in the case of the outpatient department of the inner-city American hospital, in terms of creating a "black culture" or a distinct "health-care climate."

The business enterprise is no exception.

In a pluralist society, all institutions are of necessity political institutions. All are multi-constituency institutions. All have to perform in such a way that they will not be rejected and opposed by groups in society that can veto or block them. The managers of all institutions will have to learn to think politically in such a pluralist society.

In a single-purpose institution, the basic rule for decisions is to "optimize:" to find the most favorable ratio between effort and risk on the one hand and results and opportunities on the other. "Maximization," that famous abstraction of theoretical economists, makes no sense in any institution and is not applied in any. No one in a business knows how to maximize profits or even tries. "Optimization" is the rule in the institution that has one clear goal.

In a political process, however, one does not try to optimize. One tries to "satisfice" (to use the term of formal decision theory). One tries to find the solution that will produce the minimum acceptable results rather than the optimal, let alone the maximal results. This is indeed the rule one follows in a political universe.

In a political system there are far too many constituencies to optimize; one must try to determine the one area in which optimization is required. But in all other areas—their number in a political system is always large—one tries to satisfice, that is, to find the solution in which enough of the constituencies can acquiesce. One tries to find a solution that will not create opposition, rather than one that will generate support. Satisficing is what politicians mean when they talk of an "acceptable compromise." Not for nothing is politics known as "the art of the possible," rather than the art of the desirable.

As all institutions become politicized in a pluralist society of organizations, managers will have to learn first to think through the needs and expectations of their constituencies. As long as the business operates in a market system, customer expectations have to be optimized. But most businesses look upon shareholders as a constituency that has to be satisfied. They ask: "What is the minimum return which will enable us to cover the cost of capital and to attract the capital resources we need?" The textbook question: "What is the optimal return on our capital?" is rarely taken seriously. Therefore, businessmen tend to proceed on the assumption that if they can optimize results in the market, they can satisfice the expectations of the capital market. But management will have to learn to extend the same kind of thinking to many more constituencies—employees, for instance, if only because the market for jobs and careers is as much a genuine market as the market for capital. Its expectations have to be satisficed. Then there is also a large and growing number of political constituencies that have to acquiesce if a business is to continue its economic mission and to attain economic performance.

Business managers, understandably, resent this development and consider it a perversion. It would, of course, be much easier and probably in the end socially more productive, if the single-purpose institution—whether business, hospital, or university—could concentrate on its own job, flatly rejecting demands to satisfy other social needs as illegitimate and as distractions from its competence, its mission, and its function. At the least, one needs to argue strongly, institutions should not be expected to do things for which they are basically not competent. Precisely because institutions are single-purpose, they are rarely competent to perform well outside narrow limits.

Institutions have to think through their competence. Where a manager knows he is not competent, he has to have the courage to say "No." Nothing is less responsible than good intentions where competence is lacking.

At the same time, it is no longer adequate to say: "We will stick to doing what we know how to do and resist demands to concern ourselves with anything else." This may be the most intelligent attitude, but it can no longer prevail. Today's post-industrial society is a pluralist one which has to demand from its institutions that they take responsibility beyond their own specific mission.

So managers have to distinguish between what they can and cannot do. The rules are simple, their application difficult. No one should ever take on something he is not competent to do; this is irresponsibility. No one is allowed either to take on what is likely to impair performance of the primary function of his institution—the function for the sake of which society has entrusted resources to him. That too is irresponsible. But a manager, whether of business, a hospital, a university, has to think through the impacts of the decisions he does make, for he is always responsible for his impacts. And then he needs to think through what the constituencies are that can effectively veto and block his decisions, and what their minimum expectations and needs should be.

When it comes to the performance of the primary task of an institution—whether economic goods and services in the case of the business, heath care in that of a hospital, or scholarship and higher education in that of the university—the rule is to optimize. There, managers have to base their decisions on what is right rather than on what is acceptable. But in dealing with the constituencies outside and beyond this narrow definition of the primary task, managers have to think politically—in terms of the minimum needed to placate and appease and keep quiet constituent groups that otherwise might use their power of veto. Managers cannot be politicians. They cannot confine themselves to "satisficing" decisions. But they also cannot be concerned only with optimization in the central area of performance of their institution. They have to balance both approaches in one continuous decision making process. The corporation is an economic institution. But it is also a political institution.

Part 6

The Knowledge Society

Introduction to Part 6

I began to write about the shift to knowledge as the new key resource and as the creator of wealth and jobs in my 1949 book *The New Society*. But I did not begin to use the terms knowledge society, knowledge economy, or knowledge worker until ten years later, in my 1957 book *The Landmarks of Tomorrow*—at about the same time that the Princeton economist Fritz Machlup began to write about "knowledge industries." Then, in my 1969 book *The Age of Discontinuity*, I attempted to explore the meaning of this shift from a society, economy, and polity based on manual work and manual skill to a society, economy and polity based on knowledge and knowledge workers.

The immensity of this shift is hardly fully realized as yet. From time immemorial the overwhelming majority of all people made their living working with their hands—and that was still true, as late as 1913 even in the most highly advanced country. The nineteenth and early twentieth centuries saw the movement of workers into the factory as unprecedented social revolution and as a profound change in the human condition—Marx was by no means the only one who thought so. Actually all it did, as we now realize, was to move the worker to the tool (that is to the new and not portable steam engine) instead of moving the tool to the worker. But the work itself barely changed—it remained manual and, in large part, work requiring the same tools and the same skills. Only after 1920, with the coming of "mass production" was there any significant change in work and tools.

By contrast, the shift to knowledge work and knowledge worker is a true discontinuity, a true break—and it creates both a new social condition and a new human condition.

We have barely begun to explore this change, let alone to adapt to it. Our political systems everywhere are, for instance, still based on the assumption of a preponderantly manual work force, and indeed on the assumption of a preponderantly rural work force—most extreme in Japan and France, but also still powerful in the U.S. Yet in no developed country does the rural population exceed 5 percent by now—whereas the knowledge work force already runs above 20 percent of every developed country's population. Still, so much has been written about knowledge economy, knowledge society, and knowledge worker—a good deal by me—as to make superfluous exhaustive discussion of these topics in this volume.

Part 5, "The Knowledge Society," therefore confines itself to a few fundamentals.

Its first chapter (chapter 15, "The New World-View," written fifty years ago and first published in 1957 in my book *The Landmarks of Tomorrow*), discusses the basic change in the *meaning* of knowledge—and its splintering into *knowledges*—which made possible the emergence of knowledge as a key resource and as a creator of wealth and of jobs. The change was not just an accumulation of more and more knowledge but a change in *world-view*.

The following chapter (chapter 16, "From Capitalism to Knowledge Society," from my 1993 book *Post Capitalist Society*) tries to anticipate the social and political theory of a knowledge society. The concluding chapters (chapter 17, "The Productivity of the Knowledge Worker" from my 1999 book *Management Challenges of the 21st Century*; and chapter 18, "From Information to Communication," (first delivered at the 1969 Tokyo meeting of the International Academy of Management), deal with the new and as yet still untackled—challenges—the challenge to make knowledge work productive where it is largely abysmally unproductive as yet; and the challenge to turn information into communication and thereby into social cohesion and community.

15

The New World-View

(from *The Landmarks of Tomorrow*, 1957)

Some years ago two brothers—intelligent, well educated, graduate students in their twenties—went to see a play, *Inherit the Wind*. This was a dramatization of the notorious Scopes "Monkey" trial of 1925 in which a schoolteacher in rural Tennessee was convicted of teaching Darwin's Theory of Evolution, and in which the great nineteenth-century conflict between science and religion reached a climax of total absurdity. When the brothers came home they said they were much impressed by the acting but baffled by the plot. What, they wanted to know, was all the excitement about? Their father, when their age, had been so deeply stirred by the trial that he had given up the ministry to become a lawyer. But when he tried to explain its meaning and its excitement to his sons they both exclaimed, "You are making this up. Why, it makes no sense at all."

The point of this story is that one of the sons is a graduate geneticist, the other one a theological student in a Presbyterian and strictly Calvinist seminary. Yet the "conflict between science and religion" could not even be explained to either of them.

It is almost frightening how fast the obvious of yesteryear is turning incomprehensible. An intelligent and well-educated man of the first modern generation—that of Newton, Hobbes, and Locke—might have still been able to understand and to make himself understood across the whole army of knowledge. This was still largely true up to World War II. There was still the "Educated Man," but it is unlikely that this Educated Man could still communicate with the world of today, only twenty years later. We ourselves, after all, have seen in recent elections how rapidly the issues, slogans, concerns, and alignments of as recent a period as the thirties have become irrelevant, if not actually incomprehensible.

But what matters most for us—the first post-modern generation—
is the change in *fundamental world-view*.

We still profess and we still teach the world-view of the past three
hundred years. But we no longer see it. We have as yet no name for
our new vision, no tools, no method and no vocabulary. But a world-
view is, above all, an experience. It is the foundation of artistic perception, philosophical analysis, and technical vocabulary. And we
have acquired this new foundation, all of a sudden, within these last
fifteen or twenty years.

The world-view of the modern West can be called a Cartesian
world-view. Few professional philosophers during these last three
hundred years have followed René Descartes, the early seventeenth-
century Frenchman, in his answers to the major problems of systematic philosophy. Yet the modern age took its vision from him. More
than Galileo or Calvin, Hobbes, Locke or Rousseau, far more even
than Newton, he determined, for three hundred years, what problems would appear important or even relevant, the scope of modern
man's vision, his basic assumptions about himself and his universe,
and above all, his concept of what is rational and plausible.

His was a twofold contribution.

First, Descartes gave to the modern world its basic axiom about
the nature of the universe and its order. The best-known formulation
is that in which the Académie Française, a generation after Descartes'
death, defined science as "The certain and evident knowledge of
things by their causes." Expressed less elegantly and less subtly, this
says, "The whole is the result of its parts"—the oversimplification of
the ordinary man who is neither scientist nor philosopher.

Second, Descartes provided the method to make his axiom effective in organizing knowledge, and the search for it. Whatever the significance of his Analytical Geometry for mathematics, it established a
universal, quantitative logic concerned with relationship between concepts, and capable of serving as universal symbol and universal language. Two hundred years later Lord Kelvin could redefine the world-
view of Cartesianism by saying, "I know what I can measure."

That the whole is equal to the sum of its parts had been an axiom
of arithmetic for almost two thousand years before Descartes (though
it no longer is an axiom of all arithmetic today). But Descartes' formulation also implied that the whole is determined by the parts, and
that, therefore, we can know the whole only by identifying and knowing the parts. It implied that the behavior of the whole is caused by

the motion of the parts. It implied above all that there is no "whole" altogether as apart from the different sums, structures, and relationships of parts.

These statements are likely to sound obvious today; they have been taken for granted for three hundred years—even though they were the most radical innovations when first propounded.

But though most of us still have the conditioned reflex of familiarity toward these assertions, there are few scientists today who would still accept the definition of the Académie Française—at least not for what they call "science" in their own field. Every one of our disciplines, sciences and arts today bases itself on concepts which are incompatible with the Cartesian axiom and with the world-view of the modern West developed there from.

Every one of our disciplines has moved from cause to configuration.

Every discipline has as its center today a concept of a whole that is not the result of its parts, not equal to the sum of its parts, and not identifiable, knowable, measurable, predictable, effective, or meaningful through identifying, knowing, measuring, predicting, moving or understanding the parts. The central concepts in every one of our modern disciplines, sciences, and arts are patterns and configurations.

Biology shows this more dramatically perhaps than any other science. The tremendous development of biology in the last fifty years is the result of the application of strict Cartesian method—the methods of classical mechanics, of analytical chemistry or of mathematical statistics—to the study of the living organism. But the more "scientific" the biologist has become, the more has he tended to talk in terms such as "immunity" and "metabolism," "ecology" and "syndrome," "homeostasis" and "pattern"—every one of them describing not so much a property of matter or quantity itself, as it describes harmonious order, every one therefore essentially an aesthetic term.

The psychologist today talks about "*Gestalt,*" "ego," "personality," or "behavior"—terms that could not be found in serious works before 1910. The social sciences talk about "culture," about "integration" or about the "informal group." We all talk about "forms." These are all concepts of a whole, of a pattern or of a configuration which can be understood only as a whole.

These configurations can never be reached by starting with the parts—just as the ear will never hear a melody by hearing individual sounds. Indeed, the parts in any pattern or configuration exist only, and can only be identified, in contemplation of the whole and from the understanding of the whole. Just as we hear the same sound in a tune rather than C# or A$_b$, depending on the key we play in, so the parts in any configuration—whether the "drives" in a personality, the complex of chemical, electrical, and mechanical actions within a metabolism, the specific rites and customs in a culture, or the particular colors and shapes in a nonobjective painting—can only be understood, explained or even identified from their place in the whole, that is, in the configuration.

Similarly, we have a *"Gestalt"* pattern as the center of our economic life, the business enterprise. "Automation" is merely a particularly ugly word to describe a new view of the process of physical production as a configuration and true entity. "Management," similarly, is a configuration term. In government we talk today about "administration" or "political process"; the economist talks about "national income," "productivity," or "economic growth," much as the theologian talks about "existence." Even the physical sciences and engineering, the most Cartesian of all our disciplines in their origins and basic concepts, talk about "systems" or—the least Cartesian term of them all—about "quantum" in which, in one measurement, are expressed mass and energy, time and distance, speed and direction, all absorbed into a single, indivisible process.

The most striking change perhaps is to be found in our approach to the study of speech and language—the most basic and most familiar symbol and tool of man. Despite the anguished pleas of teachers and parents, we talk less and less about "grammar"—the study of the *parts* of speech—and more and more about "communications." It is the *whole* of speech, including not only the words left unsaid but the atmosphere in which words are said and heard, that alone communicates. It is only this whole that has any existence at all in communications. One must not only know the whole of the message, one must also be able to relate to the pattern of behavior, personality, situation, and even culture in which communication takes place.

These terms and concepts are brand new. Not a single one of them had any scientific meaning fifty years ago, let alone any standing and respectability in the vocabulary of scholar and scientist. All of them are *qualitative*; quantity in no way characterizes them. A culture is not defined by the number of people who belong to it, or by any other quantity; nor is a business enterprise defined by size. Quantitative change matters only in these configurations when it becomes qualitative transformation—when, in the words of the Greek riddle, the grains of sand have become a sand pile. This is not a continuous but a discontinuous event, a sudden jump over a qualitative threshold at which sounds turn into recognizable melody, words and motions into behavior, procedures into management philosophy, or the atom of one element into that of another. Finally, none of these configurations is as such measurable quantitatively or capable of being represented and expressed—except in the most distorted manner—through the traditional symbols of quantitative relationships.

None of these new concepts, let me emphasize, conforms to the axiom that the whole is the result of its parts. On the contrary, they all conform to a new and by no means yet axiomatic assertion, namely that the *parts exist in contemplation of the whole*.

Moreover, none of these new concepts has any *causality* to it. Causation, that unifying axis of the Cartesian world-view, has disappeared. Yet it has not, as is so often said, been replaced by random and happenstance. Einstein was quite right when he said that he could not accept the view that the Lord plays dice with the universe. What Einstein was criticizing was only the inability of the physicists—including himself—to visualize any concept of order except causality, that is, their inability to free themselves of their own Cartesian blinders. Underlying the new concepts, including the new concepts of modern physics, is a unifying idea of order. *It is not causality, though, but purpose.*

Every one of these new concepts expresses purposeful unity. One might even state as a general principle of all these post-modern concepts that the elements (for we can no longer really talk of "parts") will be found so to arrange themselves as to serve the purpose of the whole. This, for instance, is the assumption that underlies the biologist's attempts to study and to understand organs and their functions. As a distinguished biologist, Edmund W. Sinnott, puts it (in his *The Biology of the Spirit*): "Life is the imposition of organization on matter." It is this arrangement in contemplation of the purpose of the whole that we mean today when we talk of "order." This universe of ours is thus once again a universe ruled by purpose—as was the one which the Cartesian world-view overthrew and replaced three hundred years ago.

But our idea of purpose is a very different one from that of Middle Ages and Renaissance. Their purpose lay outside of the material, social, psychological, or philosophical universe, if not entirely outside of anything man himself could be, could do or could see. Our purpose, by sharp contrast, is in the configurations themselves; it is not metaphysical but physical, it is not purpose *of* the universe, but purpose *in* the universe.

I read a while ago a piece by a leading physicist in which he talked about the "characteristics of subatomic particles." A slip of the pen, to be sure, but a revealing one. Only a half-century ago it would not have been possible for any physicist, no matter how slipshod, to write of anything but the "properties" of matter. For atomic particles to have "characteristics," the atom—if not matter and energy together—must have a "character"; and that presupposes that matter must have a purposeful order within itself.

The new world-view, in addition, assumes *process*. Every single one of these new concepts embodies in it the idea of growth, development, rhythm or becoming. These are all *irreversible* processes—whereas all events in the Cartesian universe were as reversible as the symbols on either side of an equation. Never, except in fairy tales, does the grown man become a boy again, never does lead change back to uranium, never does business enterprise return to family partnership. All these changes are irreversible because the process changes its own character; it is in other words self-generated change.

Only seventy-five years ago the last remnant of pre-Cartesian thinking, the idea of spontaneous generation of living beings, was finally laid to rest by the researches of Louis Pasteur. Now it comes back to us in the research of respectable biologists who look for clues to the origin of life in the action of sunlight and cosmic particles on amino acids. Now respectable mathematical physicists seriously talk about something even more shocking to the Cartesian world-view; a theory of constant and spontaneous generation of matter in the form of new universes and new galaxies. And a leading biochemist, Sir Macfarlane Burnet, the Australian pioneer of virus research, recently (in the *Scientific American* of February, 1957) defined a virus as "not an individual organism in the ordinary sense of the term but something that could almost be called a stream of biological pattern."

In this new emphasis on process may well lie the greatest departure from the world-view of the modern West that has been ruling us for the last three hundred years. For the Cartesian world was not only a mechanical one, in which all events are finitely determined; it was a static one. Inertia, in the strict meaning of classical mechanics, was the assumed norm. In this one point the Cartesians, otherwise such daring innovators, were the strictest of traditionalists.

In *our* idea of process we assume—and are increasingly conscious of the assumption—that it is growth, change and development that are normal and real, and that it is the absence of change, development, or growth that is imperfection, decay, corruption and death. We are breaking, therefore, not only with the "obvious" common sense of the world-view of the modern West, but with much older and much more fundamental Western traditions.

16

From Capitalism to Knowledge Society
(from *Post Capitalist Society*, 1993)

Every few hundred years in Western history there occurs a sharp transformation. We cross what I call a "divide." Within a few short decades, society rearranges itself—its worldview; its basic values; its social and political structure; its arts; its key institutions. Fifty years later, there is a new world. And the people born then cannot even imagine the world in which their grandparents lived and into which their own parents were born.

We are currently living through just such a transformation. It is creating a post-capitalist society—the Knowledge Society.

We are far enough advanced into the new post-capitalist society to review and revise the social, economic, and political history of the Age of Capitalism. But to foresee what the post-capitalist world itself will look like is risky still. What new questions will arise and where the big issues will lie, we can, I believe, already discover with some degree of probability. In many areas we can also describe what will not work. "Answers" to most questions are still largely hidden in the womb of the future. The one thing we can be sure of is that the world that will emerge from the present rearrangement of values, beliefs, social and economic structures, of political concepts and systems, indeed, of world-views, will be different from anything anyone today imagines. In some areas—and especially in society and its structure—basic shifts have already happened.

That the new society will be both a non-socialist and a post-capitalist society is practically certain. And it is certain also that its primary resource will be knowledge. This also means that it will have to be a society of organizations.

To understand the present transformation we have to look at the last such major transformation.

Within one hundred fifty years, from 1750 to 1900, capitalism and technology conquered the globe and created a world civilization. Neither capitalism nor technical innovations were new; both had been common, recurrent phenomena throughout the ages, in West and East alike. What was brand new was their speed of diffusion and their global reach across cultures, classes, and geography. And it was this speed and scope that converted capitalism into "Capitalism" and into a "system," and technical advances into the "Industrial Revolution."

This transformation was driven by a radical change in the meaning of knowledge. In both West and East, knowledge had always been seen as applying to *being*. Then, almost overnight, it came to be applied to *doing*.

It became a resource and a utility. Knowledge had always been a private good. Almost overnight it became a public good.

For a hundred years—during the first phase—knowledge was applied to tools, processes, products. This created the Industrial Revolution. But it also created what Karl Marx (1818-1883) called "alienation," new classes and class war, and with them Communism. In its second phase, beginning around 1880 and culminating around the end of World War II, knowledge in its new meaning came to be applied to work. This ushered in the *Productivity Revolution*, which in seventy-five years converted the proletarian into a middle-class bourgeois with near-upper-class income. The Productivity Revolution thus defeated class war and Communism.

The last phase began after World War II. Today, knowledge is being applied to *knowledge* itself. This is the *Management Revolution*. Knowledge is now fast becoming the sole factor of production, sidelining both capital and . It may be premature (and certainly would be presumptuous) to call ours a "knowledge society"; so far, we have only a knowledge economy. But our society is surely "post-capitalist."

Unlike those "terrible simplifiers," the nineteenth-century ideologues such as Hegel and Marx, we now know that major historical events rarely have just one cause and just one explanation. They typically result from the convergence of a good many separate and independent developments.

Many separate developments—most of them probably quite un-connected with each other—went for instance into turning capital-ism into Capitalism and technical advance into the Industrial Revo-lution. The best-known theory—that Capitalism was the child of the "Protestant Ethic"—was expounded in the opening years of this cen-tury by the German sociologist Max Weber (1864-1920). It has now been largely discredited; there just is not enough evidence for it. There is only a little more evidence to support Karl Marx's earlier thesis that the steam engine, the new prime mover, required such enormous capital investment that craftsmen could no longer finance their "means of production" and had to cede control to the capitalist.

There is one critical element, however, without which well-known phenomena—capitalism and technical advance—could not possi-bly have turned into a social and worldwide pandemic. That is the radical change in the *meaning of knowledge* that occurred in Europe around the year 1700, or shortly thereafter.

There are as many theories as to what we can know and how we know it as there have been metaphysicians, from Plato in 400 B.C. to Ludwig Wittgenstein and Karl Popper in our own day. But since Plato's time there have only been two theories in the West—and since around the same time, two theories in the East—regarding the meaning and function of knowledge. Plato's spokesman, the wise Socrates, holds that the sole function of knowledge is self-knowl-edge: the intellectual, moral, and spiritual growth of the person. His ablest opponent, the brilliant and learned Protagoras, holds however that the purpose of knowledge is to make the holder effective by enabling him to know what to say and how to say it. For Protagoras, knowledge meant logic, grammar, and rhetoric—later to become the *trivium*, the core of learning in the Middle Ages, and still very much what we mean by a "liberal education" or what the Germans mean by *"Allgemeine Bildung."* In the East, there were pretty much the same two theories of knowledge. Knowledge for the Confucian mean knowing what to say and how to say it as the route to advancement and earthly success. Knowl-edge for the Taoist and the Zen monk meant self-knowledge, and the road to enlightenment and wisdom. But while the two sides thus sharply disagreed about what knowledge actually meant, they were in total agreement as to what it did not mean. It did not mean *ability to do*. It did not mean *utility*. Utility was not knowledge; it was *skill*—the Greek word is *techne*.

Unlike their Far Eastern contemporaries, the Chinese Confucians with their infinite contempt for anything but book learning, both Socrates and Protagoras respected *techne.*

But even to Socrates and Protagoras, *techne,* however commendable, was not knowledge. It was confined to one specific application and had no general principles. What the shipmaster knew about navigating from Greece to Sicily could not be applied to anything else. Furthermore, the only way to learn a *techne* was through apprenticeship and experience. A *techne* could not be explained in words, whether spoken or written; it could only be demonstrated. As late as 1700, or even later, the English did not speak of "crafts." They spoke of "mysteries"—not just because the possessor of a craft skill was sworn to secrecy but also because a craft by definition was inaccessible to anyone who had not been apprenticed to a master and thus learned by example.

But then, beginning after 1700—and within an incredibly short fifty years—technology was invented. The very word is a manifesto in that it combines *"techne,"* that is, the mystery of a craft skill, with "logy," organized, systematic, purposeful knowledge.

The great document of this dramatic shift from skill to technology—one of the most important books in history—was the *Encyclopédie,* edited between 1751 and 1772 by Denis Diderot (1713-1784) and Jean d'Alembert (1717-1783). This famous work attempted to bring together in organized and systematic form the knowledge of all crafts, in such a way that the non-apprentice could learn to be a "technologist." It was by no means accidental that articles in the *Encyclopédie* that describe an individual craft, such as spinning or weaving, were not written by craftsmen. They were written by "information specialists": people trained as analysts, as mathematicians, as logicians—both Voltaire and Rousseau were contributors. The underlying thesis of the *Encyclopédie* was that effective results in the material universe—in tools, processes, and product—are produced by systematic analysis, and by the systematic, purposeful application of knowledge.

But the *Encyclopédie* also preached that principles which produced results in one craft would produce results in any other. That was anathema, however, to both the traditional man of knowledge and the traditional craftsman.

None of the original technical schools of the eighteenth and nineteenth century aimed at producing *new* knowledge, nor did the

Encyclopédie. None even talked of the application of *science* to tools, processes, and products, that is, to technology. This idea had to wait for another hundred years, until 1830 or so, when a German chemist, Justus von Liebig (1803-1873), applied science to invent, first, artificial fertilizers, and then a way to preserve animal protein: meat extract. What the early technical schools and the *Encyclopédie* did do, however, was perhaps more important. They brought together, codified, and published the *techne,* the craft mystery, as it had been developed over millennia. They converted experience into knowledge, apprenticeship into textbook, secrecy into methodology, doing into applied knowledge. These are the essentials of what we have come to call the "Industrial Revolution"— the transformation by technology of society and civilization worldwide.

It was this change in the meaning of knowledge which then made modern Capitalism inevitable and dominant. Above all, the speed of technical change created demand for capital way beyond anything the craftsman could possibly supply. The new technology also required concentration of production, that is, the shift to the factory. Knowledge could not be applied in tens of thousands of small individual workshops and in the cottage industries of the rural village. It required concentration of production under one roof.

The new technology also required a large-scale energy, whether water power or steam power, which could not be decentralized. But, though important, these energy needs were secondary. The central point was that production almost overnight moved from being craft-based to being technology-based. As a result, the capitalist moved almost overnight into the center of the economy and society. Before, he had always been "supporting cast."

As late as 1750, large-scale enterprise was governmental rather than private. The earliest, and for many centuries the greatest, of all manufacturing enterprises in the Old World was the famous arsenal owned and run by the government of Venice. And the eighteenth-century "manufactories" such as the porcelain works of Meissen and Sèvres were still government-owned. But by 1830, large-scale private capitalist enterprise dominated in the West. Another fifty years later, by the time Marx died in 1883, private capitalist enterprise had penetrated everywhere except to such remote corners of the world as Tibet or the Empty Quarter of Arabia.

The unheard-of speed with which society was transformed created the social tensions and conflicts of the new order. We now know that there is no truth in the all but universal belief that factory workers in the early nineteenth century were worse off and were treated more harshly than they had been as landless laborers in the pre-industrial countryside. They were badly off, no doubt, and harshly treated. But they flocked to the factory precisely because they were still better off there than they were at the bottom of a static, tyrannical, and starving rural society. They still experienced a much better "quality of life." "England's green and pleasant land" which William Blake (1757-1827) in his famous poem *Milton* hoped to liberate from the new "Satanic Mills," was in reality one vast rural slum.

But while industrialization, from the beginning, meant material improvement rather than Marx's famous "immiseration," the speed of change was so breathtaking as to be deeply traumatic. The new class, the "proletarians," became "alienated," to use the term Marx coined. Their alienation, he predicted, would make inevitable their exploitation. For they were becoming totally dependent for their livelihood on the access to the "means of production," which were owned and controlled by the capitalist. This in turn—so Marx predicted—would increasingly concentrate ownership in fewer and bigger hands, and increasingly impoverish a powerless proletariat—until the day at which the system would collapse under its own weight, the few remaining capitalists overthrown by proletarians who "had nothing to lose but their chains."

We know now that Marx was a false prophet—the very opposite of what he predicted has in fact happened. But this is hindsight. Most of his contemporaries shared his view of capitalism even if they did not necessarily share his prediction of the outcome. Even anti-Marxists accepted Marx's analysis of the "inherent contradictions of capitalism."

What, then, defeated Marx and Marxism? By 1950, a good many of us already knew that Marxism had failed both morally and economically. (I had said so already in 1939 in my book *The End of Economic Man*—see chapter 5 above.) But Marxism was still the one coherent ideology for most of the world, and for most of the world it looked invincible. There were "anti-Marxists" galore, but, as yet, few "non-Marxists," that is, people who thought that Marxism had become irrelevant. Even those bitterly opposed to Socialism were still convinced that it was in the ascendant.

What, then, overcame the "inevitable contradictions of capitalism," the "alienation" and "immiseration" of the working class, and with it the whole notion of the "proletarian?"

The answer is the *Productivity Revolution*. When knowledge changed its meaning two hundred fifty years ago, it began to be applied to tools, processes, and products. This is still what "technology" means to most people and what is being taught in engineering schools. But two years before Marx's death, the Productivity Revolution had already begun. In 1881, an American, Frederick Winslow Taylor (1856-1915), first applied knowledge to the study of *work*, the analysis of work, and the engineering of work.

It was by pure accident that F. W. Taylor, a well-to-do, educated man, became a worker. Poor eyesight forced him to give up going to Harvard and instead to take a job in an iron foundry. Being extremely gifted, Taylor very soon rose to be one of the bosses. And his metal-working inventions made him a rich man very early. What got Taylor to start on the study of work was his shock at the mutual and growing hatred between capitalists and workers, which had come to dominate the late nineteenth century. Taylor, in other words, saw what Marx saw—and Disraeli and Bismarck and Henry James. But he also saw what they failed to see: that the conflict was unnecessary. He set out to make workers productive so that they would earn decent money.

Taylor's motivation was not efficiency. It was not the creation of profits for the owners. To his very death, he maintained that the major beneficiary of the fruits of productivity had to be the worker, not the owner. His main motivation was the creation of a society in which owners and workers, capitalists and proletarians could share a common interest in productivity and could build a harmonious relationship on the application of knowledge to work. The people who have come closest to understanding this so far are Japan's post-World War II employers and Japan's post-World War II union leaders.

Few figures in intellectual history have had greater impact than Taylor—and few have been so willfully misunderstood or so assiduously misquoted.

In part, Taylor has suffered because history has proven him right and the intellectuals wrong. In part, he is ignored because contempt for work still lingers, above all among the intellectuals. Surely shoveling sand (the most publicized of Taylor's analyses) is not something an "educated man" would appreciate, let alone consider important.

Taylor's assertion that all manual work, skilled or unskilled, could be analyzed and organized by the application of knowledge seemed preposterous to his contemporaries. And the fact that there was a mystique to craft skill was still universally accepted for many, many years. It was this belief that encouraged Hitler, as later as 1941, to declare war on the United States. For the United States to field an effective force in Europe would require a large fleet to transport troops. America at that time had almost no merchant marine and no destroyers to protect it. Modern warfare, Hitler further argued, required precision optics in large quantities; and there were no skilled optical workers in America.

Hitler was absolutely right. The United States did not have much of a merchant marine, and its destroyers were few and ludicrously obsolete. It also had almost no optical industry. But by applying Taylor's Scientific Management, the U.S. industry trained totally unskilled workers, many of them former sharecroppers raised in a pre-industrial environment, and converted them in sixty to ninety days into first-rate welders and shipbuilders. Equally, the United States trained the same kind of people within a few months to turn out precision optics of better quality than the Germans ever did—and on an assembly line to boot.

Taylor's greatest impact all told was probably in training. A hundred years before Taylor, Adam Smith had taken for granted that at least fifty years of experience (and more likely a full century) were required for a region to gain the necessary skills to turn out high-quality products—his examples were the production of musical instruments in Bohemia and Saxony, and of silk fabrics in Scotland. Seventy years after Smith, around 1840, a German, August Borsig (1804-1854)—one of the first people outside England to build a steam locomotive—invented the German system of apprenticeship, which combines practical plant experience under a master with theoretical grounding in school.

It is still the foundation of Germany's industrial productivity. But even Borsig's apprenticeship took three to five years. Then, first in World War I but above all in World War II, the United States systematically applied Taylor's approach to training "first-class men" in a few month's time. This, more than any other factor, explains why the United States was able to defeat both Japan and Germany.

All earlier economic powers in modern history—Great Britain, the United States, Germany—emerged through leadership in new technology. The post-World War II economic powers—first Japan, then South Korea, Taiwan, Hong Kong, Singapore—all owe their rise to Taylor's training. It enabled them to endow a still largely pre-industrial and therefore still low-wage work force with world-class productivity in practically no time. In the post-World War II decades, Taylor-based training became the one truly effective engine of economic development.

The application of knowledge to work explosively increased productivity. For hundreds of years there had been no increase in the ability of workers to turn out goods or to move goods. Machines created greater capacity. But workers themselves were no more productive than they had been in the workshops of ancient Greece, in building the roads of Imperial Rome, or in producing the highly prized woolen cloth which gave Renaissance Florence its wealth.

But within a few years after Taylor began to apply knowledge to work, productivity began to rise at a rate of 3.5 to 4 percent compound a year—which means doubling every eighteen years or so. Since Taylor began, productivity has increased some fifty-fold in all advanced countries. On this unprecedented expansion rest all the increases in both standard of living and quality of life in the developed countries.

Half of this additional productivity has been taken in the form of increased purchasing power; in other words, in the form of a higher standard of living. But between one third and one half has been taken in the form of increased leisure. As late as 1910, workers in developed countries still worked as much as they had ever worked before, that is, at least 3,000 hours a year. Today, the Japanese work 2,000 hours a year, the Americans around 1,850, the Germans at most, 1,600—and they all produce fifty times as much per hour as they produced eighty years ago. Other substantial shares of increased productivity have been taken in the form of health care, which has grown from something like zero percent of the gross national product to 8-10 percent in developed countries, and in the form of education, which has grown from around two percent GNP to 10 percent or more.

Most of this increase—just as Taylor predicted—has been taken by the workers, that is, by Marx's proletarians.

Henry Ford (1863-1947) brought out the first cheap automobile, the Model T, in 1907. It was "cheap," however, only by comparison with all other automobiles on the market, which, in terms of average incomes, cost as much as a twin-engine private plane costs today. At $750, Henry Ford's Model T cost what a fully employed industrial worker in the United States earned in three to four *years*—for 80 cents was then a good day's wage, and there were no "benefits." Even an American physician in those years rarely earned more than $500 a year. Today, a unionized automobile worker in the United States, Japan, or Germany, working only forty hours a week, earns roughly eight times what a cheap new car costs today.

By 1930, Taylor's Scientific Management—despite resistance from unions and from intellectuals—had swept the developed world. As a result, Marx's "proletarian" became a "bourgeois." The blue-collar worker in manufacturing industry, the "proletarian" rather than the "capitalist," became the true beneficiary of capitalism and Industrial Revolution. This explains the total failure of Marxism in the highly developed countries for which Marx had predicted "revolution" by 1900. It explains why, after 1918, there was no "Proletarian Revolution" even in the defeated countries of Central Europe where there was misery, hunger, and unemployment. It explains why the Great Depression did not lead to a Communist revolution, as Lenin and Stalin—and practically all Marxists—had confidently expected. By that time, Marx's proletarians had not yet become affluent, but they had already become middle class. They had become productive.

"Darwin, Marx, Freud" form the trinity often cited as the "makers of the modern world." Marx would be taken out and replaced by Taylor if there were any justice in the world. But that Taylor is not given his due is a minor matter.

It is a serious matter, however, that far too few people realize that the application of knowledge to work created developed economies by setting off the productivity explosion of the last hundred years. Technologists give credit to machines, economists to capital investment. Yet both were as plentiful in the first hundred years of the capitalist age, before 1880, as they have been since. With respect to technology or to capital, the second hundred years differed very little from the first one hundred. But there was absolutely no increase in worker productivity during the first hundred years—and consequently very little increase in workers' real incomes or any decrease in their working hours. What made the second hundred years so critically different can only be explained as the result of *applying knowledge to work.*

Now, however, we are moving into a new, a third, stage. From now on progress, productivity, social cohesion will require *the application of knowledge to knowledge.* This is the third and perhaps the ultimate step in the transformation of knowledge. Supplying knowledge to find out how existing knowledge can best be applied to reproduce results is, in effect, what we mean by management.

But knowledge is now also being applied systematically and purposefully to define what *new* knowledge is needed, whether it is feasible, and what has to be done to make knowledge effective. It is being applied, in other words, to systematic innovation.

Like its two predecessors—knowledge applied to tools, processes, and products, and knowledge applied to human work—the new Knowledge Revolution has swept the earth. It took a hundred years, from the middle of the eighteenth century to the middle of the nineteenth century, for the Industrial Revolution to become dominant and worldwide. It took some seventy years, from 1880 to the end of World War II, for the Productivity Revolution to become dominant and world-wide. It has taken less than fifty years—from 1945 to 1990—for the Knowledge Revolution to become dominant and worldwide.

The Knowledge Revolution has made knowledge the essential resource. Land and Capital are important chiefly as restraints. And so is Labor in the traditional meaning of the term. All three are "costs" rather than "factors of production." Without them, knowledge cannot produce; without them, management cannot perform. But where there is effective management, that is, application of knowledge to knowledge, we can always obtain the other resources.

That knowledge has become *the* resource, rather than *a* resource, is what makes our society "post-capitalist." This fact changes—fundamentally—the structure of society. It creates new politics. It creates new social and economic dynamics.

17

The Productivity of the Knowledge Worker
(from *Management Challenges for the 21ˢᵗ Century*, 1991)

The most important, and indeed the truly unique, contribution of management in the twentieth century was the fifty-fold increase in the productivity of the manual worker in manufacturing.

The most important contribution management needs to make in the twenty-first century is similarly to increase the productivity of knowledge work and the knowledge worker.

The most valuable assets of a twentieth-century company were its *production equipment*. The most valuable asset of a twenty-first-century institution, whether business or non-business, will be its *knowledge workers* and their *productivity*.

Work on the productivity of the knowledge worker has barely begun.

In terms of actual work on knowledge worker productivity we are, in the year 2000, roughly where we were in the year 1900, a century ago, in terms of the productivity of the manual worker. But we already know infinitely more about the productivity of the knowledge worker than we did then about that of the manual worker. We even know a good many of the answers. But we also know the challenges to which we do not yet know the answers, and on which we need to go to work.

Six major factors determine knowledge-worker productivity.

1. Knowledge worker productivity demands that we ask the question: *"What is the task?"*

2. It demands that we impose the responsibility for their productivity on the individual knowledge workers themselves. Knowledge workers *have* to manage themselves. They have to have *autonomy*.

3.   Continuing innovation has to be part of the work, the task and the responsibility of knowledge workers.

4.   Knowledge work requires continuous learning on the part of the knowledge worker, but equally continuous teaching on the part of the knowledge worker.

5.   Productivity of the knowledge worker is not—at least not primarily— a matter of the *quantity* of output. *Quality* is at least as important.

6.   Finally, knowledge-worker productivity requires that the knowledge worker is both seen and treated as an "asset" rather than a "cost." It requires that knowledge workers *want* to work for the organization in preference to all other opportunities.

Each of these requirements—except perhaps the last one—is almost the exact opposite of what is needed to increase the productivity of the manual worker.

In manual work quality also matters. But lack of quality is a restraint. There has to be a certain minimum quality standard. The achievement of Total Quality Management, that is, of the application of twentieth-century statistical theory to manual work, is the ability to cut (though not entirely to eliminate) production that falls below this minimum standard.

But in most knowledge work, quality is not a minimum and a restraint. Quality is the essence of the output. In judging the performance of a teacher, we do not ask how many students there can be in his or her class. We ask how many students learn anything—and that's a quality question. In appraising the performance of a medical laboratory, the question of how many tests it can run through its machines is quite secondary to the question of how many test results are valid and reliable. And this is true even for the work of the file clerk.

Productivity of knowledge work therefore has to aim first at obtaining quality—and not minimum quality but optimum if not maximum quality. Only then can one ask: "What is the volume, the quantity of work?"

This not only means that we approach the task of making productive the knowledge worker from the quality of the work rather than the quantity. It also means that we will have to learn to define quality.

The crucial question in knowledge-worker productivity is the first one: *What is the task?* It is also the one most at odds with manual-worker productivity. In manual work the key question is always: *How should the work be done?* In manual work the task is always given. None of the people who work on manual-worker productivity ever asked: "What is the manual worker supposed to do?" Their only question was: "How does the manual worker best do the job?"

But in knowledge work the key question is: "What is the task?"

One reason for this is that knowledge work, unlike manual work, does not program the worker. The worker on the automobile assembly line who puts on a wheel is programmed by the simultaneous arrival of the car's chassis on one line and of the wheel on the other line. The farmer who plows a field in preparation for planting does not climb out of his tractor to take a telephone call, to attend a meeting, or to write a memo. *What* is to be done is always obvious in manual work.

But in knowledge work the task does not program the worker.

A major crisis in the hospital, for example, when a patient suddenly goes into coma, does of course control the nurse's task and programs her.

But otherwise, it is largely the nurse's decision whether to spend time at the patient's bed or whether to spend time filling out papers. Engineers are constantly being pulled off their tasks by having to write a report or rewrite it, by being asked to attend a meeting and so on. The job of the salesperson in the department store is to serve the customer and to provide the merchandise the customer is interested in or should become interested in. Instead the salesperson spends an enormous amount of time on paperwork, on checking whether merchandise is in stock, on checking when and how it can be delivered and so on—all the things that take salespeople away from the customer and do not add anything to their productivity in doing what salespeople are being paid for, which is to sell and to satisfy the customer.

The first requirement in tackling knowledge work is to find out what the task is so as to make it possible to concentrate knowledge workers on the task and to eliminate everything else—at least as far as it can possibly be eliminated. But this then requires that the knowledge workers themselves define what the task is or should be. And only the knowledge workers themselves can do that.

Work on knowledge-worker productivity therefore begins with asking the knowledge workers themselves:

What is your task? What should it be? What should you be expected to contribute? and What hampers you in doing your task and should be eliminated?

Knowledge workers themselves almost always have thought through these questions and can answer them. Still, it then usually takes time and hard work to restructure their jobs so that they can actually make the contribution they are already being paid for. But asking the questions and taking action on the answers usually doubles or triples knowledge-worker productivity, and quite fast.

This was the result of questioning the nurses in a major hospital. They were actually sharply divided as to what their task was, with one group saying "patient care" and another one saying "satisfying the physicians." But they were in complete agreement on the things that made them unproductive—they called them "chores": paperwork, arranging flowers, answering the phone calls of patient's relatives, answering the patients' bells, and so on. And all—or nearly all—of these could be turned over to a nonnurse floor clerk, paid a fraction of a nurse's pay. The productivity of the nurses on the floor immediately more than doubled, as measured by the time nurses spent at the patient's beds. Patient satisfaction more than doubled. And turnover of nurses, which had been catastrophically high, almost disappeared—all within four months.

And once the *task* has been defined, the next requirements can be tackled—and will be tackled by the knowledge workers themselves. They are:

1. Knowledge workers' *responsibility* for their own contribution—the knowledge worker's decision what he or she should be held accountable for in terms of quality and quantity, in respect to time and in respect to costs. Knowledge workers have to have autonomy, and that entails responsibility.

2. Continuous innovation has to be built into the knowledge worker's job.

3. Continuous learning and continuous teaching have to be built into the job.

But one central requirement of knowledge-worker productivity is then still left to be satisfied. We have to answer the question: *What is quality?*

In some knowledge work—especially in some work requiring a high degree of knowledge—we already measure quality. Surgeons, for instance, are routinely measured, especially by their colleagues, by their success rates in difficult and dangerous procedures, for example, by the survival rates of their open-heart surgical patients or the full recovery rates of their orthopedic-surgery patients. But by and large we have, so far, mainly judgments rather than measures regarding the quality of a great deal of knowledge work. The main trouble is, however, not the difficulty of measuring quality. It is the difficulty—and more particularly the sharp disagreements—in defining what the task is and what is should be.

The best example I know is the American school. As everyone knows, public schools in the American inner city have become disaster areas. But next to them—in the same location and serving the same kind of children—are private (mostly Christian) schools in which the kids behave well and learn well. There is endless speculation to explain these enormous quality differences. But a major reason is surely that the two kinds of schools define their tasks differently. The typical public school defines its task as "helping the underprivileged"; the typical Christian school (and especially the parochial schools of the Catholic Church) define their task as "enabling those who want to learn, to learn." One therefore is governed by its scholastic failures, the other one by its scholastic successes.

But similarly: There are two research departments of major pharmaceutical companies that have totally different results because they define their tasks differently. One sees its task as not having failures, that is, in working steadily on fairly minor but predictable improvements in existing products and for established markets. The other one defines its task as producing "breakthroughs" and therefore courts risks. Both are considered fairly successful—by themselves, by their own top managements and by outside analysts. But each operates quite differently and quite differently defines its own productivity and that of its research scientists.

To define quality in knowledge work and to convert the definition into knowledge-worker productivity is thus to a large extent a matter of defining the task. It requires the difficult, risk-taking and always-controversial definition as to what "results" are for a given enterprise and a given activity. We actually *know* how to do it. Still, the question is a totally new one for most organizations, and also for most knowledge workers. And to answer it *requires* controversy, *requires* dissent.

Knowledge workers must be considered a *capital asset*. Costs need to be controlled and reduced. Assets need to be made to grow.

In managing manual workers we learned fairly early that high turnover, that is, losing workers, is very costly. The Ford Motor Company, as is well known, increased the pay of skilled workers from eighty cents a day to five dollars a day in January, 1914. It did so because its turnover had been so excessive as to make its costs prohibitively high; it had to hire sixty thousand people a year to keep ten thousand. Even so, everybody, including Henry Ford himself (who had at first been bitterly opposed to this increase) was convinced that the higher wages would greatly reduce the company's profits. Instead, in the very first year, profits almost doubled. Paid five dollars a day, practically no workers left—in fact, the Ford Motor Company soon had a waiting list.

But short of the costs of turnover, rehiring or retraining and so on, the manual worker is still being seen as a cost. This is true even in Japan, despite the emphasis on lifetime employment and on building a "loyal," permanent workforce. And short of the cost of turnover, the management of people at work, based on millennia of work being almost totally manual work, still assumes that with the exception of a few highly skilled people one manual worker is like any other manual worker.

This is definitely not true for knowledge work.

Employees who do manual work do not own the means of production. They may, and often do, have a lot of valuable experience. But that experience is valuable only at the place where they work. It is not portable.

But knowledge workers *own* the means of production. It is the knowledge between their ears. And it is a totally portable and enormous capital asset. Because knowledge workers own their means of production, they are mobile. Manual workers need the job much more than the job needs them. It may still not be true for all knowledge workers that the organization needs them more than they need the organization. But for most of them it is a symbiotic relationship in which they need each other in equal measure.

Management's duty is to preserve the assets of the institution in its care. What does this mean when the knowledge of the individual knowledge worker becomes an asset and, in more and more cases, the *main* asset of an institution? What does this mean for personnel policy? What is needed to attract and to hold the highest-producing knowledge workers? What is needed to increase their productivity and to convert their increased productivity into performance capacity for the organization?

A very large number of knowledge workers do both knowledge work *and* manual work. I call them "technologists."

This group includes people who apply knowledge of the highest order.

Surgeons preparing for an operation to correct a brain aneurysm before it produces a lethal brain hemorrhage spend hours in diagnosis *before* they cut—and that requires specialized knowledge of the highest order. And then again, during the surgery, an unexpected complication may occur that calls for theoretical knowledge and judgment, both of the very highest order. But the surgery itself is manual work—and manual work consisting of repetitive manual operations in which the emphasis is on speed, accuracy, uniformity. And these operations are studied, organized, learned, and practiced exactly like any manual work.

But the technologist group also contains large numbers of people in whose work knowledge is relatively subordinate—though it is always crucial.

The file clerk's job—and that of her computer-operator successor—requires knowledge of the alphabet that no experience can teach. This knowledge is a small part of an otherwise manual task. But it is the foundation and absolutely critical.

Technologists may be the single biggest group of knowledge workers. They may also be the fastest-growing group. They include the great majority of health care workers: lab technicians; rehabilitation technicians; technicians in imaging such as X-ray, ultrasound, magnetic-resonance imaging, and so on. They include dentists and all dental support people. They include automobile mechanics and all kinds of repair and installation people. In fact, the technologist may be the true successor to the nineteenth- and twentieth-century skilled workers.

Technologists are also the one group in which developed countries can have a true and long-lasting competitive advantage.

When it comes to truly high knowledge, no country can any longer have much of a lead, the way nineteenth-century Germany had through its university. Among theoretical physicists, mathematicians, economic theorists and the like, there is no "nationality." And any country can, at fairly low costs, train a substantial number of high-knowledge people. India, for instance, despite her poverty, has been training fairly large numbers of first-rate physicians and first-rate computer programmers. Only in educating technologists can the developed countries still have a meaningful competitive edge, and for some time to come.

The United States is the only country that has actually developed this advantage—through its so far unique nationwide systems of community colleges. The community college was actually *designed* (beginning in the 1920s) to educate technologists who have *both* the needed theoretical knowledge *and* the manual skill. On this, I am convinced, rests both the still huge productivity advantage of the American economy and the—so far unique—American ability to create, almost overnight, new and different industries.

Nothing quite like the American community college exists anywhere else so far. The famous Japanese school system produces either people prepared for only manual work or people prepared only for knowledge work. Only in the year 2003 is the first Japanese institution devoted to training technologists supposed to get started. Even more famous is the German apprenticeship system. Started in the 1830s, it was one of the main factors in Germany's becoming the world's leading manufacturer. But it focused—and still focuses—primarily on manual skills and slights theoretical knowledge. It is thus in danger of becoming rapidly obsolete.

But these other developed countries should be expected to catch up with the United States fairly fast. Other countries—"emerging ones" or "Third World" ones—are, however, likely to be decades behind—in part because educating technologists is expensive, in part because in these countries people of knowledge still look down with disdain, if not with contempt, on working with one's hands. "That's what we have servants for," is still their prevailing attitude. In developed countries, however—and again foremost in the United States—more and more manual workers are going to be technologists. In increasing knowledge-worker productivity, increasing the productivity of the technologists therefore deserves to be given high priority.

Productivity of the knowledge worker will almost always require that the *work itself* be restructured and be made part of a *system.*

One example is servicing expensive equipment, such as huge and expensive earth-moving machines. Traditionally, this had been seen as distinct and separate from the job of making and selling the machines. But when the U.S. Caterpillar Company, the world's largest producer of such equipment, asked "What are we getting paid for?" the answer was, "We are not getting paid for machinery. We are getting paid for what the machinery does at the customer's place of business. That means keeping the equipment running, since even one hour during which the equipment is out of operation may cost the customer far more than the equipment itself." In other words, the answer to "What is our businesses?" was "Service." This then led to a total restructuring of operations all the way back to the factory, so that the customer can be guaranteed continuing operations and immediate repairs or replacements. And the service representative, usually a technologist, has become the true "decision maker."

What to do about knowledge worker productivity is thus largely known. So is *how* to do it.

Knowledge-worker productivity is a *survival requirement* for developed countries. In no other way can they hope to maintain themselves, let alone to maintain their leadership and their standards of living.

In the last hundred years, that is, in the twentieth century, this leadership very largely depended on making the manual worker productive. Any country, any industry, any business can do that today—using the methods that the developed countries have worked out and put into practice in the 120 years since Frederick Winslow Taylor first looked at manual work. Anybody today, anyplace, can apply those policies to training, to the organization of the work and to the productivity of workers, even if they are barely literate, if not illiterate, and totally unskilled.

The only possible advantage developed countries can hope to have is in the supply of people prepared, educated and trained for knowledge work. There, for another fifty years, the developed countries can expect to have substantial advantages, both in quality and in quantity. But whether this advantage will translate into performance depends on the ability of the developed countries—and of every industry in it, of every company in it, of every institution in it—to raise the productivity of the knowledge worker and to raise it as fast as the developed countries, in the last hundred years, have raised the productivity of the manual worker.

The countries and the industries that have emerged as the leaders in the last hundred years in the world are the countries and the industries that have led in raising the productivity of the manual worker: the United States first, Japan and Germany second. Fifty years from now—if not much sooner—the leadership in the world economy will have moved to the countries and to the industries that have most systematically and most successfully raised knowledge-worker productivity.

18

From Information to Communication
(Originally a paper for the International Academy of Management, 1969)

Concern with "information" and "communication" started shortly before World War I. Russell and Whitehead's *Principia Mathematica*, which appeared in 1910, is still one of the foundation books. And a long line of illustrious successors—from Ludwig Wittgenstein through Norbert Wiener and Noam Chomsky's "mathematical linguistics" today—has continued the work on the *logic* of information.

Roughly contemporaneous is the interest in the *meaning* of communication; Alfred Korzybski started on the study of "general semantics," that is, on the meaning of communication, around the turn of the century. It was World War I, however, which made the entire Western world communication-conscious.

When the diplomatic documents of 1914 in the German and Russian archives were published, soon after the end of the fighting, it became appallingly clear that the catastrophe had been caused, in large measure, by communications failure despite copious and reliable information. And the war itself—especially the total failure of its one and only strategic concept, Winston Churchill's Gallipoli campaign in 1915-16—was patently a tragicomedy of noncommunications. At the same time, the period immediately following World War I—a period of industrial strife and total noncommunication between Westerners and "revolutionary" communists (and a little later, equally revolutionary fascists)—showed both the need for, and the lack of, a valid theory or functioning practice of communications, inside existing institutions, inside existing societies, and between various leadership groups and their various "publics."

As a result, communications suddenly became, forty to fifty years ago, a consuming interest of scholars as well as of practitioners.

Above all, communications in management has this last half-century been a central concern to students and practitioners in all institutions—business, the military, public administration, hospital administration, university administration, and research administration. In no other area have intelligent men and women worked harder or with greater dedication than psychologists, human relations experts, managers, and management students have worked on improving communications in our major institutions.

Yet communications has proven as elusive as the unicorn. The noise level has gone up so fast that no one can really listen any more to all that babble about communications. But there is clearly less and less communicating. The communications gap within institutions and between groups in society has been widening steadily—to the point where it threatens to become an unbridgeable gulf of total misunderstanding.

In the meantime, there is an information explosion. Every professional and every executive—in fact, everyone except the deaf-mute—suddenly has access to data in inexhaustible abundance. All of us feel—and overeat—very much like the little boy who has been left alone in the candy store. But what has to be done to make this cornucopia of data redound to information, let alone to knowledge? We get a great many answers. But the one thing clear so far is that no one really has an answer. Despite "information theory" and "data processing," no one yet has actually seen, let alone used, an "information system," or a "data base." The one thing we do know, though, is that the abundance of information changes the communications problem and makes it both more urgent and even less tractable.

Despite the sorry state of communications in theory and practice, we have, however, learned a good deal about information and communications. Most of it, though, has not come out of the work on communications to which we have devoted so much time and energy. It has been the byproduct of work in a large number of seemingly unrelated fields, from learning theory to genetics and electronic engineering. We equally have a lot of experience—though mostly of failure—in a good many practical situations in all kinds of institutions. Communications we may, indeed, never understand. But communications in organizations—call it *managerial communications*—we do know something about by now. We increasingly know what does not work and, sometimes, why it does not work. Indeed, we can say bluntly that most of today's brave attempts at communication in organization—whether business, unions, government agencies, or universities—are based on assumptions that have been proven to be invalid—and that, therefore, these efforts cannot have results. And perhaps we can even anticipate what might work.

We have learned, mostly through doing the wrong things, the following four fundamentals of communications;

1.   Communication is perception,

2.   Communication is expectations,

3.   Communication is involvement,

4.   Communication and information are totally different, but information presupposes functioning communications.

1.   An old riddle asked by the mystics of many religions—the Zen Buddhists, the Sufis of Islam, or the rabbis of the Talmud—asks: "Is there a sound in the forest if a tree crashes down and no one is around to hear it?" We now know that the right answer to this is "no." There are sound waves. But there is no sound unless someone perceives it. Sound is created by perception. Sound is communication.

This may seem trite; after all, the mystics of old already knew this, for they, too, always answered that there is no sound unless someone can hear it. Yet the implications of this rather trite statement are great indeed.

a.   First, it means that it is the recipient who communicates. The so-called communicator, that is, the person who emits the communication, does not communicate. He utters. Unless there is someone who hears, there is no communication. There is only noise. The communicator speaks or writes or sings—but he does not communicate. Indeed he cannot communicate. He can only make it possible, or impossible, for a recipient—or rather percipient—to perceive.

b.   Perception, we know, is not logic. It is experience. This means, in the first place, that one always perceives a configuration. One cannot perceive single specifics. They are always part of a total picture. *The Silent Language* (as Edward T. Hall called it in the title of his pioneering work)—that is, the gestures, the tone of voice, the environment all together, not to mention the cultural and social referents—cannot be dissociated from the spoken language. In fact, without them the spoken word has no meaning and cannot communicate. It is not only that the same words, for example, "I enjoyed meeting you," will be heard as having a wide variety of meanings. Whether they are heard as warm or as icy cold, as endearment or as rejection, depends on their setting in the silent language, such as the tone of voice or the occasion. More important is that by themselves, that is, without being part of the total configuration of occasion, silent language, and so on, the phrase has no meaning at all. By itself it cannot make possible communication. It cannot be understood. Indeed it cannot be heard. To paraphrase an old proverb of the Human Relations school: "One cannot communicate a word; the whole man always comes with it."

c.   But we know about perception also that one can only perceive what one is capable of perceiving. Just as the human ear does not hear sounds above a certain pitch, so does human perception all together not perceive what is beyond its range of perception. It may, of course, hear physically, or see visually, but it cannot accept. The stimulus cannot become communication.

This is a very fancy way of stating something the teachers of rhetoric have known for a very long time. In Plato's *Phaedrus*, which among other things, is also the earliest extant treatise on rhetoric, Socrates points out that one has to talk to people in terms of their own experience, that is, that one has to use a carpenter's metaphors when talking to carpenters, and so on. One can only communicate in the recipient's language or altogether on his terms. And the terms have to be experience-based. It, therefore, does very little good to try to explain terms to people. They will not be able to receive them if the terms are not of their own experience. They simply exceed their perception capacity.

The connection between experience, perception, and concept formation, that is, cognition, is, we now know, infinitely subtler and richer than any earlier philosopher imagined. But one fact is proven and comes out strongly. Percept and concept in the learner, whether child or adult, are not separate. We cannot perceive unless we also conceive. But we also cannot form concepts unless we can perceive. To communicate a concept is impossible unless the recipient can perceive it, that is, unless it is within his perception.

There is a very old saying among writers: "Difficulties with a sentence always mean confused thinking. It is not the sentence that needs straightening out, it is the thought behind it." In writing we attempt to communicate with ourselves. An unclear sentence is one that exceeds our own capacity for perception. Working on the sentence, that is, working on what is normally called communications, cannot solve the problem. We have to work on our own concepts first to be able to understand what we are trying to say—and only then can we write the sentence.

In communicating, whatever the medium, the first question has to be, "Is this communication within the recipient's range of perception? Can he receive it?

The "range of perception" is, in fact, physiological and largely (though not entirely) set by physical limitations of man's animal body. When we speak of communications, however, the most important limitations on perception are usually cultural and emotional rather than physical. That fanatics are not being convinced by rational arguments, we have known for thousands of years.

Now we are beginning to understand that it is not "argument" that is lacking. Fanatics do not have the ability to perceive a communication which goes beyond their range of emotions. Before this is possible, their emotions would have to be altered. In other words, no one is really "in touch with reality," if by that we mean complete openness to evidence. The distinction between sanity and paranoia is not in the ability to perceive, but in the ability to learn, that is, in the ability to change one's emotions on the basis of experience.

That perception is conditioned by what we are capable of perceiving was realized forty years ago by the most quoted but probably least heeded of all students of organization, Mary Parker Follett. Follett taught that a disagreement or conflict is likely not to be about the answers, or, indeed, about anything ostensible. It is, in most cases, the result of incongruity in perceptions. What A sees so vividly, B does not see at all. And, therefore, what A argues has no pertinence to B's concerns, and vice versa. Both, Follett argued, are likely to see reality. But each is likely to see a different aspect thereof. The world, and not only the material world, is multidimensional. Yet one can only see one dimension at a time. One rarely realizes that there could be other dimensions, and that something that is so obvious to us and so clearly validated by our emotional experience has other dimensions, a back and sides, which are entirely different and which, therefore, lead to entirely different perception. The old story about the blind men and the elephant in which every one of them, upon encountering this strange beast, feels one of the elephant's parts, his leg, his trunk, his hide, and reports an entirely different conclusion, each held tenaciously, is simply a story of the human condition. And there is no possibility of communication until this is understood and until he who has felt the hide of the elephant goes over to him who felt the leg and feels the leg himself. There is no possibility of communications, in other words, unless we first know what the recipient, the true communicator, can see and why.

2. We perceive, as a rule, what we expect to perceive. We see largely what we expect to see, and we hear largely what we expect to hear. That the unexpected may be resented is not the important thing—though most of the writers on communications in business or government think it is. What is truly important is that the unexpected is usually not received at all. It is either not seen or heard but ignored. Or is it misunderstood, that is, mis-seen as the expected or misheard as the expected.

On this we now have a century or more of experimentation. The results are quite unambiguous. The human mind attempts to fit impressions and stimuli into a frame of expectations. It resists vigorously any attempts to make it "change its mind," that is, to perceive what it does not expect to perceive or not to perceive what it expects to perceive. It is, of course, possible to alert the human mind to the fact that what it perceives is contrary to its expectations. But this first requires that we understand what it expects to perceive. It then requires that there be an unmistakable signal— "this is different," that is, a shock which breaks continuity. A "gradual" change in which the mind is supposedly led by small, incremental steps to realize that what is perceived is not what it expects to perceive, rarely works.

Before we can communicate, we must, therefore, know what the recipient expects to see and to hear. Only then can we know whether communication can utilize his expectations—and what they are—or whether there is need for the "shock of alienation," for an "awakening" that breaks through the recipient's expectations and forces him to realize that the unexpected is happening.

3. Many years ago psychologists stumbled on a strange phenomenon in their studies of memory, a phenomenon that, at first, upset all their hypotheses. In order to test memory, the psychologists compiled a list of words to be shown to their experimental subjects for varying times as a test of their retention capacity. As control, a list of nonsense words, mere jumbles of letters, were devised to find out to what extent understanding influenced memory. Much to the surprise of these early experimenters almost a century ago or so, their sub-

jects (mostly students, of course) showed totally uneven memory retention of individual words. More surprising, they showed amazingly high retention of the nonsense words. The explanation of the first phenomenon is fairly obvious. Words are not mere information. They do carry emotional charges. And, therefore, words with unpleasant associations were not retained. In fact, this selective retention by emotional association has since been used to construct tests for emotional disorders and for personality profiles.

The relatively high retention rate of nonsense words was a greater problem. It was expected, after all, that no one would really remember words that had no meaning at all. But it has become clear over the years that the memory for these words, though limited, exists precisely because these words have no meaning. For this reason, they also make no demand. They are truly neuter. In respect to them, memory could be said to be truly mechanical, showing neither emotional preference nor emotional rejection.

A similar phenomenon, known to every newspaper editor, is the amazingly high readership and retention of the fillers, the little three- or five-line bits of irrelevant incidental information that are being used to balance a page. Why should anybody want to read, let alone remember, that it first became fashionable to wear different-colored hose on each leg at the court of some long-forgotten duke? Why should anybody want to read, let alone remember, when and where baking powder was first used? Yet there is no doubt that these little tidbits of irrelevancy are read and, above all, that they are remembered far better than almost anything in the daily paper except the great screaming headlines of the catastrophes. The answer is that these fillers make no demands. It is precisely their total irrelevancy that accounts for their being remembered.

Communication is always propaganda. The emitter always wants "to get something across." Propaganda, we now know, is both a great deal more powerful than the rationalists with their belief in "open discussion" believe, and a great deal less powerful than the myth-makers of propaganda, for example, a Dr. Goebbels in the Nazi régime, believed and wanted us to believe. Indeed, the danger of total propaganda is not that the propaganda will be believed. The danger is that nothing will be believed and that every communication becomes suspect. In the end, no communication is being received any more. Everything anyone says is considered a demand and is resisted, resented, and in effect not heard at all. The end results of total propaganda are not fanatics, but cynics—but this, of course, may be even greater and more dangerous corruption.

Communication always demands that the recipient become somebody, do something, believe something. It always appeals to motivation If, in other words, communication fits in with the aspirations, the values, the purposes of the recipient, it is powerful. If it goes against his aspirations, his values, his motivations, it is likely not to be received at all, or, at best, to be resisted. Of course, at its most powerful, communication brings about conversion, that is, a change of personality, of values, beliefs, aspirations. But this is the rare, existential event, and one against which the basic psychological forces of every human being are strongly organized. Even the Lord, the Bible reports, first had to strike Saul blind before he could raise him as Paul. Communications aiming at conversion demand surrender. By and large, therefore, there is no communication unless the message can key in to the recipient's own values, at least to some degree.

Where communication is perception, information is logic. As such, information is purely formal and has no meaning. It is impersonal rather than interpersonal. The more it can be freed of the human component, that is, of such things as emotions and values, expectations and perceptions, the more valid and reliable does it become. Indeed, it becomes increasingly informative.

All through history, the problem has been how to glean a little information out of communications, that is, out of relationships between people, based on perception. All through history, the problem has been to isolate the information content from an abundance of perception. Now, all of a sudden, we have the capacity to provide information—both because of the conceptual work of the logicians, especially the symbolic logic of Russell and Whitehead, and because of the technical work on data processing and data storage, that is, of course, especially because of the computer and its tremendous capacity to store, manipulate, and transmit data. Now, in other words, we have the opposite problem from the one mankind has always been struggling with. Now we have the problem of handling information per se, devoid of any communication content.

The requirements for effective information are the opposite of those for effective communication. Information is, for instance, always specific. We perceive a configuration in communications; but we convey specific individual data in the information process. Indeed, information is, above all, a principle of economy. The fewer data needed, the better the information. And an overload of information, that is, anything much beyond what is truly needed, leads to a complete information blackout. It does not enrich, but impoverishes.

At the same time, information presupposes communication. Information is always encoded. To be received, let alone be used, the code must be known and understood by the recipient. This requires prior agreement, that is, some communication. At the very least, the recipient has to know what the data pertain to. Are the figures on a piece of computer tape the height of mountain tops or the cash balances of Federal Reserve member banks? In either case, the recipient would have to know what mountains are or what banks are to get any information out of the data.

The prototype information system may well have been the peculiar language known as *Armee Deutsch* (Army German), which served as language of command in the Imperial Austrian Army prior to 1918. A polyglot army in which officers, noncommissioned officers, and men often had no language in common, it functioned remarkably well with fewer than two hundred specific words, "fire," for instance, or "at ease," each of which had only one totally unambiguous meaning. The meaning was always an action. And the words were learned in and through actions, that is, in what behaviorists now call operant conditioning. The tensions in the Austrian Army after many decades of nationalist turmoil were very great indeed. Social intercourse between members of different nationalities serving in the same unit became increasingly difficult, if not impossible. But to the very end, the information system functioned. It was completely formal, completely rigid, completely logical in that each word had only one possible meaning; and it rested on preestablished communication regarding the specific response to a certain set of sound waves. This example, however, shows also that the effectiveness of an information system depends on the willingness and ability to think through carefully what information is needed by whom and for what purposes, and then on the systematic creation of communication between the various parties to the system as to the meaning of each specific input and output. The effectiveness, in other words, depends on the preestablishment of communication.

Communication communicates better the more levels of meaning it has and the less possible it is, therefore, to quantify it.

Medieval aesthetics held that a work of art communicates on a number of levels, at least three if not four: the literal, the metaphorical, the allegorical, and the symbolic. The work of art that most consciously converted this theory into artistic practice was Dante's *Divina Commedia*. If, by information we mean something that can be quantified, then the *Divina Commedia* is without any information content whatever. But it is precisely the ambiguity, the multiplicity of levels on which this book can be read, from being a fairy tale to being a grand synthesis of metaphysics, that makes it the overpowering work of art it is, and the immediate communication which it has been to generations of readers.

Communications, in other words, may not be dependent on information. Indeed, the most perfect communications may be purely shared experiences, without any logic whatever. Perception has primacy rather than information.

What, then, can our knowledge and our experience teach us about communications in organizations, about the reasons for our failures, and about the prerequisites for success in the future?

For centuries we have attempted communication downwards. This, however, cannot work, no matter how hard and how intelligently we try. It cannot work, first, because it focuses on what we want to say. It assumes, in other words, that the utterer communicates. But we know that all he does is utter. Communication is the act of the recipient. What we have been trying to do is to work on the emitter, specifically on the manager, the administrator, the commander, to make him capable of being a better communicator. But all one can communicate downwards are commands, that is, prearranged signals.

On cannot communicate downwards anything connected with understanding, let alone with motivation. This requires communication upwards; from those who perceive to those who want to reach their perception.

But "listening" does not work either. The Human Relations school of Elton Mayo, forty years ago, recognized the failure of the traditional approach to communications. Its answer—especially as developed in Mayo's two famous books, *The Human Problems of an Industrial Civilization* and *The Social Problems of an Industrial Civilization*—was to enjoin listening. Instead of starting out with what I, that is, the executive, want to get across, the executive should start out by finding out what subordinates want to know, are interested in, are, in other words, receptive to. To this day, the human relations prescription, though rarely practiced, remains the classic formula.

Of course, listening is a prerequisite to communication. But it is not adequate, and it cannot, by itself, work. Perhaps the reason why it is not being used widely, despite the popularity of the slogan, is precisely that, where tried, it has failed to work. Listening first assumes that the superior will understand what he is being told. It assumes, in other words, that the subordinates can communicate. It is hard to see, however, why the subordinate should be able to do what his superior cannot do. In fact, there is no reason for assuming he can. There is no reason, in other words, to believe that listening results any less in misunderstanding and miscommunications than does talking. In addition, the theory of listening does not take into account that communication is involvement. It does not bring out the subordinate's preferences and desires, his values and aspirations. It may explain the reasons for misunderstanding.

But it does not lay down a basis for understanding. This is not to say that listening is wrong, any more than the futility of downward communications furnishes any argument against attempts to write well, to say things clearly and simply, and to speak the language of those whom one addresses rather than one's own jargon. Indeed, the realization that communications have to be upward—or rather that they have to start with the recipient, rather than the emitter, which underlies the concept of listening—is absolutely sound and vital. But listening is only the starting point.

More and better information does not solve the communications problem, does not bridge the communications gap. On the contrary, the more information the greater is the need for functioning and effective communication. The more information, in other words, the greater is the communications gap likely to be.

The more personal and formal the information process in the first place, the more will it depend on prior agreement on meaning and application, that is, on communications. In the second place, the more effective the information process, the more impersonal and formal it will become, the more will it separate human beings and thereby require separate, but also much greater, efforts, to reestablish the human relationship, the relationship of communication. It may be said that the effectiveness of the information process will depend increasingly on our ability to communicate, and that, in the absence of effective communication—that is, in the present situation—the information revolution cannot really produce information. All it can produce is data.

It can also be said—and this may well be more important—that the test of an information system will increasingly be the degree to which it frees human beings from concern with information and allows them to work on communications. The test, in particular, of the computer will be how much time it gives executives and professionals on all levels for direct, personal, face-to-face relationships with other people.

It is fashionable today to measure the utilization of a computer by the number of hours it runs during one day. But this is not even a measurement of the computer's efficiency. It is purely a measurement of input. The only measurement of output is the degree to which availability of information enables human beings not to control, that is, not to spend time trying to get a little information on what happened yesterday. And the only measurement of this, in turn, is the amount of time that becomes available for the job only human beings can do, the job of communication. By this test, of course, almost no computer today is being used properly. Most of them are being misused, that is, are being used to justify spending even more time on control rather than to relieve human beings from controlling by giving them information. The reason for this is quite clearly the lack of prior communication, that is, of agreement and decision on what information is needed, by whom and for what purposes, and what it means operationally. The reason for the misuse of the computer is, so to speak, the lack of anything comparable to the *Armee Deutsch* of yesterday's much-ridiculed Imperial Austrian Army with its two hundred words of command which even the dumbest recruit could learn in two weeks' time.

The Information Explosion, in other words, is the most impelling reason to do to work on communication. Indeed, the frightening communications gap all around us—between management and workers; between business and government; between faculty and students, and between both of them and university administration; between producers and consumers; and so on—may well reflect in some measure the tremendous increase in information without a commensurate increase in communication.

Can we then say anything constructive about communication? Can we do anything? We can say that we have to go from Information to Communication. We can say that communication has to start from the intended recipient of communication rather than from the emitter. In terms of traditional organization we have to start upward. Downward communication cannot work and does not work. It comes *after* upward communication has successfully been established. It is reaction rather than action, response rather than initiative.

Finally, there will be no communication if it is conceived as going from the "I" to the "thou." Communication only works from one member of "us" to another. Communication—and this may be the true lesson of our communication failure and the true measure of our communication need—is not a *means* of organization. It is a *mode* of organization.

Part 7

The Next Society

Introduction to Part 7

"The Next Society," written in the summer of 2001, was scheduled to be published in the *Economist* in the week of the terrorist attack on New York and Washington on September 11th. It had to be postponed for two months until November 3, 2001. The September 11 attack fundamentally changed world politics. But it did not change the equally drastic changes in society, especially in the society of the developed countries, with which this part deals. It is therefore published here in its entirety.

19

The Next Society

(originally published in *The Economist*, 2001)

The new economy may or may not materialize, but there is no doubt that the next society will be with us shortly. In the developed world, and probably in the emerging countries as well, this new society will be a good deal more important than the new economy (if any). It will be quite different from the society of the late twentieth century, and also different from what most people expect. Much of it will be unprecedented. And most of it is already here, or is rapidly emerging.

In the developed countries, the dominant factor in the next society will be something to which most people are only just beginning to pay attention: the rapid growth in the older population and the rapid shrinking of the younger generation. Politicians everywhere still promise to save the existing pensions system, but they—and their constituents—know perfectly well that in another twenty-five years people will have to keep working until their mid-seventies, health permitting.

What has not yet sunk in is that a growing number of older people—say those over fifty—will not keep on working as traditional full-time nine-to-five employees, but will participate in the labor force in many and different ways: as temporaries, as part-timers, as consultants, on special assignments and so on. What used to be personnel departments and are now known as human-resources departments still assume that those who work for an organization are full-time employees. Employment laws and regulations are based on the same assumption. Within twenty or twenty-five years, however, perhaps as many as half the people who work for an organization will not be employed by it, certainly not on a full-time basis. This will be especially true for older people. New ways of working

197

with people at arm's length will increasingly become the central managerial issue of employing organizations, and not just of businesses.

The shrinking of the younger population will cause an even greater upheaval, if only because nothing like this has happened since the dying centuries of the Roman Empire. In every single developed country, but also in China and Brazil, the birth rate is now well below the replacement rate of 2.2 live births per woman of reproductive age. Politically, this means that immigration will become an important—and highly divisive—issue in all rich countries. It will cut across all traditional political alignments. Economically, the decline in the young population will change markets in fundamental ways. Growth in family formation has been the driving force of all domestic markets in the developed world, but the rate of family formation is certain to fall steadily unless bolstered by large-scale immigration of younger people. The homogeneous mass market that emerged in all rich countries after the Second World War has been youth-determined from the start. It will now become middle-age-determined, or perhaps more likely it will split into two: a middle-age-determined mass market and a much smaller youth-determined one. And because the supply of young people will shrink, creating new employment patterns to attract and hold the growing number of older people (especially older educated people) will become increasingly important.

The next society will be a knowledge society. Knowledge will be its key resource, and knowledge workers will be the dominant group in its workforce.

Its three main characteristics will be:

- Borderlessness, because knowledge travels even more effortlessly than money

- Upward mobility, available to everyone through easily acquired formal education

- The potential for failure as well as success. Anyone can acquire the "means of production," that is, the knowledge required for the job, but not everyone can win.

Together, those three characteristics will make the knowledge society a highly competitive one, for organizations and individuals alike. Information technology, although only one of many new features of the next society, is already having one hugely important effect: it is allowing knowledge to spread near-instantly, and making it accessible to everyone. Given the ease and speed at which information travels, every institution in the knowledge society—not only businesses, but also schools, universities, hospitals and increasingly government agencies too—has to be globally competitive, even though most organizations will continue to be local in their activities and in their markets. This is because the Internet will keep customers everywhere informed on what is available anywhere in the world, and at what price.

This new knowledge economy will rely heavily on knowledge workers.

At present, this term is widely used to describe people with considerable theoretical knowledge and learning: doctors, lawyers, teachers, accountants, chemical engineers. But the most striking growth will be in "knowledge technologists": computer technicians, software designers, analysts in clinical labs, manufacturing technologists, paralegals. These people are as much manual workers as they are knowledge workers; in fact, they usually spend far more time working with their hands than with their brains. But their manual work is based on a substantial amount of theoretical knowledge which can be acquired only through formal education, not through an apprenticeship. They are not, as a rule, much better paid than traditional skilled workers, but they see themselves as "professionals." Just as unskilled manual workers in manufacturing were the dominant social and political force in the twentieth century, knowledge technologists are likely to become the dominant social—and perhaps also political—force over the next decades.

Structurally, too, the next society is already diverging from the society almost all of us still live in. The twentieth century saw the rapid decline of the sector that had dominated society for 10,000 years: agriculture. In volume terms, farm production now is at least four or five times what it was before the First World War. But in 1913 farm products accounted for 70 percent of world trade, whereas now their share is at most 17 percent. In the early years of the twentieth century, agriculture in most developed countries was the largest single contributor to GDP; now in rich countries its contribution has dwindled to the point of becoming marginal.

And the farm population is down to a tiny proportion of the total.

Manufacturing has traveled a long way down the same road. Since the Second World War, manufacturing output in the developed world has probably tripled in volume. But inflation-adjusted manufacturing prices have fallen steadily, whereas the cost of prime knowledge products—health care and education—has tripled, again adjusted for inflation. The relative purchasing power of manufactured goods against knowledge products is now only one-fifth or one-sixth of what it was fifty years ago. Manufacturing employment in America has fallen from 35 percent of the workforce in the 1950s to less than half that now, without causing much social disruption. But it may be too much to hope for an equally easy transition in countries such as Japan or Germany, where blue-collar manufacturing workers still make up 25-30 percent of the labor force.

The decline of farming as a producer of wealth and of livelihoods has allowed farm protectionism to spread to a degree that would have been unthinkable before the Second World War. In the same way, the decline of manufacturing will trigger an explosion of manufacturing protectionism—even as lip service continues to be paid to free trade. This protectionism may not necessarily take the form of traditional tariffs, but of subsidies, quotas and regulations of all kinds. Even more likely, regional blocks will emerge that trade freely internally but are highly protectionist externally. The European Union, NAFTA and Mercosur already point in that direction.

Statistically, multinational companies play much the same role in the world economy as they did in 1913. But they have become very different animals. Multinationals in 1913 were domestic firms with subsidiaries abroad, each of them self-contained, in charge of a politically defined territory, and highly autonomous. Multinationals now tend to be organized globally along product or service lines, but like the multinationals of 1913, they are held together and controlled by ownership. By contrast, the multinationals of 2025 are likely to be held together and controlled by strategy. There will still be ownership, of course, but alliances, joint ventures, minority stakes, know-how agreements and contracts will increasingly be the building blocks of a confederation. This kind of organization will need a new kind of top management.

In most countries, and even in a good many large and complex companies, top management is still seen as an extension of operating management. Tomorrow's top management, however, is likely to be a distinct and separate organ: it will stand for the company. One of the most important jobs ahead for the top management of the big company of tomorrow, and especially of the multinational, will be to balance the conflicting demands on business being made by the need for both short-term and long-term results, and by the corporation's various constituencies: customers, shareholders (especially institutional investors and pension funds), knowledge employees, and communities.

Against that background, this survey will seek to answer two questions: what can and should managements do now to be ready for the next society? And what other big changes may lie ahead of which we are as yet unaware?

By 2030, people over sixty-five in Germany, the world's third-largest economy, will account for almost half the adult population, compared with one-fifth now. And unless the country's birth rate recovers from its present low of 1.3 per woman, over the same period its population, now 82 million, will decline to 70-73 million. The number of people of working age will fall by a full quarter, from 40 million to 30 million.

The German demographics are far from exceptional. In Japan, the world's second-largest economy, the population will peak in 2005, at around 125 million. By 2050, according to the more pessimistic government forecasts, the population will have shrunk to around 95 million. Long before that, around 2030, the share of the over-sixty-fives in the adult population will have grown to about half. And the birth rate in Japan, as in Germany, is down to 1.3 per woman.

The figures are pretty much the same for most other developed countries—Italy, France, Spain, Portugal, the Netherlands, Sweden—and for a good many emerging ones, especially China. In some regions, such as central Italy, southern France, or southern Spain, birth rates are even lower than in Germany or Japan.

Life expectancy—and with it the number of older people—has been going up steadily for 300 years. But the decline in the number of young people is something new. The only developed country that has so far avoided this fate is America. But even there the birth rate is well below replacement level, and the proportion of older people in the adult population will rise steeply in the next thirty years.

All this means that winning the support of older people will become a political imperative in every developed country. Pensions have already become a regular election issue. There is also a growing debate about the desirability of immigration to maintain the population and workforce. Together these two issues are transforming the political landscape in every developed country.

By 2030 at the latest, the age at which full retirement benefits start will have risen to the mid-seventies in all developed countries, and benefits for healthy pensioners will be substantially lower than they are today. Indeed, fixed retirement ages for people in reasonable physical and mental condition may have been abolished to prevent the pensions burden on the working population from becoming unbearable. Already young and middle-aged people at work suspect that there will not be enough pension money to go round when they themselves reach traditional retirement age. But politicians everywhere continue to pretend that they can save the current pensions system.

Immigration is certain to be an even hotter issue. The respected DIW research institute in Berlin estimates that by 2020 Germany will have to import one million immigrants of working age each year simply to maintain its workforce. Other rich European countries are in the same boat. And in Japan there is talk of admitting 500,000 Koreans each year—and sending them home five years later. For all big countries but America, immigration on such a scale is unprecedented.

The political implications are already being felt. In 1999 fellow Europeans were shocked by the electoral success in Austria of a xenophobic right-wing party whose main plank is no immigration. Similar movements are growing in Flemish-speaking Belgium, in traditionally liberal Denmark and in northern Italy. Even in America, immigration is upsetting long-established political alignments. American trade unions' opposition to large-scale immigration has put them in the anti-globalization camp that organized violent protests during the Seattle meeting of the World Trade Organization in 1999. A future Democratic candidate for the American presidency may have to choose between getting the union vote by opposing immigration, or getting the vote of Latinos and other newcomers by supporting it. Equally, a future Republican candidate may have to choose between the support of business, which is clamoring for workers, and the vote of a white middle class that increasingly opposes immigration.

Even so, America 's experience of immigration should give it a lead in the developed world for several decades to come. Since the

1970s it has been admitting large numbers of immigrants, either legally or illegally. Most immigrants are young, and the birth rates of first-generation immigrant women tend to be higher than those of their adopted country. This means that for the next thirty or forty years America 's population will continue to grow, albeit slowly, whereas in some other developed countries it will fall.

But it is not numbers alone that will give America an advantage.

Even more important, the country is culturally attuned to immigration, and long ago learned to integrate immigrants into its society and economy. In fact, recent immigrants, whether Hispanics or Asians, may be integrating faster than ever. One-third of all recent Hispanic immigrants, for instance, are reported to be marrying non-Hispanics and non-immigrants. The one big obstacle to the full integration of recent immigrants in America is the poor performance of American public schools.

Among developed countries, only Australia and Canada have a tradition of immigration similar to America's. Japan has resolutely kept foreigners out, except for a spate of Korean immigrants in the 1920s and 1930s, whose descendants are still being discriminated against. The mass migrations of the nineteenth century were either into empty, unsettled spaces (such as the United States, Canada, Australia, Brazil), or from farm to city within the same country.

By contrast, immigration in the twenty-first century is by foreigners in nationality, language, culture and religion who move into settled countries. European countries have so far been less than successful at integrating such foreigners.

The biggest effect of the demographic changes may be to split hitherto homogenous societies and markets. Until the 1920s or 30s, every country had a diversity of cultures and markets. They were sharply differentiated by class, occupation and residence, for example, "the farm market" or "the carriage trade," both of which disappeared some time between 1920 and 1940. Yet since the Second World War, all developed countries have had only one mass culture and one mass market. Now that demographic forces in all the developed countries are pulling in opposite directions, will that homogeneity survive?

The markets of the developed world have been dominated by the values, habits and preferences of the young population. Some of the most successful and most profitable businesses of the past half-century, such as Coca-Cola and Procter & Gamble in America, Unilever in Britain and Henckel in Germany, owe their prosperity in large measure to the growth of the young population and to the high rate of family formation between 1950 and 2000. The same is true of the car industry over that period.

Now there are signs that the market is splitting. In financial services, perhaps America 's fastest-growing industry over the past twenty-five years, it has split already. The bubble market of the 1990s,with its frantic day-trading in high-tech stocks, belonged mainly to the under-forty-fives. But the customers in the markets for investments, such as mutual funds or deferred annuities, tend to be over fifty, and that market has also been growing apace. The fastest-growing industry in any developed country may turn out to be the continuing education of already well-educated adults, which is based on values that are all but incompatible with those of the youth culture.

But it is also conceivable that some youth markets will become exceedingly lucrative. In the coastal cities of China, where the government was able to enforce its one-child policy, middle-class families are now reported to spend more on their one child than earlier middle-class families spent on their four or five children together. This seems to be true in Japan too. Many American middle-class families are spending heavily on the education of their single child, mainly by moving into expensive suburban neighborhoods with good schools. But this new luxury youth market is quite different from the homogeneous market of the past fifty years. That mass market is rapidly weakening because of the decline in the numbers of young people reaching adulthood.

In future there will almost certainly be two distinct workforces, broadly made up of the under-fifties and the over-fifties respectively. These two workforces are likely to differ markedly in their needs and behavior, and in the jobs they do. The younger group will need a steady income from a permanent job, or at least a succession of full-time jobs. The rapidly growing older group will have much more choice, and will be able to combine traditional jobs, non-conventional jobs and leisure in whatever proportion suits them best.

The split into two workforces is likely to start with women knowledge technologists. A nurse, a computer technologist or a paralegal can take fifteen years out to look after her children and then return to full-time work. Women, who now outnumber men in American higher education, increasingly look for work in the new knowledge technologies. Such jobs are the first in human history to be well adapted to the special needs of women as childbearers, and to their increasing longevity. That longevity is one of the reasons for the split in the job market.

A fifty-year working life unprecedented in human history is simply too long for one kind of work.

The second reason for the split is a shrinking life expectancy for businesses and organizations of all kinds. In the past, employing organizations have outlived employees. In future, employees, and especially knowledge workers, will increasingly outlive even successful organizations. Few businesses, or even government agencies or programs, last for more than thirty years. Historically, the working lifespan of most employees has been less than thirty years because most manual workers simply wore out. But knowledge workers who enter the labor force in their twenties are likely to be still in good physical and mental shape fifties years later.

"Second career" and "second half of one's life" have already become buzz-words in America. Increasingly, employees there take early retirement as soon as their pension and Social Security rights are guaranteed for the time when they reach traditional retirement age; but they do not stop working. Instead, their "second career" often takes an unconventional form. They may work freelance (and often forget to tell the taxman about their work, thus boosting their net income), or part-time, or as "temporaries," or for an outsourcing contractor, or as contractors themselves. Such "early retirement to keep on working" is particularly common among knowledge workers, who are still a minority among people now reaching fifty or fifty-five, but will become the largest single group of older people in America from about 2030.

Population predictions for the next twenty years can be made with some certainty because almost everybody who will be in the workforce in 2020 is already alive. But, as American experience in the past couple of decades has shown, demographic trends can change quite suddenly and unpredictably, with fairly immediate effects. The American baby boom of the late 1940s, for instance, triggered the housing boom of the 1950s.

In the mid-1920s America had its first "baby bust." Between 1925 and 1935 the birth rate declined by almost half, dipping below the replacement rate of 2.2 live births per woman. In the late 1930s,

President Roosevelt's Commission on American Population (consisting of the country's most eminent demographers and statisticians) confidently predicted that America's population would peak in 1945 and would then start declining. But an exploding birth rate in the late 1940s proved it wrong. Within ten years, the number of live births per woman doubled from 1.8 to 3.6. Between 1947 and 1957, America experienced an astonishing baby boom. The number of babies born rose from 2.5 million to 4.1 million.

Then, in 1960-61, the opposite happened. Instead of the expected second-wave baby boom as the first boomers reached adulthood, there was a big bust. Between 1961 and 1975, the birth rate fell from 3.7 to 1.8. The number of babies born went down from 4.3 million in 1960 to 3.1 million in 1975.

The next surprise was the "baby boom echo" in the late 1980s and early 1990s. The number of live births went up quite sharply, surpassing even the numbers of the first baby boom's peak years. With the benefit of hindsight, it is now clear that this echo was triggered by large-scale immigration into America, beginning in the early 1970s. When the girls born to these early immigrants started having children of their own in the late 1980s, their birth rates were still closer to those of their parents' country of origin than to those of their adopted country. Fully one-fifth of all children of school age in California in the first decade of this century have at least one foreign-born parent.

But nobody knows what caused the two baby busts, or the baby boom of the 1940s. Both busts occurred when the economy was doing well, which in theory should have encouraged people to have lots of children. And the baby boom should never have happened, because historically birth rates have always gone down after a big war. The truth is that we simply do not understand what determines birth rates in modern societies. So demographics will not only be the most important factor in the next society, it will also be the least predictable and least controllable one.

A century ago, the overwhelming majority of people in developed countries worked with their hands: on farms, in domestic service, in small craft shops and (at that time still a small minority) in factories. Fifty years later, the proportion of manual workers in the American labor force had dropped to around half, and factory workers had become the largest single section of the workforce, making up 35 percent of the total. Now, another fifty years later, fewer than a quarter of American workers make their living from manual jobs. Factory workers still account for the majority of the manual workers, but their share of the total workforce is down to around 15 percent, more or less back to what it had been 100 years earlier.

Of all the big developed countries, America now has the smallest proportion of factory workers in its labor force. Britain is not far behind. In Japan and Germany their share is still around a quarter, but it is shrinking steadily.

To some extent this is a matter of definition. Data-processing employees of a manufacturing firm, such as the Ford Motor Company, are counted as employed in manufacturing, but when Ford outsources its data processing, the same people doing exactly the same work are instantly redefined as service workers. However, too much should not be made of this. Many studies in manufacturing businesses have shown that the decline in the number of people who actually work in the plant is roughly the same as the shrinkage reported in the national figures.

Before the First World War there was not even an English word for people who made their living other than by manual work. The term service worker was coined around 1920s, but it has turned out to be rather misleading. These days, fewer than half of all non-manual workers are actually service workers. The only fast-growing group in the workforce, in America and in every other developed country, are knowledge workers, people whose jobs require formal and advanced schooling. They now account for a full third of the American workforce, outnumbering factory workers by two to one. In another twenty years or so, they are likely to make up close to two-fifths of the workforce of all rich countries.

The terms "knowledge industries," "knowledge work," and "knowledge worker" are only forty years old. They were coined around 1960, simultaneously but independently; the first by a Princeton economist, Fritz Machlup, the second and third by this writer. Now everyone uses them, but as yet hardly anyone understands their implications for human values and human behavior, for managing people and making them productive, for economics and for politics. What is already clear, however, is that the emerging knowledge society and knowledge economy will be radically different from the society and economy of the late twentieth century, in the following ways.

Knowledge workers, collectively, are the new capitalists. Knowledge has become the key resource, and the only scarce one. This means that knowledge workers collectively own the means of production. But as a group, they are also capitalists in the old sense: through their stakes in pension funds and mutual funds, they have become majority shareholders and owners of many large businesses in the knowledge society.

Effective knowledge is specialized. That means knowledge workers need access to an organization—a collective that brings together an array of knowledge workers and applies their specialisms to a common end-product.

The most gifted mathematics teacher in a secondary school is effective only as a member of the faculty. The most brilliant consultant on product development is effective only if there is an organized and competent business to convert her advice into action. The greatest software designer needs a hardware producer. But in turn the high school needs the mathematics teacher, the business needs the expert on product development, and the PC manufacturer needs the software programmer. Knowledge workers therefore see themselves as equal to those who retain their services, as professionals rather than as employees.

The knowledge society is a society of seniors and juniors rather than of bosses and subordinates.

All this has important implications for the role of women in the labor force. Historically women 's participation in the world of work has always equaled men's. The lady of leisure sitting in her parlor was the rarest of exceptions even in a wealthy nineteenth-century society. A farm, a craftsman's business or a small shop had to be run by a couple to be viable. As late as the beginning of the twentieth century, a doctor could not start a practice until he had got married; he needed a wife to make appointments, open the door, take patients' histories and send out the bills.

But although women have always worked, since time immemorial the jobs they have done have been different from men's. There was men 's work and there was women's work. Countless women in the Bible go to the well to fetch water, but not one man. There never was a male spinster. Knowledge work, on the other hand, is unisex, not because of feminist pressure but because it can be done equally well by both sexes. That said, the first modern knowledge jobs were still designed for only one or the other sex. Teaching as a profession was invented in 1794, the year the Ecole Normale was founded in Paris, and was seen strictly as a man 's job. Sixty years later, during the Crimean war of 1854-56, Florence Nightingale founded the second new knowledge profession, nursing. This was considered as exclusively women 's work. But by 1850 teaching everywhere had become unisex, and in 2000 two-fifths of America 's students at nursing schools were men.

There were no women doctors in Europe until the 1890s. But one of the earliest European women to get a medical doctorate, the great Italian educator Maria Montessori, reportedly said: I am not a woman doctor; I am a doctor who happens to be a woman. The same logic applies to all knowledge work. Knowledge workers, whatever their sex, are professionals, applying the same knowledge, doing the same work, governed by the same standards and judged by the same results.

High-knowledge workers such as doctors, lawyers, scientists, clerics and teachers have been around for a long time, although their number has increased exponentially in the past 100 years. The largest group of knowledge workers, however, barely existed until the start of the twentieth century, and took off only after the Second World War. They are knowledge technologists people who do much of their work with their hands (and to that extent are the successors to skilled workers), but whose pay is determined by the knowledge between their ears, acquired in formal education rather than through apprenticeship. They include X-ray technicians, physiotherapists, ultrasound specialists, psychiatric caseworkers, dental technicians and scores of others. In the past thirty years, medical technologists have been the fastest-growing segment of the labor force in America, and in Britain as well.

In the next twenty or thirty years the number of knowledge technologists in computers, manufacturing and education is likely to grow even faster. Office technologists such as paralegals are also proliferating. And it is no accident that yesterday's secretary is rapidly turning into an assistant, having become the manager of the boss's office and of his work. Within two or three decades, knowledge technologists will become the dominant group in the workforce in all developed countries, occupying the same position that unionized factory workers held at the peak of their power in the 1950s and 60s.

The most important thing about these knowledge workers is that they do not identify themselves as workers but as professionals. Many of them spend a good deal of their time doing largely unskilled work, for example, straightening out patients' beds, answering the telephone or filing. However, what identifies them in their own and in the public's mind is the part of their job that involves putting their formal knowledge to work. That makes them full-fledged knowledge workers.

Such workers have two main needs: formal education that enables them to enter knowledge work in the first place, and continuing education throughout their working lives to keep their knowledge up to date. For the old high-knowledge professionals such as doctors, clerics and lawyers, formal education has been available for many centuries. But for knowledge technologists, only a few countries so far provide systematic and organized preparation. Over the next few decades, educational institutions to prepare knowledge technologists will grow rapidly in all developed and emerging countries, just as new institutions to meet new requirements have always appeared in the past. What is different this time is the need for the continuing education of already well-trained and highly knowledgeable adults. Schooling traditionally stopped when work began. In the knowledge society it never stops.

Knowledge is unlike traditional skills, which change very slowly. A museum near Barcelona in Spain contains a vast number of the hand tools used by the skilled craftsmen of the late Roman Empire which any craftsman today would instantly recognize, because they are very similar to the tools still in use. For the purposes of skill training, therefore, it was reasonable to assume that whatever had been learned by age seventeen or eighteen would last for a lifetime.

Conversely, knowledge rapidly becomes obsolete, and knowledge workers regularly have to go back to school. Continuing education of already highly educated adults will therefore become a big growth area in the next society. But most of it will be delivered in non-traditional ways, ranging from weekend seminars to online training programs, and in any number of places, from a traditional university to the student 's home. The information revolution, which is expected to have an enormous impact on traditional schools and universities, will probably have an even greater effect on the continuing education of knowledge workers.

Knowledge workers of all kinds tend to identify themselves with their knowledge. They introduce themselves by saying, "I am an anthropologist" or "I am a physiotherapist." They may be proud of the organization they work for, be it a company, a university or a government agency, but they "work at the organization;" they do not "belong to it." They feel that they have more in common with someone who practices the same specialism in another institution than with their colleagues at their own institution who work in a different knowledge area.

Although the emergence of knowledge as an important resource increasingly means specialization, knowledge workers are highly mobile within their specialism. They think nothing of moving from one university, one company or one country to another, as long as they stay within the same field of knowledge. There is a lot of talk about trying to restore knowledge workers' loyalty to their employing organization, but such efforts will get nowhere. Knowledge workers may have an attachment to an organization and feel comfortable with it, but their primary allegiance is likely to be to their specialized branch of knowledge.

Knowledge is non-hierarchical. Either it is relevant in a given situation, or it is not. An open-heart surgeon may be much better paid than, say, a speech therapist, and enjoy a much higher social status, yet if a particular situation requires the rehabilitation of a stroke victim, then in that instance the speech therapist's knowledge is greatly superior to that of the surgeon. This is why knowledge workers of all kinds see themselves not as subordinates but as professionals, and expect to be treated as such.

Money is as important to knowledge workers as to anybody else, but they do not accept it as the ultimate yardstick, nor do they consider money as a substitute for professional performance and achievement. In sharp contrast to yesterday's workers, to whom a job was first of all a living, most knowledge workers see their job as a life.

The knowledge society is the first human society where upward mobility is potentially unlimited. Knowledge differs from all other means of production in that it cannot be inherited or bequeathed. It has to be acquired anew by every individual, and everyone starts out with the same total ignorance.

Knowledge has to be put in a form in which it can be taught, which means it has to become public. It is always universally accessible, or quickly becomes so. All this makes the knowledge society a highly mobile one. Anyone can acquire any knowledge at a school, through a codified learning process, rather than by serving as an apprentice to a master.

Until 1850 or perhaps even 1900, there was little mobility in any society. The Indian caste system, in which birth determines not only an individual's status in society but his occupation as well, was only an extreme case. In most other societies too, if the father was a peasant, the son was a peasant, and the daughters married peasants. By and large, the only mobility was downward, caused by war or disease, personal misfortune or bad habits such as drinking or gambling.

Even in America, the land of unlimited opportunities, there was far less upward mobility than is commonly believed. The great majority of professionals and managers in America in the first half of the twentieth century were still the children of professionals and managers rather than the children of farmers, small shopkeepers or factory workers. What distinguished America was not the amount of upward mobility but, in sharp contrast to most European countries, the way it was welcomed, encouraged and cherished.

The knowledge society takes this approval of upward mobility much further: it considers every impediment to such mobility a form of discrimination. This implies that everybody is now expected to be a success—an idea that would have seemed ludicrous to earlier generations. Naturally, only a tiny number of people can be outstanding successes; but a very large number are expected to be adequately successful.

In 1958 John Kenneth Galbraith first wrote about *"The Affluent Society."* This was not a society with many more rich people, or in which the rich were richer, but one in which the majority could feel financially secure. In the knowledge society, a large number of people, perhaps even a majority, have something even more important than financial security: social standing, or "social affluence."

The upward mobility of the knowledge society, however, comes at a high price: the psychological pressures and emotional traumas of the rat race. There can be winners only if there are losers. This was not true of earlier societies.

The son of the landless laborer who became a landless laborer himself was not a failure. In the knowledge society, however, he is not only a personal failure but a failure of society as well.

Japanese youngsters suffer sleep deprivation because they spend their evenings at a crammer to help them pass their exams. Otherwise they will not get into the prestige university of their choice, and thus into a good job. These pressures create hostility to learning.

They also threaten to undermine Japan's prized economic equality and turn the country into a plutocracy, because only well-off parents can afford the prohibitive cost of preparing their youngsters for university. Other countries, such as America, Britain, and France, are also allowing their schools to become viciously competitive. That this has happened over such a short time—no more than thirty or forty years—indicates how much the fear of failure has already permeated the knowledge society.

Given this competitive struggle, a growing number of highly successful knowledge workers of both sexes: business managers, university teachers, museum directors, doctors, "plateau" in their forties. They know they have achieved all they will achieve. If their work is all they have, they are in trouble. Knowledge workers therefore need to develop, preferably while they are still young, a noncompetitive life and community of their own, and some serious outside interest be it working as a volunteer in the community, playing in a local orchestra or taking an active part in a small town's local government. This outside interest will give them the opportunity for personal contribution and achievement.

In the closing years of the twentieth century, the world price of the steel industry 's biggest single product, hot rolled coil, the steel for automobile bodies, plunged from $460 to $260 a ton. Yet these were boom years in America and prosperous times in most of continental Europe, with automobile production setting records. The steel industry 's experience is typical of manufacturing as a whole. Between 1960 and 1999, the share of manufacturing in America's GDP, as well as its share of total employment, roughly halved, to about 15 percent. Yet in the same forty years manufacturing 's physical output probably tripled. In 1960, manufacturing was the center of the American economy, and of the economies of all other developed countries. By 2000, as a contributor to GDP it was easily out- ranked by the financial sector.

The relative purchasing power of manufactured goods (what economists call the terms of trade) has fallen by three-quarters in the past forty years. Whereas manufacturing prices, adjusted for inflation, are down by 40 percent, the prices of the two main knowledge products, health care and education, have risen about three times as fast as inflation. In 2000, therefore, it took five times as many units of manufactured goods to buy the main knowledge products as it had done forty years earlier.

The purchasing power of workers in manufacturing has also gone down, although by much less than that of their products. Their productivity in terms of physical output has risen so sharply that most of their real income has been preserved. Forty years ago, labor costs in manufacturing typically accounted for around 30 percent of total manufacturing costs; now they are generally down to 12-15 percent. Even in cars, still the most labor-intensive of the engineering industries, labor costs in the most advanced plants are no higher than 20 percent. Manufacturing workers, especially in America, have ceased to be the backbone of the consumer market. At the height of the crisis in America 's rust belt, when employment in the big manufacturing centers was ruthlessly slashed, national sales of consumer goods barely budged.

What has changed manufacturing, and sharply pushed up productivity, are new concepts. Information and automation are less important than new theories of manufacturing, which are an advance comparable to the arrival of mass production eighty years ago. Indeed, some of these theories, such as Toyota 's lean manufacturing, do away with robots, computers and automation. One highly publicized example involved replacing one of Toyota 's automated and computerized paint-drying lines by half a dozen hairdryers bought in a supermarket.

Manufacturing is following exactly the same path that farming trod earlier. Beginning in 1920,and accelerating after the Second World War, farm production shot up in all developed countries. Before the First World War, many Western European countries had to import farm products. Now there is only one net farm importer left: Japan. Every single European country now has large and increasingly unsaleable farm surpluses. In quantitative terms, farm production in most developed countries today is probably at least four times what it was in 1920 and three times what it was in 1950 (except in Japan). But whereas at the beginning of the twentieth century farmers were the largest single group in the working population in most developed countries, now they account for no more than 3-5 percent. And whereas at the beginning of the twentieth century agriculture was the largest single contributor to national income in most developed countries, in 2000 America it contributed less than 2 percent to GDP.

Manufacturing is unlikely to expand its output in volume terms as much as agriculture did, or to shrink as much as a producer of wealth and of jobs. But the most believable forecast for 2020 suggests that manufacturing output in the developed countries will at least double, while manufacturing employment will shrink to 10-12 percent of the total workforce.

In America, the transition has largely been accomplished already, and with a minimum of dislocation. The only hard-hit group has been African Americans, to whom the growth in manufacturing jobs after the Second World War offered quick economic advancement, and whose jobs have now largely gone. But by and large, even in places that relied heavily on a few large manufacturing plants, unemployment remained high only for a short time. Even the political impact in America has been minimal.

But will other industrial countries have an equally easy passage? In Britain, manufacturing employment has already fallen quite sharply without causing any unrest, although it seems to have produced social and psychological problems. But what will happen in countries such as Germany or France, where labor markets remain rigid and where, until very recently, there has been little upward mobility through education? These countries already have substantial and seemingly intractable unemployment, for example, in Germany's Ruhr area and in France's old industrial area around Lille. They may face a painful transition period with severe social upheavals.

The biggest question mark is over Japan. To be sure, it has no working-class culture, and it has long appreciated the value of education as an instrument of upward mobility. But Japan 's social stability is based on employment security, especially for blue-collar workers in big manufacturing industry, and that is eroding fast. Yet before employment security was introduced for blue-collar workers in the 1950s, Japan had been a country of extreme labor turbulence. Manufacturing's share of total employment is still higher than in almost any other developed country—around one-third of the total—and Japan has practically no labor market and little labor mobility.

Psychologically, too, the country is least prepared for the decline in manufacturing. After all, its owed its rise to great-economic-power status in the second half of the twentieth century to becoming the world 's manufacturing virtuoso. One should never underrate the Japanese. Throughout their history they have shown unparalleled ability to face up to reality and to change practically overnight. But the decline in manufacturing as the key to economic success confronts Japan with one of the biggest challenges ever.

The decline of manufacturing as a producer of wealth and jobs changes the world 's economic, social, and political landscape. It makes "economic miracles" increasingly difficult for developing countries to achieve. The economic miracles of the second half of the twentieth century—Japan, South Korea, Taiwan, Hong Kong, Singapore—were based on exports to the world's richest countries of manufactured goods that were produced with developed-country technology and productivity but with emerging-country labor costs. This will no longer work. One way to generate economic development may be to integrate the economy of an emerging country into a developed region—which is what Vicente Fox, the new Mexican president, envisages with his proposal for total integration of "North America," that is, the United States, Canada, and Mexico. Economically this makes a lot of sense, but politically it is almost unthinkable. The alternative—which is being pursued by China—is to try to achieve economic growth by building up a developing country's domestic market. India, Brazil, and Mexico also have large enough populations to make home-market-based economic development feasible, at least in theory. But will smaller countries, such as Paraguay or Thailand, be allowed to export to the large markets of emerging countries such as Brazil?

The decline in manufacturing as a creator of wealth and jobs will inevitably bring about a new protectionism, once again echoing what happened earlier in agriculture. For every 1 percent by which agricultural prices and employment have fallen in the twentieth century, agricultural subsidies and protection in every single developed country, including America, have gone up by at least 1 percent, often more. And the fewer farm voters there are, the more important the "farm vote" has become. As numbers have shrunk, farmers have become a unified special-interest group that carries disproportionate clout in all rich countries.

Protectionism in manufacturing is already in evidence, although it tends to take the form of subsidies instead of traditional tariffs. The new regional economic blocks, such as the European Union, NAFTA, or Mercosur, do create large regional markets with lower internal barriers, but they protect them with higher barriers against producers outside the region. And non-tariff barriers of all kinds are steadily growing. In the same week in which the 40 percent decline in sheet-steel prices was announced in the American press, the American government banned sheet-steel imports as "dumping." And no matter how laudable their aims, the developed countries' insistence on fair labor laws and adequate environmental rules for manufacturers in the developing world acts as a mighty barrier to imports from these countries.

Politically, too, manufacturing is becoming more influential the fewer manufacturing workers there are, especially in America. In last year's presidential election the labor vote was more important than it had been forty or fifty years earlier, precisely because the number of trade-union members has become so much smaller as a percentage of the voting population. Feeling endangered, they have closed ranks. A few decades ago, a substantial minority of American union members voted Republican, but in last year's election more than 90 percent of union members are thought to have voted Democrat (though their candidate still lost).

For over 100 years, America's trade unions have been strong supporters of free trade, at least in their rhetoric. But in the past few years they have become staunchly protectionist and declared enemies of "globalization." No matter that the real threat to manufacturing jobs is not competition from abroad, but the rapid decline of manufacturing as a creator of work: it is simply incomprehensible that manufacturing production can go up while manufacturing jobs go down, and not only to trade unionists but also to politicians, journalist, economists and the public at large. Most people continue to believe that when manufacturing jobs decline, the country's manufacturing base in threatened and has to be protected. They have great difficulty in accepting that, for the first time in history, society and economy are no longer dominated by manual work, and a country can feed, house and clothe itself with only a small minority of its population engaged in such work.

The new protectionism is driven as much by nostalgia and deep-seated emotion as by economic self-interest and political power. Yet it will achieve nothing, because "protecting" ageing industries does not work. That is the clear lesson of seventy years of farm subsidies. The old crops—corn, wheat, cotton—into which America has pumped countless billions since the 1930s have all done poorly, whereas unprotected and unsubsidized new crops such as soy beans have flourished. The lesson is clear: policies that pay old industries to hold on to redundant people can only do harm. Whatever money is being spent should instead go on subsidizing the incomes of older laid-off workers, and to retraining and redeploying younger ones.

For most of the time since the corporation was invented around 1870, the following five basic points have been assumed to apply:

1.   The corporation is the "master," the employee is the "servant." Because the corporation owns the means of production without which the employee could not make a living, the employee needs the corporation more than the corporation needs the employee.

2.   The great majority of employees work full time for the corporation. The pay they get for the job is their only income and provides their livelihood.

3.   The most efficient way to produce anything is to bring together under one management as many as possible of the activities needed to turn out the product.

The theory underlying this was not developed until after the Second World War, by Ronald Coase, an Anglo-American economist, who argued that bringing together activities into one company lowers transactional costs, and especially the cost of communications (for which theory he received the 1991 Nobel prize in economics). But the concept itself was discovered and put into practice seventy or eighty years earlier by John D. Rockefeller. He saw that to put exploration, production, transport refining and selling into one corporate structure results in the most efficient and lowest-cost petroleum operation. On this insight he built the Standard Oil Trust, probably the most profitable large enterprise in business history. The concept was carried to an extreme by Henry Ford in the early 1920s. The Ford Motor Company not only produced all parts of the automobile and assembled it, but it also made its own steel, its own glass and its own tires. It owned the plantations in the Amazon that grew the rubber trees, owned and ran the railroad that carried supplies to the plant and carried the finished cars from it, and planned eventually to sell and service Ford cars too (though it never did).

4.   Suppliers and especially manufacturers have market power because they have information about a product or a service that the customer does not and cannot have, and does not need if he can trust the brand. This explains the profitability of brands.

5. To any one particular technology pertains one and only one industry, and conversely, to any one particular industry pertains one and only one technology. This means that all technology needed to make steel is peculiar to the steel industry; and conversely, that whatever technology is being used to make steel comes out of the steel industry itself. The same applies to the paper industry, to agriculture or to banking and commerce.

On this assumption were founded the industrial research labs, beginning with Siemens's, started in Germany in 1869, and ending with IBM's, the last of the great traditional labs, founded in America in 1952. Each of them concentrated on the technology needed for a single industry, and each assumed that its discoveries would be applied in that industry.

6. Similarly, everybody took it for granted that every product or service had a specific application, and that for every application there was a specific product or material. So beer and milk were sold only in glass bottles; car bodies were made only from steel; working capital for a business was supplied by a commercial bank through a commercial loan; and so on. Competition therefore took place mainly within an industry. By and large, it was obvious what the business of a given company was and what its markets were.

Every one of these assumptions remained valid for a whole century, but from 1970 onwards every one of them has been turned upside down. The list now reads as follows:

1. The means of production is knowledge, which is owned by knowledge workers and is highly portable. This applies equally to high-knowledge workers such as research scientists and to knowledge technologists such as physiotherapists, computer technicians and paralegals. Knowledge workers provide capital just as much as does the provider of money. The two are dependent on each other. This makes the knowledge worker an equal, an associate or a partner

2. Many employees, perhaps a majority, will still have full-time jobs with a salary that provides their only or main income. But a growing number of people who work for an organization will not be full-time employees but part-timers, temporaries, consultants or contractors. Even of those who do have a full-time job, a large and growing number may not be employees of the organization for which they work, but employees of, for example, an outsourcing contractor.

3. There always were limits to the importance of transactional costs. Henry Ford 's all-inclusive Ford Motor Company proved unmanageable and became a disaster. But now the traditional axiom that an enterprise

should aim for maximum integration has become almost entirely in-validated. One reason is that the knowledge needed for any activity has become highly specialized.

It is therefore increasingly expensive, and also increasingly difficult, to maintain enough critical mass for every major task within an enterprise. And because knowledge rapidly deteriorates unless it is used constantly, maintaining within an organization an activity that is used only intermittently guarantees incompetence.

4.   The second reason why maximum integration is no longer needed is that communications costs have come down so fast as to become in-significant.

This decline began well before the information revolution. Perhaps its biggest cause has been the growth and spread of business literacy. When Rockefeller built his Standard Oil Trust, he had great difficulty finding people who knew even the most elementary bookkeeping or had heard of the most common business terms. At the time there were no business textbooks or business courses, so the transactional costs of making oneself understood were extremely high. Sixty years later, by 1950 or 1960, the large oil companies that succeeded the Standard Oil Trust could confidently assume that their more senior employees were business literate.

By now the new information technology—Internet and email—have practically eliminated the physical costs of communications. This has meant that the most productive and most profitable way to organize is to disintegrate.

This is being extended to more and more activities. Outsourcing the management of an institution's information technology, data processing, and computer system has become routine. In the early 1990s most American computer firms, for example, Apple, even outsourced the production of their hardware to manufacturers in Japan or Singapore. In the late 1990s practically every Japanese consumer-electronics company repaid the compliment by outsourcing the manufacturing of its products for the American market to American contract manufacturers.

In the past few years the entire human-relations management of more than 3 million American workers—hiring, firing, training, benefits and so on—has been outsourced to professional employee organizations. This sector, which ten years ago barely existed, is now growing at a rate of 30 percent a year. It originally concentrated on small and medium-sized companies, but the biggest of the firms, Exult, founded only in 1998, now manages employment issues for a number of *Fortune 500* companies, including BP Amoco, a British-American oil giant, and Unisys, a computer maker. According to a study by McKinsey, a consultancy, outsourcing human-relations management in this way can save up to 30 percent of the cost, and increase employee satisfaction as well.

5.   The customer now has the information. As yet, the Internet lacks the equivalent of a telephone book that would make it easy for users to find what they are looking for. It still requires pecking and hunting. But the information is somewhere on a website, and search firms to find it for a fee are rapidly developing. Whoever has the information has the power. Power is thus shifting to the customer, be it another business or the ultimate consumer. Specifically, that means the supplier, for example, the manufacturer, will cease to be a seller and instead become a buyer for the customer. This is already happening.

General Motors (GM), still the world's largest manufacturer and for many years its most successful selling organization, last year announced the creation of a major business that will buy for the ultimate car consumer. Although wholly owned by GM, the business will be autonomous, and will buy not only General Motors cars, but whatever car and model most closely fits the individual customer's preferences, values, and wallet.

6.   Lastly, there are few unique technologies any more. Increasingly, the knowledge needed in a given industry comes out of some totally different technology with which, very often, the people in the industry are unfamiliar.

No one in the telephone industry knew anything about fiberglass cables.

They were developed by a glass company, Corning. American finance has been transformed by the credit card and commercial paper, neither of which came out of traditional banking. More than half the important inventions developed since the Second World War by the most productive of the great research labs, the Bell Laboratory, have been applied mainly outside the telephone industry.

The Bell Lab 's most significant invention of the past fifty years was the transistor, which created the modern electronics industry. But the telephone company saw so little use for this revolutionary new device that it practically gave it away to anybody who asked

for it which is what put Sony, and with it the Japanese, into the consumer-electronics business.

Research directors, as well as high-tech industrialists, now tend to
believe that the company-owned research lab, that proud nineteenth-
century invention, has become obsolete. This explains why, increasingly, development and growth of a business is taking place not
inside the corporation itself but through partnerships, joint ventures,
alliances, minority participation and know-how agreements with institutions in different industries and with a different technology. Something that only fifty years ago would have been unthinkable is becoming common: alliances between institutions of a totally different
character, say a profit-making company and a university department,
or a city or state government and a business that contracts for a
specific service such as cleaning the streets or running prisons.

Practically no product or service any longer has either a single
specific end-use or application, or its own market. Commercial paper competes with the banks' commercial loans. Cardboard, plastic,
and aluminum compete with glass for the bottle market. Glass is
replacing copper in cables. Steel is competing with wood and plastic
in providing the studs around which the American one-family home
is constructed. The deferred annuity is pushing aside traditional life
insurance—but, in turn, insurance companies rather than financial-
service institutions are becoming the managers of commercial risks.

A "glass company" may therefore have to redefine itself by what
it is good at doing rather than by the material in which it has specialized in the past.

One of the world 's largest glass makers, Corning, sold its profitable business making traditional glass products to become the number one producer and supplier of high-tech materials. Merck,
America's largest pharmaceutical company, diversified from making drugs into wholesaling every kind of pharmacy product, most of
them not even made by Merck, and a good many by competitors.

The same sort of thing is happening in the non-business sectors
of the economy. One example is the free-standing "birthing center"
run by a group of obstetricians that competes with the American
hospital's maternity ward.

And Britain, long before the Internet, created the "Open University," which allowed people to get a university education and obtain a
degree without ever setting foot in a classroom or attending a lecture.

One thing is almost certain: in future there will be not one kind of corporation but several different ones. The modern company was invented simultaneously (around 1870) but independently in three countries: America, Germany and Japan. It was a complete novelty and bore no resemblance to the economic organization that had been the "economic enterprise" for millennia: the small, privately owned and personally run firm. As late as 1832, England's McLane Report—the first statistical survey of business—found that nearly all firms were privately owned and had fewer than ten employees. The only exceptions were quasi-governmental organizations such as the Bank of England or the East India Company. Forty years later a new kind of organization with thousands of employees had appeared on the scene, for example, the American railroads, and Germany's Deutsche Bank.

Wherever the corporation went, it acquired some national characteristics and adapted to different legal rules in each country. Moreover, very large corporations everywhere are being run quite differently from the small owner-managed kind. And there are substantial internal differences in culture, values and rhetoric between corporations in different industries. Banks everywhere are very much alike, and so are retailers or manufacturers. But banks everywhere are different from retailers or manufacturers. Otherwise, however, the differences between corporations everywhere are more of style than of substance. The same is true of all other organizations in modern society: government agencies, armed forces, hospitals, universities and so on.

The tide turned around 1970, first with the emergence of new institutional investors such as pension funds and mutual trusts as the new owners, then more decisively with the emergence of knowledge workers as the economy's big new resource and the society's representative class. The result has been a fundamental change in the corporation.

A bank in the next society will still not look like a hospital, nor be run like one. But different banks may be quite different from one another, depending on how each of them responds to the changes in its workforce, technology and markets. A number of different models is likely to emerge, especially of organization and structure, but perhaps also of recognitions and rewards.

The same legal entity—for example, a business, a government agency or a large not-for-profit organization—may well contain several different human organizations that interlock, but are managed separately and differently.

One of these is likely to be a traditional organization of full-time employees.

Yet there may also be a closely linked but separately managed human organization made up mainly of older people who are not employees but associates or affiliates. And there are likely to be "perimeter" groups such as the people who work for the organization, even full time, but as employees of an outsourcing contractor or of a contract manufacturer. These people have no contractual relationship with the business they work for, which in turn has no control over them. They may not have to be "managed," but they have to be made productive. They will therefore have to be deployed where their specialized knowledge can make the greatest contribution. Despite all the present talk of "knowledge management," no one yet really knows how to do it.

Just as important, the people in every one of these organizational categories will have to be satisfied. Attracting them and holding them will become the central task of people management. We already know what does not work: bribery. In the past ten or fifteen years many businesses in America have used bonuses or stock options to attract and keep knowledge workers. It always fails.

According to an old saying, you cannot hire a hand: the whole man always comes with it. But you cannot hire a man either; the spouse almost always comes with it. And the spouse has already spent the money when falling profits eliminate the bonus or falling stock prices make the option worthless. Then both the employee and the spouse feel bitter and betrayed.

Of course knowledge workers need to be satisfied with their pay, because dissatisfaction with income and benefits is a powerful disincentive.

The incentives, however, are different. The management of knowledge workers should be based on the assumption that the corporation needs them more than they need the corporation. They know they can leave. They have both mobility and self-confidence. This means they have to be treated and managed as volunteers, in the same way as volunteers who work for not-for-profit organizations. The first thing such people want to know is what the company is trying to do and where it is going. Next, they are interested in personal achievement and personal responsibility, which means they have to be put in the right job. Knowledge workers expect continuous learning and continuous training. Above all, they want respect, not so much for themselves but for their area of knowledge. In that regard, they have moved several steps beyond traditional workers, who used to expect to be told what to do, even though lately they have increasingly come to expect to participate. Knowledge workers, by contrast, expect to *make* the decisions in their own area.

Eighty years ago, GM first developed both the organizational concepts and the organizational structure on which today 's large corporations everywhere are based. It also invented the idea of a distinct top management. Now it is experimenting with a range of new organizational models. It has been changing itself from a unitary corporation held together by control through ownership into a group held together by management control, with GM often holding only a minority stake. GM now controls but does not own Fiat, itself one of the oldest and largest car makers. It also controls Saab in Sweden and two smaller Japanese car makers, Suzuki and Isuzu.

At the same time GM has divested itself of much of its manufacturing by spinning off into a separate company, called Delphi, the making of parts and accessories that together account for 60-70 percent of the cost of producing a car. Instead of owning or at least controlling the suppliers of parts and accessories, GM will in future buy them at auction and on the Internet. It has joined up with its American competitors, Ford and Daimler Chrysler, to create an independent purchasing co-operative that will buy for its members from whatever source offers the best deal. All the other carmakers have been invited to join. GM will still design its cars, it will still make engines, and it will still assemble. It will also still sell its cars through its dealer network. But in addition to selling its own cars, GM intends to become a car merchant and a buyer for the ultimate consumer, finding the right car for the buyer no matter who makes it.

GM is still the world 's largest car manufacturer, but for the past twenty years Toyota has been the most successful one. Like GM, Toyota is building a worldwide group, but unlike GM, Toyota has organized its group round its core competence in manufacturing. The company is moving away from having multiple suppliers of parts and accessories, ultimately aiming for no more than two suppliers for any one part. These suppliers will be separate and independent companies, owned locally, but Toyota will in effect run their manufacturing operation for them. They will get the Toyota business only if they agree to being inspected and advised by a special Toyota manufacturing consulting organization. And Toyota will also do most of the design work for the suppliers.

This is not a new idea. Sears Roebuck did the same for its suppliers in the 1920s and 1930s. Britain's Marks & Spencer, although in deep trouble now, was the world's most successful retailer for fifty years, maintaining its pre-eminence largely by keeping an iron grip on its suppliers. It is rumored in Japan that Toyota intends ultimately to market its manufacturing consultancy to non-car companies, turning its manufacturing core competence into a separate big business.

Yet another approach is being explored by a large European manufacturer of branded and packaged consumer goods. Some 60 percent of the company's products are sold in the developed countries through some 150 retail chains. The company plans to create a worldwide website that will take orders direct from customers in all countries, either to be picked up in the retail store nearest to them, or to be delivered by that store to their home. But—and this is the true innovation—the website will also take orders for non-competing packaged and branded consumer products made by other, and especially smaller, firms.

Such firms have great difficulty in getting their wares on to increasingly crowded supermarket shelves. The multinational's website could offer them direct access to customers and delivery through an established large retailer. The pay-off for the multinational and the retailer would be that both get a decent commission without having to invest any money of their own, without risk and without sacrificing shelf space to slow-moving items.

There are already a good many variations on this theme: the American contract manufacturers, already mentioned, who now make the products for half a dozen competing Japanese consumer-electronics firms; a few independent specialists who design software for competing information-hardware makers; the independent specialists who design credit cards for competing American banks and also often market and clear the cards for the bank. All the bank does is the financing.

These approaches, however different, still all take the traditional corporation as their point of departure. But there are also some new ideas that do away with the corporate model altogether. One example is a "syndicate" being tested by several non-competing manufacturers in the European Union. Each of the constituent companies is medium-sized, family-owned and owner-managed. Each is a leader in a narrow, highly engineered product line.

Each is heavily export dependent. The individual companies intend to remain independent, and to continue to design their products separately. They will also continue to make them in their own plants for their main markets, and to sell them in these markets. But for other markets, and especially for emerging or less developed countries, the syndicate will arrange for the making of the products, either in syndicate-owned plants producing for several of the members or by local contract manufacturers. The syndicate will handle the delivery of all members' products and service them in all markets. Each member will own a share of the syndicate, and the syndicate, in turn, will own a small share of each member 's capital.

If this sounds familiar, it is. The model is the nineteenth-century farmers' co-operative.

As the corporation moves towards a confederation or a syndicate, it will increasingly need a *top management* that is separate, powerful and accountable. This top management's responsibilities will cover the entire organization's direction, planning, strategy, values and principles; its structure and its relationship between its various members; its alliances, partnerships and joint ventures; and its research, design and innovation. It will have to take charge of the management of the two resources common to all units of the organization: key people and money. It will represent the corporation to the outside world and maintain relationships with governments, the public, the media and organized labor. But it will not "operate" anything.

An equally important task for top management in next society's corporation will be to balance the three dimensions of the corporation: as an economic organization, as a human organization and as an increasingly important social organization. Each of the three models of the corporation developed in the past half-century stressed one of these dimensions and subordinated the other two. The German model of the social market economy put the emphasis on the social dimension, the Japanese one on the human dimension and the American one ("shareholder sovereignty") on the economic dimension.

None of the three is adequate on its own. The German model achieved both economic success and social stability, but at the price of high unemployment and dangerous labor-market rigidity. The Japanese model was strikingly successful for twenty years, but faltered at the first serious challenge; indeed it has become a major obstacle to recovery from Japan's present recession. Shareholder sovereignty is also bound to flounder. It is a fair-weather model that works well only in times of prosperity. Obviously the enterprise can fulfill its human and social functions only if it prospers as a business. But now that knowledge workers are becoming the key employees, a company also needs to be a desirable employer to be successful.

Crucially, the claim to the absolute primacy of business gains that made shareholder sovereignty possible has also highlighted the importance of the corporation's social function. The new shareholders whose emergence since 1960 or 1970 produced shareholder sovereignty are not "capitalists." They are employees who own a stake in the business through their retirement and pension funds. By 2000, pension funds and mutual funds had come to own the majority of the share capital of America 's large companies. This has given shareholders the power to demand short-term rewards. But the need for a secure retirement income will increasingly focus people 's minds on the future value of the investment. Corporations, therefore, will have to pay attention both to their short-term business results and to their long-term performance as providers of retirement benefits. The two are not irreconcilable, but they are different, and they will have to be balanced.

Over the past decade or two, managing a large corporation has changed out of all recognition. That explains the emergence of the "CEO superman," such as Jack Welch of GE, Andrew Grove of Intel, or Sanford Weil of Citigroup.

But organizations cannot rely on supermen to run them; the supply is both unpredictable and far too limited. Organizations survive only if they can be run by competent people who take their job seriously. That it takes genius today to be the boss of a big organization clearly indicates that top management is in crisis.

The recent failure rate of chief executives in big American companies points in the same direction. A large proportion of CEOs of such companies appointed in the past ten years were fired as failures within a year or two.

But each of these people had been picked for his proven competence, and each had been highly successful in his previous jobs. This suggests that the jobs they took on had become undoable. The American record suggests not human failure, but systems failure. Top management in big organizations needs a new concept.

Some elements of such a concept are beginning to emerge. For instance, Jack Welch at GE built a top-management team in which the company's chief financial officer and its chief human-resources officer are near-equals to the chief executive, and are both excluded from the succession to the top job. He has also given himself and his team a clear and publicly announced priority task on which to concentrate. During his twenty years in the top job, Mr. Welch has had three such priorities, each occupying him for five years or more. Each time he has delegated everything else to the top managements of the operating businesses within the GE confederation.

A different approach has been taken by Asea Brown Boveri (ABB), a huge Swedish-Swiss engineering multinational. Goran Lindahl, who retired as chief executive earlier this year, went even further than GE in making the individual units within the company into separate worldwide businesses and building up a strong top management team of a few non-operating people. But he also defined for himself a new role as a one-man information system for the company, traveling incessantly to get to know all the senior managers personally, listening to them and telling them what went on within the organization.

A largish financial-services company tried another idea: appointing not one CEO but six. The head of each of the five operating businesses is also CEO for the whole company in one top management area, such as corporate planning and strategy, or human resources. The company's chairman represents the company to the outside world and is also directly concerned with obtaining, allocating and managing capital. All six people meet twice a week as the top management committee. This seems to work well, but only because none of the five operating CEOs wants the chairman's job; each prefers to stay in operations. Even the man who designed the system, and then himself took the chairman's job, doubts that the system will survive once he is gone.

In their different ways, the top people at all of these companies were trying to do the same thing: to establish their organization's unique personality.

And that may well be the most important task for top management in the next society 's big organizations. In the half-century after the Second World War, the business corporation has brilliantly proved itself as an economic organization, that is a creator of wealth and jobs. In the next society, the biggest challenge for the large company especially for the multinational may be its social legitimacy: its values, its mission, its vision. Increasingly, in the next society 's corporation, top management will, in fact, be the company. Everything else can be outsourced.

Will the corporation survive? Yes, after a fashion. Something akin to a corporation will have to coordinate the next society's economic resources. Legally and perhaps financially, it may even look much the same as today's corporation. But instead of there being a single model adopted by everyone, there will be a range of models to choose from.

The next society has not quite arrived yet, but it has got far enough for action to be considered in the following areas:

1. *The future corporation.* Enterprises—including a good many non-businesses, such as universities—should start experimenting with new corporate forms and to conduct a few pilot studies, especially in working with alliances, partners and joint ventures, and in defining new structures and new tasks for top management. New models are also needed for geographical and product diversification for multinational companies, and for balancing concentration and diversification.

2. *People policies.* The way people are managed almost everywhere assumes that the workforce is still largely made up of people who are employed by the enterprise and work full-time for it until they are fired, quit, retire, or die. Yet already in many organizations as many as two-fifths of the people who work there are not employees and do not work full time.

Today's human-resources managers also still assume that the most desirable and least costly employees are young ones. In America, especially, older people, and particularly older managers and professionals, have been pushed into early retirement to make room for younger people who are believed to cost less or to have more up-to-date skills. The results of this policy have not been encouraging. After two years wage costs per employee tend to be back where they were before the "oldies" were pushed out, if not higher. The number of salaried employees seems to be going up at least as fast as production or sales, which means that the new young hires are no more productive than the old ones were. But in any event, demography will make the present policy increasingly self-defeating and expensive.

The first need is for a people policy that covers all those who work for an enterprise, whether they are employed by it or not. After all, the performance of every single one of them matters. So far, no one seems to have devised a satisfactory solution to this problem. Second, enterprises must attract, hold and make productive people who have reached official retirement age, have become independent outside contractors or are not available as full-time permanent employees. For example, highly skilled and educated older people, instead of being retired, might be offered a choice of continuing relationships that convert them into long-term "inside outsiders," preserving their skill and knowledge for the enterprise and yet giving them the flexibility and freedom they expect and can afford.

There is a model for this, but it comes from academia rather than business: the professor emeritus, who has vacated his chair and no longer draws a salary. He remains free to teach as much as he wants, but gets paid only for what he does. Many emeriti do retire altogether, but perhaps as many as half continue to teach part-time, and many continue to do full-time research.

A similar arrangement might well suit senior professionals in a business. A big American corporation is currently trying out such an arrangement for older top- level people in its law and tax departments, in research and development, and in staff jobs. But for people in operating work, for example, sales or manufacturing, something different needs to be developed.

3. *Outside information.* It can be argued that the information revolution has caused managements to be less well informed than they were before. They have more data, to be sure, but most of the information so readily made available by IT is about internal company matters. But the most important changes affecting an institution today are likely to be outside ones, about which present information systems offer few clues.

One reason is that information about the outside world is not usually available in computer-useable form. It is not codified, nor is it usually quantified. This is why IT people, and their executive customers, tend to scorn information about the outside world as "anecdotal." Moreover, far too many managers assume, wrongly, that the society they have known all their lives will remain the same forever.

Some outside information is now becoming available on the Internet. Although this is still in totally disorganized form, it is now possible for managements to ask what outside information they need, as a first step towards devising a proper information system for collecting relevant information about the outside world.

4.   *Change agents.* To survive and succeed, every organization will have to turn itself into a change agent. The most effective way to manage change is to create it. But experience has shown that grafting innovation on to a traditional enterprise does not work. The enterprise has to become a change agent. This requires the organized abandonment of things that become outdated or have been unsuccessful, and the organized and continuous improvement of every product, service and process within the enterprise (which the Japanese call *kaizen*). It requires the exploitation of successes, especially unexpected and un-planned-for ones, and it requires systematic innovation. The point of becoming a change agent is that it changes the mindset of the entire organization. Instead of seeing change as a threat, its people will come to consider it as an opportunity.

What about future trends and events we are not even aware of yet? If there is one thing that can be forecast with confidence, it is that the future will turn out in unexpected ways.

Take, for example, the information revolution. Almost everybody is sure of two things about it: first, that it is proceeding with unprecedented speed; and second, that its effects will be more radical than anything that has gone before.

Wrong, and wrong again. Both in its speed and its impact, the information revolution uncannily resembles its two predecessors within the past 200 years, the first industrial revolution of the later eighteenth and early nineteenth centuries and the second industrial revolution in the late nineteenth century.

The first industrial revolution, triggered by James Watt's improved steam engine in the mid-1770s, immediately had an enormous impact on the West's imagination, but it did not produce many social and economic changes until the invention of the railroad in 1829, and of pre-paid postal service and of the telegraph in the decade thereafter. Similarly, the invention of the computer in the mid-1940s, the information revolution's equivalent of the steam engine, stimulated people's imagination, but it was not until forty years later, with the spread of the Internet in the 1990s, that the information revolution began to bring about big economic and social changes.

We are puzzled and alarmed today by the growing inequality in income and wealth and by the emergence of the "super-rich," such as Microsoft's Bill Gates. Yet the same sudden and inexplicable growth in inequality, and the same emergence of the super-rich of their day, characterized both the first and the second industrial revolutions. Relative to the average income and average wealth of their time and country, those earlier super-rich were a good deal richer than a Bill Gates is relative to today's average income and wealth in America.

These parallels are close and striking enough to make it almost certain that, as in the earlier industrial revolutions, the main effects of the information revolution on the next society still lie ahead. The decades of the nineteenth century following the first and second industrial revolutions were the most innovative and most fertile periods since the sixteenth century for the creation of new institutions and new theories. The first industrial revolution turned the factory into the central production organization and the main creator of wealth. Factory workers became the first new social class since the appearance of knights in armor more than 1,000 years earlier.

The House of Rothschild, which emerged as the world's dominant financial power after 1810, was not only the first investment bank but also the first multinational company since the fifteenth century Hanseatic League and the Medici. The first industrial revolution brought forth, among many other things, intellectual property, universal incorporation, limited liability, the trade union, the co-operative, the technical university and the daily newspaper. The second industrial revolution produced the modern civil service and the modern corporation, the commercial bank, the business school, and the first non-menial jobs outside the home for women.

The two industrial revolutions also bred new theories and new ideologies. *The Communist Manifesto* was a response to the first industrial revolution; the political theories that together shaped the twentieth-century democracies—Bismarck's welfare state, Britain's Christian Socialism and Fabians, America's regulation of business— were all responses to the second one. So was Frederick Winslow Taylor's scientific management (starting in 1881), with its productivity explosion. And so was the invention of professional management a few years later.

Following the information revolution, once again we see the emergence of new institutions and new theories. The new economic regions—the European Union, NAFTA, and the proposed Free-Trade Area of the Americas—are neither traditionally free-trade nor traditional protectionist. They attempt a new balance between the two, and between the economic sovereignty of the national state and supranational economic decision-making. Equally, there is no real precedent for the Citigroups, Goldman Sachses or ING Barings that have come to dominate world finance. They are not multinational but transnational.

The money they deal in is almost totally beyond the control of any country's government or central bank.

And then there is the upsurge in interest in Joseph Schumpeter's postulates of "dynamic disequilibrium" as the economy's only stable state; of the innovator's "creative destruction" as the economy 's driving force; and of new technology as the main, if not the only, economic change agent. They are the very antithesis of all earlier and still prevailing economic theories based on the idea of equilibrium as a healthy economy's norm, monetary and fiscal policies as the drivers of a modern economy, and technology as an "externality."

All this suggests that the greatest changes are almost certainly still ahead of us. We can also be sure that the society of 2030 will be very different from that of today, and that it will bear little resemblance to that predicted by today's best-selling futurists. It will not be dominated or even shaped by information technology. IT will, of course, be important, but it will be only one of several important new technologies. The central feature of the next society, as of its predecessors, will be new institutions and new theories, ideologies, and problems.

Index